A Historical Theology of Worship

Princeton Theological Monograph Series
K. C. Hanson, Charles M. Collier, D. Christopher Spinks,
and Robin A. Parry, Series Editors

Recent volumes in the series:

Robert A. Hand
Theological Epistemology in Immanuel Kant's Transcendental Idealism and Karl Barth's Theology

Scott P. Rice
Trinity and History: The God-World Relation in the Theology of Dorner, Barth, Pannenberg, and Jenson

Hakbong Kim
Person, Personhood, and the Humanity of Christ: Christocentric Anthropology and Ethics in Thomas F. Torrance

Lisanne Winslow
A Trinitarian Theology of Nature

Matthew T. Prior
Confronting Technology: The Theology of Jacques Ellul

Edmund Fong
Obedience from First to Last: The Obedience of Jesus Christ in Karl Barth's Doctrine of Reconciliation

Chad Michael Rimmer
Greening the Children of God: Thomas Traherne and Nature's Role in the Ecological Formation of Children

Steven Schafer
Marriage, Sex, and Procreation: Contemporary Revisions to Augustine's Theology of Marriage

Matthew Hutton Hartline
Crowned with Immortal Glory: Eschatological Hope in the Spirituality of William Perkins

A Historical Theology of Worship
Understanding Freedom, Order, and Participation from the Perspective of a Free Church Tradition.

Elaine Sarah Colechin

Foreword by David Cornick

☙PICKWICK *Publications* · Eugene, Oregon

A HISTORICAL THEOLOGY OF WORSHIP
Understanding Freedom, Order, and Participation from the Perspective of a Free Church Tradition

Princeton Theological Monograph Series

Copyright © 2024 Elaine Sarah Colechin. All rights reserved. Except for brief quotations in critical publications or reviews, no part of this book may be reproduced in any manner without prior written permission from the publisher. Write: Permissions, Wipf and Stock Publishers, 199 W. 8th Ave., Suite 3, Eugene, OR 97401.

Pickwick Publications
An Imprint of Wipf and Stock Publishers
199 W. 8th Ave., Suite 3
Eugene, OR 97401

www.wipfandstock.com

PAPERBACK ISBN: 979-8-3852-0344-4
HARDCOVER ISBN: 979-8-3852-0345-1
EBOOK ISBN: 979-8-3852-0346-8

Cataloguing-in-Publication data:

Names: Colechin, Elaine Sarah [author]. | Cornick, David [foreword]

Title: A historical theology of worship : understanding freedom, order, and participation from the perspective of a Free Church tradition / Elaine Sarah Colechin.

Description: Eugene, OR: Pickwick Publications, 2024 | Series: Princeton Theological Monograph Series | Includes bibliographical references and index.

Identifiers: ISBN 979-8-3852-0344-4 (paperback) | ISBN 979-8-3852-0345-1 (hardcover) | ISBN 979-8-3852-0346-8 (ebook)

Subjects: LCSH: Liturgics. | Public worship. | Public worship—Congregational Church—History. | Public worship—Presbyterian Church—History. | Free churches—Liturgy—Theology. | Dissenters, Religious—England.

Classification: BV178 C654 2024 (print) | BX9185 (ebook)

Scripture quotations are from New Revised Standard Version Bible, copyright © 1989 National Council of the Churches of Christ in the United States of America. Used by permission. All rights reserved worldwide.

Prayer "From our hearts to yours" by Karen Campbell, copyright © 2020, words by Karen Campbell, Prayer Handbook; Prayers from the Heart, United Reformed Church. Used by permission.

To family and friends who have supported me along the way.

Contents

List of Tables ix
Foreword by David Cornick xi
Acknowledgements xiii

1. Introduction 1
2. Puritan and Nonconformist Worship 18
3. Worship in Congregationalism 64
4. Worship in Presbyterianism 99
5. A Theology of Freedom, Order, and Participation 133
6. Conclusion 160

Bibliography 169
Name/Subject Index 181
Scripture Index 186

List of Tables

Table 1. Comparison of rubrics for a service of the Word in the services books of the Congregational Union in England and Wales

Table 2. Comparison of rubrics for a service of the Word in the service books of the Presbyterian Church of England

Foreword

ONCE, ON HIS WAY to Jerusalem, Jesus encountered ten lepers who begged for mercy and healing. Jesus healed them, and they went away to show themselves to the priests. But only one turned back, praised God and fell at Jesus's feet in thanksgiving (Luke 17:11–19). The church of Jesus Christ is, as it were, the company of "tenth lepers," those called to return creation's thanks to the Creator for the wonder of being, the gift of life and the sheer generosity of redemption. The church's vocation is worship, and worship is the church's heartbeat and *raison d'être*. It is what the church *does*. In a sense it is the simplest and most beautiful of activities, yet its very simplicity reveals its profundity—a meeting space between God and human beings; the inanimate things of creation, bread and wine, lent sacramental power; human words becoming the vehicle for the work of the Holy Spirit. Thought, art, music, imagination, skill, prayer, devotion – all mixed in the crucible of praise and meditation. And that crucible itself, which will probably involve a community of people and a building, is itself the product of the vagaries and idiosyncrasies of history, as well as the influence of theological ideas.

Elaine Colechin sets out in this book to unravel some of that complexity and help us understand more of the dynamics of worship. She begins from a small canvas, the United Reformed Church, formed in 1972 from the union of the Congregational Church in England and Wales and the Presbyterian Church of England, and later unions with the Re-formed Association of the Churches of Christ and some churches of the Congregational Union of Scotland in 1981 and 2000 respectively. That canvas provides a vista into the Reformed Communion worldwide which allows her to trace the tensions between "freedom," "order," and "participation" (key ingredients of Reformed worshipping experience) from Martin Bucer's 1539 *Psalter* to the present day. As she does so, we note the evolution of central theological concepts like freedom according to the intellectual and spiritual pre-occupations of the day. This is subtle and persuasive church history.

Yet church history can never be divorced from theology. Dietrich Bonhoeffer, Jürgen Moltmann, Frances Young, and Jeremy Begbie become Elaine's conversation partners as she explores freedom, order, and participation through analogies with music and performance, and as the work of the Holy Spirit.

This exploration begins with a small canvas. "Freedom," "order," and "participation" are factors that have shaped the worship of the United Reformed Church and its predecessor traditions. Yet in different ways and weightings, they are also part of the worshipping life of the church universal, and all who come to this book from whatever tradition will find themselves enriched by Elaine's scholarship (as I have been) and encouraged to begin their own explorations of why and how they belong to the ecumenical company of "tenth lepers."

David Cornick
Emeritus Fellow
Robinson College, Cambridge

Acknowledgements

THIS BODY OF WORK would not have been achieved if it were not for the guidance of my doctoral supervisors, Revd. Dr. John Bradbury, Revd. Dr. David Cornick, and Revd. Dr. Robert Pope. My thanks to them and many others who have encouraged me to turn my doctoral thesis into this book charting some of the history and theology behind the worship that I offer on a weekly basis as a Minister of Word and Sacraments in the United Reformed Church. In addition, I am very grateful to Dr. Mike Colechin who proofread my PhD dissertation and this manuscript, ensuring its readability for all who may be interested. And my thanks go to the Archives, Libraries, and their staff across the country that preserve and protect manuscripts and documents, making them accessible to researchers like myself. If it had not been for the sources particularly held by the Westminster College Archive and Library, Cambridge University Library, and some local County Archives, I would not have been able to substantiate what might be best described as "folk-law" within the church.

Introduction

> Let the word of Christ dwell in you richly; teach and admonish
> one another in all wisdom, and with gratitude in your hearts sing
> psalms, hymns, and spiritual songs. (Col 3:16)

THE DISTINCTIVE CHARACTER OF the church that sets it apart from other forms of community in society is its gathering for corporate worship. Many commentators have observed how worship is the definitive and central activity of Christian community.[1] Worship is where community can be expressed and created; it is where the church finds an ethic and lifestyle that it can embody and sustain.[2] It is in worship that the church "is gathered by God and becomes *ekklesia*"; it is in worship where "God's Word is encountered communally" and the church "is confronted by its divine vocation."[3] Therefore, the church's worship and theology are in "dynamic interaction," grounded in the living faith of a community.[4] This is demonstrated by the observation made by Aidean Kavanagh, Benedictine monk and Professor of Liturgics, of worship as transacting "the church's faith in God under the condition of God's real presence in both church and world."[5] This means that in worship the church should be most fully itself, revealing its nature to the

---

1. Allmen, *Worship*, 42; Schmemann, *Introduction*, 14; Ellis, *Gathering*, 1–2; Dryness, *Primer*, 5; see Duncan B. Forrester, "In Spirit and in Truth: Christian Worship in Context," in Forrester and Gay, *Worship and Liturgy*, 3.
2. See Forrester, "In Spirit and in Truth," 3.
3. Ellis, *Gathering*, 5.
4. Duck, *Worship*, 3.
5. Kavanagh, *Liturgical Theology*, 8.

world.[6] For many traditions, however, worship has come to be understood more as a "bestowal of spiritual experience instead of the epiphany of the church's being."[7] Practice and doctrine are perceived as unconnected. Yet, a worshipping community that encounters God in Word and Sacrament will be shaped by that encounter. Consequently, the practices of worship should both reflect and inform what a community believes about God, themselves, and the world.[8] Worship cannot be seen as just an activity of the church. It shapes the church's identity: who the church says it is in the world. In worship, Christians learn how to be Christian, exploring the nature and claim of faith.[9] As the British Methodist theologian and liturgical scholar, Geoffrey Wainwright observed: worship can establish doctrine as well as doctrine institute worship.[10]

The centrality of worship in the life and being of the church might be universal; how the church worships is not. The approach taken to worship differs between denominations because of doctrinal differences. Through the Liturgical and Ecumenical Movements of the late-nineteenth and twentieth centuries there has been the encouragement for there to be common features. There has been the promotion of shared language in practices that are universal in the whole church (e.g., the ecumenical drafting of ancient liturgical prayer for use in the Eucharist) to elevate what unites the church—its nature as the one body of Christ.[11] Essentially, though, the identity of a congregation gathered for worship defines how that worship is offered to God. Therefore, given the juxtaposition of the human and divine, as well as doctrine and practice, in worship, how does a church understand its worship? How does a church's corporate worship impact its theology? How does a church's nature, faith, and order influence how it perceives and undertakes worship? These are the questions this book will attempt to answer giving a distinct way of considering the theology of worship which could be applied to individual congregations and the universal church alike.

---

6. Moore-Keish, *Do This*, 83.
7. Schmemann, *Introduction*, 25; Moore-Keish, *Do This*, 83.
8. Moore-Keish, *Do This*, 69.
9. See Forrester, "In Spirit and in Truth," 4.
10. Wainwright, "Theology of Worship," 456.
11. Rom 12:5.

Introduction

Liturgical Theology

The exploration of the interplay between theology and worship has led to the development of the discipline "liturgical theology." It is a method of drawing theological conclusions about a church from how it worships, therefore elucidating the meaning of worship.[12] Through the analysis of liturgies in prayer books and missals, the "theological meaning of [a] church's symbolic action in various rites, including the interrelation of word and sacramental action," is interpreted highlighting "the implications for doctrine and the faith experience of the church in the world."[13] As a principle, liturgical theology has been predominantly applied to worship in traditions which have prescribed liturgy. This is because, although liturgical theology considers the whole rite of worship, the methodological starting point is the words and instructions of a liturgy.[14] Christopher Ellis, British Baptist theologian, however, demonstrated the application of liturgical theology in traditions which are described as liturgically free. Through the lens of Baptist worship, Ellis showed that even when a denomination has no prescribed liturgy, its worship both forms and expresses the Christian faith of those worshipping. Ellis established that even without a prescribed liturgy there is a recognized "cannon" of fundamental elements, an *ordo*, that encompasses a church's worship which, in turn, undergirds all historical developments.[15] The *ordo*, in its simplest form is a collection of rules and rubrics which regulate how a church worships, such as those found in a prayer book or missal. In liturgical theology, consideration of the *ordo* goes beyond rules and rubrics. It considers the origins of the basic structure of worship, its development, and the theological content as the *lex ordandi* (the law of prayer) of the church.[16] This allowed Ellis to interpret the *ordo* for worship in a liturgically free church in the following way:

> On one hand . . . the pattern of worship services and the meaning implicit in their ordering. On the other hand . . . the overall shape of worship practices and the dynamic interaction between various concerns in the life and witness of a congregation.[17]

---

12. Schmemman, *Introduction*, 16.
13. Saliers, "Liturgical Theology," 336.
14. Fagerberg, *Theologia Prima*, 41.
15. Ellis, *Gathering*, 36; Saliers, "Liturgical Theology," 337.
16. Schememann, *Introduction*, 40.
17. Ellis, *Gathering*, 43.

Using this interpretation in his analysis of Baptist worship, Ellis concluded:

> Christian worship occurs when, with attention to Scripture, in openness to the Spirit of God and in covenant community, disciples gather in the name of Jesus to meet God and to seek [God's] Kingdom.[18]

This suggests a discipleship model that sees the Church as a community of disciples who yearn for the Kingdom of God, seek to express the Lordship of Jesus Christ in their common life and worship with its creative tension between Word and Spirit, between scriptural command and loving encounter.

Corporate worship, Ellis's work identified, is an entwinement of freedom, order, and participation. The study of their theological and historical understanding can offer a theology of worship that reflects the identity of the church and informs what the church should be in its relationship with God.

Freedom, Order, and Participation

The theological basis of freedom is the Holy Spirit. The apostle Paul wrote in his second letter to the church in Corinth: "where the Spirit of the Lord is, there is freedom."[19] Ernest Payne, Baptist historian and defender of the Free Church tradition, interpreted this to mean in the church:

> Freedom of inspiration, freedom from set and uniform liturgical forms in worship, freedom from imposition of binding credal formularies, freedom from any confining of the grace of God to a particular form of Church order, to a priestly succession, or even to the channels of the sacraments, sacred as they are generally held to be. The liberty of the Christian . . . has meant liberty of conscience. The liberty of the Church has meant an assertion of "the Crown Rights of the Redeemer" against any claim to authority over it by the state.[20]

In worship, as Payne alludes to, a congregation has the freedom to order their worship as they feel best reflects their community. A worshipping community is free to respond to a revelation of God that comes from the

---

18. Ellis, *Gathering*, 256.
19. 2 Cor 3:17.
20. Payne, *Free Church Tradition*, 144–45.

INTRODUCTION

reading and preaching of Scripture as addressed as the living Word of God.[21] However, this should not be understood as having sole autonomy—the Holy Spirit is also at work. If the apostle Paul's perspective on freedom is adhered to by a congregation, then their worship should be understood to be under the guidance of the Holy Spirit.[22] This is interpreted in different ways and ranges from the expectation of spontaneity and/or extemporization occurring in worship to the acknowledgement of the Holy Spirit leading the hand that penned the liturgy. In some traditions, though, freedom implies more than the Holy Spirit in action. It relates to the identity of the church.

Payne referred to the "liberty of conscience" in his expounding of the apostle Paul's words to the Corinthians. Although this is grounded in a theology of the Holy Spirit, in Free Church traditions "liberty of conscience" represents a distinct understanding of the relationship between church and state. Free churches share the conviction that the church should be separate to the state. From the fifteenth century onwards, this led to more and more division in the Western church and in the British context, eventually, brought into being the Free Church movement. British denominations who are recognized within the movement include the churches which would be historically called "the old dissent" (the Congregationalists, Presbyterians, Baptists, and Quakers), the Methodists, the Churches of Christ, Brethren, Independent Methodists, Pentecostal, and Independent Evangelical Church. In addition, there are numerous newer groups that emerged from the charismatic and restoration movements of the 1970s and 1980s who would be classified as free churches as they do not align with other strands of the world church, such the Orthodox, Roman Catholic, Anglican, and Lutheran churches.[23]

The fact there is the categorization of "denominations" within the Free Church movement recognizes that freedom does not rule out order. A denomination will have a polity and culture that differentiates it from others and influences the character and nature of its worship. Although not observed by all denominations in these terms, ritual, symbol, sacrament, and sacrifice are gathered and expressed in particular ordered actions in worship as a means of response to God. Therefore, if freedom in worship highlights the participation of the divine in worship, order reflects humanity's

---

21. Ellis, *Gathering*, 27.
22. 2 Cor 3:17.
23. Ellis, *Gathering*, 25–26.

participation in worship. The theologian Evelyn Underhill suggested that worship should be seen as a purely responsive action of humanity. In response to the revelation of God in the visible world, worship should weave "every aspect of... human personality, physical, mental, and spiritual, into [humanity's] adoring recognition of the beauty and perfection of God."[24] Dom Gregory Dix, Anglican Benedictine monk and liturgical scholar, in his analysis of the Anglican Eucharist liturgy, demonstrated how familiar order enables participation of the congregation.[25] Both Underhill and Dix, although emphasizing worship as humanity's response to God, recognized the interrelationship with the divine in worship and the impact of this on the rest of the life of the church and the individual congregant.[26] This observation was also made by the theologian David Fergusson who noted that God can be acknowledged and honored beyond the boundaries of worship and worship involves a wide range of activities, not all of which entirely capture the notion of acknowledging and honoring God.[27] Worship, Fergusson suggested, creates an exchange between the divine and humanity which means that God is the subject as well as the object of worship:

> Worship might be described as a performative action in which both the church and God participate. It is not merely a human acknowledgement of who God is or what Christ has done. Worship is an event by which God is known and Christ is communicated; it is not of [humanity's] making for it is dependent upon the grace of God. In this regard, the act of worship is not merely a human recollection or bearing witness although it includes these. It is also an event in which God's grace works for [humanity] in repeated, regular and dependable ways, albeit in a manner that refers [humanity] to the once and for all action of Christ.[28]

In this book freedom, order, and participation in worship will be explored in more detail to develop a theological understanding of worship and show the interrelationship of worship with the nature, faith, and order of the church. Where liturgical theology begins with order, this book

---

24. Underhill, *Worship* 343.
25. Dix, *Shape*, xiv.
26. Underhill, *Worship*, 343; Dix, *Shape*, 741.
27. See David Fergusson, "The Theology of Worship: A Reformed Perspective," in Forrester and Gay, *Worship and Liturgy*, 71.
28. See Fergusson, "Theology of Worship," 72–73.

Introduction

begins with freedom and uses the case-study of a church of the Free Church tradition.

The United Reformed Church

The United Reformed Church was formed in 1972 when most congregations belonging to the Congregational Church in England and Wales united with the Presbyterian Church of England. Although two relatively small denominations in the United Kingdom, behind their union lay an ecumenical hope for the wider union of the church. This was something that was believed to be "the will of God," demonstrated in the inaugural service of the United Reformed Church. The then Archbishop of Canterbury, the Cardinal Archbishop of Westminster and the Moderator of the Free Church Federal Council all greeted the United Reformed Church's first Moderator of General Assembly with the statement and pledge: "I give thanks with you for this union, and share your resolve to seek the wider unity which is Christ's will."[29] Despite this genuine commitment to growing unity, it has only, so far, been furthered by union with the Re-formed Association of the Churches of Christ in 1981 and around two-thirds of the churches belonging to the Congregational Union of Scotland in 2000.

The vision of the reunification of the church was not the only reason for the initial union. As many British denominations, the Congregational and Presbyterian Churches had seen decline in church membership and attendance in the immediate post-war era. From the structures of the new church, Martin Camroux, a United Reformed Church minister, in his critique of the United Reformed Church and its role in the ecumenical vision, argued that the union was a means of safeguarding traditions. The formation of the United Reformed Church was more about the unity of Congregationalists and Presbyterians, than the beginning of wider unity in the church.[30] This is further demonstrated by the choice of name for the new church. The title "United Reformed Church" was intended to show how the Church would be distinctive among the existing British denominations and so did not fully embracing the ecumenical vision. Firstly, this is

---

29. United Reformed Church, *Service of Thanksgiving*, 12–13; Huxtable, *New Hope*, 33; Camroux, *Ecumenism*, 41. It should be noted that the Moderator of General Assembly within the United Reformed Church is an office held by a Minister of Word and Sacraments, a Church Related Community Worker, or an Elder who is elected by General Assembly for a given period of time to be the denomination's representative.

30. Camroux, *Ecumenism*, 61.

shown by the finality of the name. The Basis of Union, the foundational and controlling document of the nature of the United Reformed Church, acknowledges there is only one church and that in obedience to God's call, a unity of all people should be the church's mandate.[31] However, by the Church adopting the name "United" rather than say "Uniting," the process of union is suggested as complete. If the vision was of the unity of the whole church, then every union that has occurred in the life of the United Reformed Church should only ever have been seen as a step along the way, and the process of uniting only complete when the one church is a visible reality, which is currently not the case. Secondly, there is the significance of being "Reformed," which came from the Presbyterians and Congregationalists recognizing themselves as part of the wider Reformed tradition. It should be noted that at the time of union, this was not terminology that was widely used in either denomination except by those who were part of the academy, (i.e., those engaged with the academic exploration of church history and/or theology and those exploring the context of the new church in the global landscape).[32] Yet, in uniting the Congregationalists and Presbyterians there was the hope of creating a strong Reformed church in England and Wales—a church that rediscovered, Camroux suggested, "a supposed Genevan heritage that would support the Church's mission."[33]

Freedom, Order, and Participation in the United Reformed Church

It is within an understanding of being "Reformed" that the story of the worship of the United Reformed Church begins. The Basis of Union states:

> Christ's mercy in continuing his call to the Church in all its failure and weakness has taught the Church that its life must ever be renewed and reforming according to Scripture, under the guidance of the Holy Spirit.[34]

The life of the Church has an order in which "the Word must be properly preached and the sacraments properly administered" to ensure renewal

---

31. United Reformed Church, "Basis of Union," clauses 1–4, 7–8; Thompson, *What We Believe*, 2–3.
32. Thompson, *What We Believe*, 1–2.
33. Camroux, *Ecumenism*, 60–61.
34. United Reformed Church, "Basis of Union," clause 6.

Introduction

and reform.[35] This bases the ecclesiology of the Church on the foundation of worship as it was formulated by John Calvin (1509–64) in his *Institutes of the Christian Religion* (1559).[36] Calvin was one of the sixteenth century European Reformers who are identified as being foundational for the Reformed tradition. However, the Congregationalists and Presbyterians cannot simply be described as Reformed. They have distinct histories that relate to national histories and different understandings of the relationship between church and state in Great Britain. This was reflected in the opening words to the preface of the first service book compiled for use within the United Reformed Church:

> Both the traditions which came together to form the United Reformed Church cherished freedom in worship. The publication of this book does not impugn that freedom. The orders found here are not prescribed.[37]

Despite the Church having books of liturgy (*A Book of Services* [1980], *Service Book* [1989], and *Worship: From the United Reformed Church* [2003, extended in 2004 and revised in 2024]), the worship of the United Reformed Church can be described as having a generally accepted structure while being liturgically free.[38] This reflects the Reformed nature of the Church and the belief that both worshippers and presiders "should be free to respond to the leading of the Holy Spirit."[39] Yet, it also comes from how the United Reformed Church interprets order. From the union, as demonstrated by the books of liturgy published by the Church, efforts have been made to provide the Church with liturgies, that although not prescribed, reflected the heritage and nature of the Church in worship. This is shown in how each iteration of the Church's books of liturgy has followed on from an expansion of the union.[40] The reasoning behind this was expressed by James Todd, one of the authors of the first order of worship compiled for the Church, when discussing the work:

---

35. Thompson, *What We Believe*, 5.
36. Calvin, *Institutes*, 4.1.9.
37. United Reformed Church, *Book of Services*, 7.
38. Bradbury, *Perpetually Reforming*, 188.
39. See Julian Templeton and Keith Riglin, "Ordered Freedom: English Reformed Worship," in Templeton and Riglin, *Reforming Worship*, 3.
40. Colechin, "Worship of the United Reformed Church," 42–43.

> We believe it to be an abiding principle of Reformed Church worship that the minister should never be so confined to any form of prayer that he is not at liberty to follow the leading of the Holy Spirit. But we hope that our worship will always be orderly and in obedience to the Gospel. There are dangers in freedom: there are dangers in fixity of form too. What we have tried to do is to provide our Church with the text of a service which does justice to the traditions which we have inherited, which takes into account the new liturgical insights by which all branches of the Church are being enriched, and which will enable our congregations to worship God in freedom, with confidence and joy.[41]

Full, prescribed liturgies could not be conceived as something the United Reformed Church could enforce within the worship life of its congregations. The Church cherishes "freedom and variety in worship, and above all liberty to follow the leading of the Holy Spirit, too much to allow [itself] to be bound by an invariable order."[42] Nonetheless, the production of fully scripted liturgies was a way of putting into the hands of worship leaders the constituents that fittingly express the doctrine of a church that holds the values of unity and being Reformed. Erik Routley, theologian and hymnologist, spoke of how the approach to writing liturgy in the Church followed historical principles. In the Presbyterian Church, directories of worship were not uncommon and it is this approach that has been applied in nearly all the service books and liturgies that have been written for use in the United Reformed Church. In most cases, the liturgies (and particularly those in *A Book of Services*, *Service Book*, and *Worship: From the United Reformed Church*) were never intended to be taken as "do this."[43] They were the encouragement to "do it like this."[44] Donald Hilton, Moderator of General Assembly of the United Reformed Church from 1993 to 1994, wrote in the introduction to his second collection of service for use at Lent and Easter:

> The services should be altered and adapted in the light of local needs and opportunities.[45]

---

41. Todd, "Tradition and Change," 7.
42. Todd, "Tradition and Change," 7.
43. United Reformed Church, *Book of Services*, 7; United Reformed Church, *Service Book*, ix; United Reformed Church, *Worship*, Foreword.
44. Routley, "New Book," 415.
45. Hilton, *Lent and Easter 2*, 3.

Introduction

This equal holding of order and freedom within worship the Church reflects further its nature as Reformed. Holding Scripture as central to worship and practice, the United Reformed Church heeds the words of the apostle Paul to the church in Corinth: worship should be "decent and orderly."[46] Therefore, through the liturgies that have been published, the Church has been given an understanding of form and structure that can positively affect worship. These liturgies and other worship resources written by members and worship leaders of the Church demonstrate how the Church sees that without order, freedom can lead to chaos within worship as there is nothing that is holding the action and the people together.[47] The Church recognizes that corporate worship is at its best when order and freedom are given equal consideration. The church historian, Horton Davies summarized it in this way: "form needs freedom to keep it fresh, and freedom needs form to prevent it from turning into irresponsible chaos."[48]

Another reflection of freedom in the worship of the United Reformed Church comes from the Church's description of being a "broad church." Its broadness relates both to the Church being a union of traditions and to the range of theological opinions found across the Church.[49] This has resulted in a variety of worship styles which are influenced by ecumenical engagement and the consequential cross-fertilization. David Peel, theologian and Moderator of General Assembly of the United Reformed Church from 2005 to 2006, wrote of the United Reformed Church's worship:

> We have not been afraid to take on board resources and styles which have originated in our sister churches around the world, religious communities like those at Iona and Taizé, and the Charismatic Renewal Movement.[50]

However, the broadness of the Church not only impacts the Church's worship; it is shaped by the Church's worship. Edmund Banyard, Moderator of General Assembly of the United Reformed Church from 1988 to 1989, wrote:

---

46. 1 Cor 14:40.

47. Colechin, "Praising God," 231–34; Colechin, "Worship of the United Reformed Church," 284–320.

48. Davies, *Worship and Theology*, 1:75.

49. See John Burgess, "Introduction," in Burgess, *Word and Spirit*, 3.

50. Peel, *Reforming Theology*, 269.

A Historical Theology of Worship

> Wherever we live, we are likely to have neighbors who feel uncomfortable if they need to attend church. They do not easily relate to the worship which they find there, it does little or nothing for them. That doesn't necessarily mean that what we do in our churches is wrong, but if we believe that God has entrusted us with good news to be shared, we ought to understand why we worship as we do and ask whether our worship patterns are appropriate to our day and what we might learn from those who are trying other ways.[51]

In having the freedom to adapt worship to the needs of the world around the Church, the Church begins to respond to the needs of society and engages in God's mission.

Freedom in worship to respond to the needs of the world in the present moment has been considered in terms of the Church's ability to be spontaneous. Bernard Thorogood, General Secretary of the United Reformed Church from 1980 to 1992, wrote:

> Our readiness to include in our worship whatever is most pressing in today's life. It is taking life with seriousness. So if we are caught up in quarrels it may be that true worship means dealing personally with the quarrel before we sing our praises to God.[52]

This is biblical. In the Sermon on the Mount, Jesus taught that no one should bring an offering to God while they were angry with another; if they come to the altar to offer a gift and remember they have something against another, they should leave that gift, go and reconcile with their sister or brother, and then return to make that offering.[53] This biblical nature is important as it again reflects the centrality of Scripture not only in the worship of the Church but also in the life of the Church and the congregation. This puts the onus on the congregation and why they should make themselves ready to worship God as they bring to God what is pressing in the world. This can be interpreted in the minister's or worship leader's ability to draw everyone in through extemporary prayer referencing what is pressing in life. However, this does not deal with the personal element and the need for the people to sort personal quarrels before coming to worship.

Spontaneity is about more than the people's offering to God; it is observed as being of God. Therefore, worship should be considered as flowing

---

51. Banyard, *Straws*, 79.
52. Thorogood, *Father's House*, 95.
53. Matt 5:22–24.

Introduction

out of God's activity in the congregation.[54] This is the work of the Holy Spirit. In the United Reformed Church's worship, the work of the Holy Spirit is often thought only to manifest in the words and actions of the one leading worship on behalf of those gathered.[55] However, the Holy Spirit makes God present and brings about encounter with God in the whole congregation. Accordingly, any understanding of freedom in worship must recognize that it is something of God and, as has been the case in the United Reformed Church at times, not overemphasize the place of personal freedom, whether that be of the one who is leading worship or the congregation.[56]

The concept of response sits alongside freedom. Every element of an act of worship should evoke a response in the congregation to God and Jesus Christ as incarnate God as well as Savior.[57] With the emphasis on the centrality of Scripture in worship which comes from the Reformed tradition upheld in the United Reformed Church, corporate worship has taken on the framework of being about hearing and responding to God's word. In corporate worship "God is revealed (or God's nature or God's teaching) through the reading of scripture, its exposition (in the sermon) and the sacraments (the acted word)."[58] Consequently, the nature of that response depends on how order and freedom are interpreted and used. Where the tendency is for worship to be led predominantly by the minister or worship leader, then the onus is on them to construct an act of worship which, through its content, conveys a sense of worth and purpose upon the congregation so that they feel as if they are participating.[59] In these circumstances, worship has to be seen as relevant and something which the congregation can engage with as a whole (e.g., the inclusivity of worship both in its content and the language used). This has been enabled by the array of worship resources published by the Church which have been written by members of the Church.[60] The annual *Prayer Handbook* for the United Reformed Church is a prime example of this in practice. Over the years,

---

54. See Brian Harley, "Making Room for the Spirit in Worship," in Burgess, *Word and Spirit*, 17.

55. Todd, "Tradition and Change," 17; see John Burgess, "Experiencing the Glory: Revelation in Worship," in Burgess, *Word and Spirit*, 125.

56. See Susan Durber, "Tearing Down the Temple: Deconstructing Worship," in Burgess, *Word and Spirit*, 113.

57. Owen, *Sharers*, 84.

58. See Burgess, "Experiencing the Glory," 125.

59. Tucker, *Reformed Ministry*, 119.

60. Colechin, "Worship of the United Reformed Church," 284–320.

it has commissioned and included contributions from all aspects of the Church's life.[61] Although the *Prayer Handbook*, like all worship resources published for and on behalf of the Church, is not mandated, when used, it does offer different voices and ideas which may otherwise go unheard in some congregational settings.

The worship resources published by and on behalf of the United Reformed Church have taken participation further than offering material written by others. Patterns and aspects of worship have been suggested that more actively engage the congregation.[62] The simplest interpretation of this has been through the expansion of who leads an act of worship. Teaching material on worship in the Church has encouraged congregations to take a more active part in the planning and leading of worship.[63] It has also been achieved in the content of worship. In the anthologies of prayers in the catalogue of worship resources of the United Reformed Church, verbal responses by the congregation during prayers have been promoted. There are also specific actions, like the "offertory." Bernard Thorogood wrote:

> The offertory is a critical moment in worship. It is necessary for the proper pattern of response. Even if our church should inherit a great legacy tomorrow we shall still take up an offering at each service, for we need to demonstrate that there is a personal response to the gifts of God in Christ. . . . Then we can indeed come to the offertory with conviction and joy, glad that we can offer some sign of our commitment to the life of the Spirit in the context of our praise.[64]

Then there is the singing of hymns as the church was encouraged to do by the apostle Paul in its worship.[65] In the worship of the United Reformed Church, hymns singing is seen as an essential part of an act of worship. This is borne witness to by the contributions made to modern hymnody by members of the United Reformed Church (e.g., Alan Gaunt, Jill Jenkins, Erik Routley, and Brian Wren). Hymns bring the emotions of the congregation into worship in a way that otherwise might be lost due to the other main element being that of the sermon (or the preaching of God's word).

---

61. Colechin, "Praising God," 229–31.
62. Peel, *Reforming Theology*, 65.
63. United Reformed Church, *Wholly Worship*, 39; Colechin, "Praising God," 233.
64. Thorogood, *Father's House*, 51–52.
65. Eph 5:19; Col 3:16.

Introduction

Hymns also act as a counterpoint to what can be a highly cerebral pattern of worship.[66]

These separate elements drawn together actively engage the congregation in participation. From the outset in the "call to worship," when the congregation make their approach to God, through to the end when, in the "dismissal" or "sending out," the congregation acknowledge that worship and glorification of God does not end with the act of worship, the congregation is encouraged to participate through word and/or action. Some of the published liturgies of the United Reformed Church are described as being responsive conversations—exchanges between worship leader and congregation, as well as with God. This was something that was deemed important in the first liturgies written on behalf of the United Reformed Church. One of their authors, Erik Routley, wrote in defense:

> Our new liturgy has much responsive conversation in it—we have assumed that the demand for "participation," which is to be heard so vigorously expressed in many places, is a demand our own people are anxious to make and to have granted.[67]

Discussion on participation in worship can focus very much on the practicalities. Yet, theologically, it is about a discourse between God and the people. Worship should be an encounter with God and within it there should be a "seeking for, recognition of, and response to the revelation of God."[68] The congregation often misses this point, as Susan Durber, theologian and United Reformed Church minister, observed:

> Sometimes we can be beguiled into thinking that worship should be entertaining, popular, and dramatic, partly at least because we want people to be attracted to it. We have come to think of it as the main way in which we draw people to the Gospel. But if worship is actually the staff of spiritual life for those who are part of the Christian community, it is not going to be wonderfully exciting, because the life we are being prepared to live in Christ's name is not like that. Worship is a healing and a re-shaping of our desires. It is spiritual bread.[69]

---

66. Peel, *Reforming Theology*, 278.
67. Routley, "New Book," 414.
68. See Burgess, "Experiencing the Glory," 126.
69. See Durber, "Tearing Down the Temple," 115.

Durber's comment makes the case that the people need to see worship as more, but it emphasizes the activity of worship as God's with the people being recipients. Given the attitudes to freedom and order in the Church, and the high place the reading and preaching of God's word in worship is held, this holds a level of truth. Biblically, though, worship is described as something the people offer to God. It may be concluded, then, that primarily, God should be the audience, not the congregation.[70] Worship can be seen and thought of as a one-sided conversation; development of theological ideas regarding worship through history shows that worship is a fusion of heavenly words and human response, which "makes life worship and worship alive."[71]

In the Rest of This Book

The worship of the United Reformed Church is a dynamic understanding of the interrelationship between freedom, order, and participation. Its comprehension is scriptural and bound up in tradition. However, the Church's tradition is not simply Reformed; the United Reformed Church has antecedent traditions that are influenced by events in history. Therefore, the first part of this book, chapter 2 to chapter 4, will trace the development of the understanding of freedom, order, and participation in corporate worship and how they were expressed in the antecedent traditions of the Church. It should be acknowledged that the United Reformed Church has four antecedent traditions: English Congregationalism, English Presbyterianism, Churches of Christ, and Scottish Congregationalism. The Churches of Christ and Scottish Congregationalism have impacted the worship of the United Reformed Church, however, it is English Congregationalism and English Presbyterianism that will be focused on as they are the dominant antecedent traditions in eleven of the thirteen synods of the United Reformed Church.[72] The origins of the United Reformed Church worship date back to before these traditions were established denominations. English Congregationalism and Presbyterianism have their roots in English

---

70. Marvin, *Shaping Up*, 6.

71. Thorogood, *Father's House*, 11.

72. The United Reformed Church is made up of thirteen synods: eleven in England and two national synods which cover Scotland and Wales. A synod is one of the organizational layers in the structure of the Church bringing together congregations in a geographical grouping.

Introduction

Puritanism. Therefore, beginning at the Westminster Assembly in 1643, when worship in the English church was first critically argued, chapter 2 to chapter 4 will provide a chronological historical survey charting how perspectives on freedom, order, and participation have been formulated and advanced as thoughts and ideologies have changed over the centuries. To give background to the discussion in each chapter, a short history of the tradition under consideration is included. The histories are not comprehensive, they focus on important aspects that relate to the development of worship in that tradition.

The second part of this book is the development of a theology of freedom, order, and participation in worship (chapter 5). It theologically develops some of the themes that are highlighted in the historical survey and relates them to the general experience of worship in the United Reformed Church. These observations should not be seen as exclusive, they can be witnessed in the worship of other church traditions. This will become evident in a theology of worship that will be realized through the analogy of traditional jazz music, drawing together the interaction of freedom, order, and participation in a way that shows their equal importance. Examples from the United Reformed Church will be used, but the theology of worship presented is general. The aim is to present a theology of freedom, order, and participation in which corporate worship can be understood in any tradition. Through the Holy Spirit, corporate worship will be shown to be where a community of believers encounter the Word of God and respond in a manner that glorifies God.

2

Puritan and Nonconformist Worship

PRIOR TO 1662, THE goal of a unified but reformed church in England appeared to be possible. Notable groups sought reform along lines similar to those found in Continental Europe but firmly from within a national church. However, the events of 1662 brought the vision of a united church for the nation to an end. The antecedent traditions of the United Reformed Church found themselves outside the Church of England. It is from this shift from being part of a national movement to becoming marginalized groups that the understanding of corporate worship which can be discerned in the United Reformed Church began to take shape. Freedom, order and participation characterized corporate worship before and after 1662, but their interrelationship and the meaning of the terms were shaped for the United Reformed Church by the development of theological thinking that came as a result of exclusion and ejectment from the Church of England.

Historical Context

It could be argued that the changes in theological thought that are important to how the interrelationship between freedom, order and participation is perceived in the corporate worship of the United Reformed Church were initiated by the birth of Puritanism in England. Puritanism established itself within the English church during the reign of Elizabeth I. Some of the disputes which ultimately led to dissent and finally nonconformity can be traced back at least to the Elizabethan Settlement in 1559.[1] This period of history is complex with both religious and political pressures influencing

---

1. Davies, *English Puritans*, 57–76; Winship, *Hot Protestants*, 9–81; Tomkins, *Journey of the Mayflower*, 18–33.

the nature of the church in England. Through revisions of the *Book of Common Prayer* what constituted corporate worship was considered. But it was not until the convening of the Westminster Assembly in 1643 that worship was debated in terms of freedom, order, and participation. Therefore, this historical narrative begins at the Westminster Assembly and is split into three parts : the period between the convening of the Westminster Assembly in 1643 to the Great Ejectment in 1662; the period between 1662 and the so-called Act of Toleration in 1689; and the development of nonconformity in the eighteenth century.

Westminster Assembly (1643) to the Great Ejectment (1662)

As the Long Parliament sought to take control of the governance of England, a remodeling of the church in England was sought which would make it a Protestant church that truly reflected Puritan values and theology. Parliament's *Solemn League and Covenant* with the Scottish Lords in 1643 revealed the desire to reform the English Church "according to the Word of God and the example of the best reformed churches."[2] The task of reform was given to an Assembly of divines, peers, members of parliament and commissioners from Scotland convened at Westminster Abbey between 1643 and 1652. The intention of what has become known as the Westminster Assembly was to bring together in "nearest conjunction and uniformity in religion, [a] confession of faith, form of Church government, directory of worship, and catechizing" for the "Churches of God in the three kingdoms [Scotland, England, and Ireland]."[3] To unite the English church under one confession was not a simple undertaking. There was already a movement of separation from the national church in the country. Dating back to the sixteenth century there was a radical movement, which led to individuals and congregations being labelled as "Separatists." Members of this movement were unable to accept the form the established church took as the "true" church, and consequently chose to separate themselves physically and spiritually from a church they deemed as "a church of confusion where the Lord's people may not tarry."[4] Also, there were two streams of thought

---

2. England Parliament, *Solemn League and Covenant*; Cornick, *Under God's Good Hand*, 51.

3. Rushworth, "Scotland," 197; Warfield, *Westminster Assembly*, 25–26; Ryrie, *Protestants*, 114.

4. Acheson, *Radical Puritans*, 1.

particularly over church governance, although this did impact other aspects of church life and practice. It had been hoped that the *Solemn League and Covenant* would secure, for the English church, a settlement similar to the Scottish parish-based model governed by presbyteries rather than bishops. However, a minority of the divines of the Westminster Assembly believed that the governance of the church should be led by the congregation through the "law of Christ and by mutual consultation and advice."[5]

Against this backdrop, the Westminster Divines presented five documents to the English Parliament and Church of Scotland for approval and adoption: a directory for public worship (1644), a form of church governance which was only relevant to the church in England and Ireland (1645), a confession of faith (1646), and two catechisms, a shorter and longer version (1648). The Church of Scotland adopted all relevant documents. The English Parliament, after editing, only ever adopted the form of church governance (in 1646) and approved for use in the church: the directory of worship (in 1645), the confession of faith (in 1648) and the shorter catechism (in 1648). Also, the English Parliament never vigorously applied them to the Church of England. In January 1645, Parliament issued an ordinance regarding the use of the *Directory for Public Worship of God* yet never enforced it, as demonstrated in a subsequent ordinance made in August 1645:

> Whereas by an Ordinance of Parliament made the Third Day of *January* last past, and entitled, *An Ordinance of Parliament for the taking away the Book of Common-Prayer, and for establishing and putting in execution of the Directory for the Publick Worship of God*; it was (among other things therein contained) Ordained, That the said Book of Common-Prayer should not remain or be from thenceforth used in any Church, Chappels, and Place of Publick Worship, within the Kingdom of *England*, and Dominion of *Wales*; and that the Directory for Publick Worship in the said recited Ordinance set forth, should be from thenceforth used, pursued, and observed, according to the true Intent and Meaning of the said Ordinance, in all Exercises of the Publick Worship of God, in every Congregation, Church, Chappel, and Place of Publick Worship, within this Kingdom of *England*, and Dominion of *Wales*: Yet nevertheless in regard that in or by the said recited Ordinance, there was no special Direction made or Contained for the speedy dispersing of the said Directory into the several Parishes within

---

5. Ryrie, *Protestants*, 115.

the Kingdom of *England*, and Dominion of *Wales*, and publishing of the same Directory; nor any Punishment set down either for the using of the said Book of Common-Prayer, or for the non-using or depraving of the said Directory; by Means whereof there has been as yet little Fruit of the said Ordinance.[6]

The impact of Parliament not applying the documents of the Westminster Assembly is seen in how, during the decade of the Commonwealth, the English church fragmented. The division of the church was also a consequence of the promotion of relative freedom in religious thought.[7] Despite, or perhaps because of, the ambiguities about his personal religious convictions, Oliver Cromwell, Lord Protector from September 1651, appeared to have been supportive of a comprehensive state church. Nevertheless, with the breakdown of the church authority during the Civil War and the official abolition of bishops in 1645, every parish became *de facto* independent. This led to the increased emergence of a diverse range of theological views and sects, some tolerable and others not. Church historian, Alec Ryrie observed that the resulting eruption of religious creativity in the 1640s and 1650s left behind a legacy of Protestant identities and suggested that this ended the vision of a national church in England.[8] The further diversification of the Protestant church would have made the realization of an all-inclusive state church more difficult, but there was a hope, as shown by the Westminster Divines, that there may have been the possibility of a middle way. Richard Baxter (1615–91), one of the Westminster Divines, who after the events of 1660 to 1662 lamented:

> God did so wonderfully bless the labours of this *unanimous faithful ministers* that had it not been for the faction of the Prelatists on one side that drew men off, and the factions of the giddy and turbulent sectaries on the other side. . . . England had been like in a quarter of an age to have become a land of saints and pattern of holiness to all the world, and the unmatchable paradise of the earth. Never were such fair opportunities to sanctify a nation lost and trodden as have been in this land of late. Woe to them that were the cause of it.[9]

---

6. Rushworth, "Parliamentary and Civil Occurrences," 209.

7. It should be noted that this freedom was limited or restricted. Protestant Trinitarians were tolerated; however, Catholics were not and extreme Quakers still faced persecution.

8. Ryrie, *Protestants*, 131.

9. Baxter, *Autobiography*, 84; Zakai, "Religious Toleration," 29–30.

Baxter blamed the end of the church envisioned by the Westminster Assembly on two distinct groups: those who advocated an episcopal church government; and those who had previously sought to separate from the Church of England and were spoken out against by the Westminster Divines in the pamphlet *Certaine Considerations to Dis-swade Men from Further Gathering of Churches* (1643). This would have included groups known as Brownists, Barrowists, Anabaptists, and Familists.[10]

Parliament, on Cromwell's death, was predominantly Royalist and, with the collusion of the Army which feared unrest as the result of the weak leadership of Cromwell's son and successor Richard, the opportunity was taken to restore the monarchy. But this was a monarchy that was to be controlled by Parliament. When Charles Stuart promised in the *Declaration of Breda* (1660) that, if made king, he would uphold liberty of conscience in matters of religion, Parliament saw this as a threat to its control of the church and the ability to re-establish an episcopal structure in it.[11] Parliament's solution, citing as justification the security of the realm, was to return the church to full prelacy by passing an "Act of Uniformity" and other measures which signaled an end to relative toleration and any hope for a comprehensive church settlement.[12] Parliament sought to regain control of the clergy and restore both uniformity and conformity in the practice of the church's worship through the imposition of a prayer book. Once king, Charles II attempted to honor his promise in the *Declaration of Breda* by convening the Savoy Conference in 1661 to discuss the revision of the prayer book. This was not a meeting of equals, nor was it conciliatory or constructive. The Puritan divines at the meeting (all of whom envisioned a self-governing English Church under principles that have come to be known as presbyterian) had to defend their perspective on worship, requesting modification of an already assumed order (that of the *Directory for the Public Worship of God* from the Westminster Assembly).[13] Unbeknown to the Puritans, while they were engaged at the Savoy Conference, in the genuine belief that the form of the Church was a matter of debate, Parliament appointed a separate committee. This committee's purpose was to review the legislation passed in 1641 which abolished the church courts and law, as well as consider the

---

10. Zakai, "Religious Toleration," 13.
11. Miller, *After the Civil War*, 147; Keeble, *Restoration*, 116.
12. Miller, *After the Civil War*, 148; Keeble, *Restoration*, 116.
13. Keeble, *Restoration*, 116.

content of the Church's liturgy as it was before Charles I's amendments.[14] This review led to the *Act of Uniformity*, passed in 1662, by which Parliament attempted to regain control of the English church without taking into consideration the views of the Puritan divines on its worship and practices. The Act required all clergy and teachers to give "unfeigned consent and assent" to the *Book of Common Prayer* (not complete at the time the Act became law), never praying or preaching without it, submitting to episcopal ordination and agreeing not to attempt to change the structure of the Church of England by force. All clergy who occupied a living were also required to declare that the *Solemn League and Covenant* was illegal and invalid, and that they would not take up arms against the king.[15] Ministers were expected to comply with the requirements of the Act on or before Bartholomew's Day (24 August) in 1662. Those who refused were to be ejected from their livings.

Great Ejectment (1662) to the So-Called Act of Toleration (1689)

Through the *Act of Uniformity* and preceding laws, an already divided church became more disparate in England. The potential penalty of imprisonment for openly practicing a Christian faith that was unlawful did not dissuade those who dissented from the government's attempts to control the church. This did not mean that those who sought not to conform did not do all they could to elude detection. Meeting times and places would vary, as would the size of gatherings.[16] In terms of worship, there was greater flexibility and a dislike grew of "all false dignity, pomposity, externality and formality."[17] What began as a resistance movement of the Spirit became the idea of only worshipping in the Spirit. Church historian Horton Davies stated that John Wilson's *Cultus Evangelicus—a brief Discourse concerning the Spirituality and Simplicity of New Testament Worship* (1667) demonstrated this by contrasting spiritual with carnal, corporeal and external.[18] Wilson, Horton recorded, wrote that God could not only be worshipped by

---

14. Rushworth, "December"; Keeble, *Restoration*, 117.
15. Keeble, *Restoration*, 118.
16. Watts, *Dissenters*, 230.
17. Davies, *Worship and Theology*, 2:450.
18. Davies, *Worship and Theology*, 2:451.

"body or outward man . . . but with soul or inner man, which is what [God] in all holy addresses mainly looks after."[19]

When James II came to the throne in 1685, an attempt at religious pluralism and toleration was made. Openly Roman Catholic, James II suspended laws put in place by Parliament during the reign of Charles II and through his *Declaration of Indulgence* (1688) sought to enable those who had not conformed to worship more freely.[20] Given resistance of Parliament to James II's actions, it is hard to say how much freedom there was. Historian Michael Watts suggested that the *Declaration of Indulgence* broke the back of Anglican intolerance and led eventually to the possibility of toleration.[21] This did not facilitate civil equality but it did allow the consolidation of the diverse ecclesiological landscape in England.

English Nonconformity in the Eighteenth Century

In 1689, with William of Orange and Mary II on the throne, the *Act for Exempting their Majestyes Protestant Subjects Dissenting from the Church of England from the Penalties of certain Laws* or the so-called *Act of Toleration* entered into law. This allowed Protestant, Trinitarian nonconformists, who were prepared to "take an oath of allegiance and supremacy" to the crown and "make a declaration against transubstantiation," the freedom to worship under license.[22] This Act may appear to suggest that Parliament had accepted that freedom to worship as conscience dictated was incontrovertible. Yet in what this Act required of those who agreed to it, there was also an attempt to control religious dissent. When attempts to eradicate had come to nothing, logically, Parliament looked for potential ways to control the dissenters/nonconformists. The vision of the whole English church under the control of the State had not been lost. This was demonstrated by the subsequent Acts passed during the reign of Anne. However, on the day that the *Schism Act* (1714) was to take effect, which would have resulted in the closure of nonconformist academies and ensured that education could be accessed only by those willing to be versed in the worship of the Church of England, Anne died and George I, of the House of Hanover, succeeded to

19. Davies, *Worship and Theology*, 2:451.

20. This act was opposed by the bishops and put James II on a collision course with Parliament which led to his removal from the throne in 1688.

21. Watts, *Dissenters*, 259.

22. Thompson, *Protestant Dissenting Traditions*, 270.

the throne. Through the swift and astute actions of London nonconformist ministers, favor was won with the new royal court as they publicly prayed for the new king and at the earliest opportunity presented a loyal address to the throne.[23] This, and the fact that George was himself Lutheran and Hanover had no parallel to the arguments between the Church of England and nonconformists, meant that the Act was repealed in 1718 by the *Religious Worship Act*. This did not give liberty to nonconformists in aspects of civil life. The *Corporation Act* (1661) and *Test Act* (1673, revised 1678) remained in force.[24] Attempts to persecute nonconformists did subside over the period as rifts respecting royal succession became apparent in the Church of England. While some in the Church of England accepted the change of monarch, others saw William and Mary as having deposed James II, the rightful monarch according to succession. Matters were particularly acute given the birth of an heir, James Francis Edward, who was raised Catholic and was seen, by some in the Church of England, as the rightful heir to the throne.

With less threat of suppression from the State, nonconformity developed, and specific denominational identities began to take shape with different emphases in doctrine and varying degrees of loyalty to orthodox teaching. In the early part of the eighteenth century although the strands which are now identified by historians as Presbyterian, Independent and Baptist were developing, nonconformist ministers and lay-people met collectively to discuss matters of orthodoxy regarding the free-thinking which became manifest alongside the freedom of religion. A significant debate in these settings in the early eighteenth century was over the doctrine of the Trinity.

The debate over the Trinity was not new within Christianity. In the fourth century Arians had believed that there was a time when Jesus did not exist, specifically before creation.[25] Similarly in the sixteenth century, through the interrogation of Scripture "Socinians denied both the

---

23. Thompson, *Protestant Dissenting Traditions*, 274.

24. These two Acts limited the ability of Catholics and Nonconformists to hold roles of public office without accepting the position of the Church of England in the State. The *Corporation Act* (1661) required a person to receive communion via the rite of Church of England as a precondition of taking up office. The *Test Act* (1662), which was primarily aimed at Catholic recusants, required anyone seeking a position in public office to renounce transubstantiation.

25. Cornick, *Under God's Good Hand*, 90.

pre-existence of Jesus and his divinity."[26] When such antitrinitarian views were voiced in seventeenth century England, they were stifled by provisions in the *Toleration Act* and the passing of a *Blasphemy Act* in 1698. To hold such views remained illegal until 1813 and the passing of the *Doctrine of the Trinity Act*, but there was an openness to discussion in the eighteenth century. The freedom and encouragement to question received wisdom, which was part of the new age of enlightenment, as well as the ability to do so within nonconformity because of its freedom from the State, meant that all Christian teaching was open for dispute through reasoned and/or enlightened interrogation of Scripture. The questioning of the doctrine of the Trinity at this time cannot definitively be argued as an outcome of Enlightenment rationalism, yet it is an example where testing doctrine against Scripture could logically lead to invalidation of the concept that the one God is also three persons where neither the necessary singularity compromises the apparent plurality, or vice versa. The suspicion of the Trinity, especially in its doctrinal form, came from taking *Sola Scriptura* to its logical conclusion, as the teaching of the Trinity is not explicitly articulated in Scripture. When texts questioning the divinity of Christ and doubting the validity of the Trinity found their way into the dissenting academies, the nonconformist education establishments, concerns within nonconformist communities were raised. In Exeter, this led the Assembly of Devon and Cornwall ministers resolving that their trinitarian faith should be expressed by the formula "that there is but one God; and that the Father, Word, and the Holy Spirit, is that One God," to which ministers should subscribe.[27] This was in line with statements within the catechisms drafted by the Westminster Assembly and the Thirty-Nine Articles of the Church of England. However, one of those who was being called out by the Assembly for the unorthodox views in their teaching, James Peirce (1672–1726), refused on the grounds that Scripture was the sole test of faith.[28] Unable to resolve the matter locally, advice was sought from colleagues in London who met at the Salters' Hall. This led to the "Salters' Hall controversy" of 1719 revealing the theological rifts within nonconformity. To subscribe to any credal documentation was, Erik Routley wrote, perceived by some ministers as "an act of treachery to that freedom which [was] enjoyed" because of the previous generations'

---

26. Cornick, *Under God's Good Hand*, 90.
27. Cornick, *Under God's Good Hand*, 91.
28. Cornick, *Under God's Good Hand*, 91.

"grievous and costly fighting."[29] Interestingly, when the London ministers met to vote on whether they should put their signatures to a trinitarian declaration of faith, the prominent subset in the non-subscribers were those who were described as Presbyterian. As more moderate Puritans, freedom, particularly from government and magistrate, had not been part of their early narrative. The Baptist historian John Briggs described Presbyterians as searching for an "intellectually defensible theology."[30] This could in part explain why many of the non-subscribers did not at first refute the doctrine of the Trinity, but "insisted that such matters were to be tested only by the explicit teachings found in scripture."[31] Eventually, through the development of subordinationist views of the Godhead, the doctrinal position was referred to as Arianism, while scientific inquiry and rational speculation found a Unitarian interpretation best served their expression of faith.[32]

This does not fully explain why Presbyterianism in England diminished during the eighteenth century, or why with General Baptist congregations, many Presbyterians evolved to be Unitarian. However, David Cornick, theologian, historian and General Secretary of the United Reformed Church from 2001 to 2008, argued that in combination with the lack of structured church governance as Presbyterianism understood it,[33] learned ministers had a freer hand over the direction a congregation might take because, unlike the ministers in Independent chapels, they were not answerable to the Church Meeting.[34] Interestingly, there is evidence that not all Presbyterian congregations became Unitarian through the leadership of the minister. In Bury St. Edmunds the Meeting House in Churchgate Street, now known as the town's Unitarian Church, was founded by the Reverend Samuel Bury, a Presbyterian, in 1678. Entries in the Church Book of the Independent Meeting House in Whiting Street (now Bury St. Edmunds United Reformed Church) refer to the Meeting House being Presbyterian until the late-eighteenth century.[35] Under the ministry of Evan Johns, there

---

29. Routley, *Congregationalism*, 61.

30. See John Briggs, "The Changing Shape of Nonconformity, 1662–2000," in Pope, *Nonconformity*, 8.

31. See Briggs, "Changing Shape of Nonconformity," 8.

32. Routley, *Congregationalism*, 61; Cornick, *Under God's Good Hand*, 92; see Briggs, "Changing Shape of Nonconformity," 8.

33. Trinitarian Presbyterians remained in the north-east of England and Scotland where structures had been successfully established.

34. Cornick, *Under God's Good Hand*, 93.

35. Grieve and Jones, *Three Hundred Years*, 45–46.

was a shift in the Meeting House towards Unitarianism. This move appears to have not been due to the leadership of the minister, instead led by the congregation. Historian John Duncan wrote that it may have been the case that Johns left because of the tendency of the people.[36] It is argued that Unitarianism was part of the theology of the congregation from its founding under the leadership of Samuel Bury. Unitarian defendants have tried to demonstrate this from Bury's writings. However, E. Lord, in his revision of Alexander Gordon's biography of Samuel Bury, observed from Bury's farewell letter to his congregation in Bristol that he was closer to Richard Baxter's 'middle-way' than to a unitarian faith. Bury wrote, "I never was prostituted to any party, but have endeavored to serve God as a catholic Christian," and in the letter spoke of requirements which had no justification in Scripture as making "apocryphal sins and duties."[37]

The supremacy of logic and reason in religion may have come with the Age of Enlightenment, but the importance of deep spiritual encounters with God should not be negated. Rather, experience as a way to advance an argument became an essential part of evangelism. This was encouraged by the Evangelical Revival, an international movement in the church.[38] Although the notable outcome of the Revival was the establishment of Methodism, the "Old Dissent" experienced effects of the movement.[39] The Evangelical Revival addressed some of the foundational elements of the sixteenth century European Reformation: justification by faith and the centrality of Scripture. The movement did not simply reemphasize these central beliefs, it encapsulated a way in which these beliefs could be experienced and communicated.[40] Historian David Bebbington described these as "conversionism" (the belief that lives needed to be changed) and "activism" (the expression of the gospel in effort).[41] In the existing nonconformist churches this meant the release of new energy within their ministry and mission. The Revival encouraged the growth of "practical" religion, as demonstrated by

---

36. Duncan, "Presbyterians in Bury St. Edmunds," 107.

37. See Alexander Gordon and E. Lord, "Bury Samuel (bap. 1663, d. 1730), Presbyterian Minister," in Cannadine et al., *Oxford Dictionary of National Biography*.

38. Ditchfield, *Evangelical Revival*, 33.

39. The "Old Dissent" includes the Presbyterians, Independents (subsequently referred to as Congregationalists), Baptists, and Quakers.

40. Ditchfield, *Evangelical Revival*, 27.

41. Beddington, *Evangelism*, 16.

Philip Doddridge (1702-51) through his devotional writing and hymns, which impacted the worship particularly of the Independent churches.[42]

Freedom

The nonconformist churches which existed in the eighteenth century were the product of dispute and strongly held convictions rather than the triumph of freedom. Nevertheless, central to the argument that led to their presence in the religious landscape of England was the freedom of worship as conscience dictated. How this was understood and demonstrated in the church changed and developed over the course of the seventeenth and eighteenth centuries. The foundations of thinking related to freedom of worship were set out in the Westminster Assembly's *Confession of Faith* and shown in the format and content of the Westminster Assembly's *Directory for the Public Worship of God* and can be thought of in terms of liberty of conscience and the work of the Holy Spirit. These are not independent of each other: the Holy Spirit is at work in the Christian conscience.

Freedom of Thought and Conscience

Political scientist Edward Andrew wrote that "Christian conscience presents the capacity for choice as the definitive feature of human beings."[43] In the seventeenth century, Andrew observed, this meant an individual had the capacity of moral choice to avoid those sins that would consign a person to damnation. Conscience, therefore, was not just the means of determining what was good and what was evil, it was innately linked to God's judgement.[44] For John Calvin (1509-64), conscience enabled humanity to convict itself of guilt rather than be guided by conscience on ways of sanctification.[45] Calvin wrote:

> To comprehend what conscience is; we must first seek the definition from the derivation of the word. For just as when through the mind and understanding men grasp a knowledge of things, and from this are said "to know," this is the source of the word "knowledge," so also when they have a sense of divine judgement,

---

42. Cornick, *Under God's Good Hand*, 95.
43. Andrew, *Conscience and Its Critics*, 16.
44. Bradbury, "Non-conformist Conscience?," 34.
45. Calvin, *Institutes*, 1.15.2.

as a witness joined to them, which does not allow them to hide their sins from being accused before the Judge's tribunal, this sense is called "conscience." For it is a certain mean between God and man, because it does not allow man to suppress within himself what he knows, but pursues him to the point of convicting him.[46]

Therefore, to have a free conscience was to believe the testimony of the Gospel that through Christ there is the forgiveness of sins and peace because of that knowledge of grace.[47] Consequently, a freedom of conscience was the freedom to follow Christ. For Calvin, such conscience was rooted in divine revelation of Scripture and informed by the discipline of the church and the relationship of the believer with the church.[48] It was the church that formed the Christian conscience through its proclamation of the Word and the councils of the church. The church, Calvin stated, "will have much more weight" in the interpretation of Scripture than the individual alone.[49]

It is upon this premise of Calvin that the Westminster Assembly established a position on "liberty of conscience" in the Westminster Assembly's *Confession of Faith*:

> God alone is Lord of conscience, and hath left it free from the doctrines and commandments of men which are in anything contrary to his Word, or beside it, in matters of faith or worship. . . . And because of the powers which God hath ordained, and the liberty of Christ have purchased, are not intended by God to destroy, but mutually to uphold and preserve one another; they who, upon pretence of Christian liberty, shall oppose any lawful power, or the lawful exercise of it, whether it be civil or ecclesiastical, resist the ordinance of God. And for their publishing of such opinions, or maintaining of such practices, as are contrary to the light of nature, or the known principles of Christianity, whether concerning faith, worship or conversation . . . are destructive to the external peace and order which Christ hath established in the Church; they may lawfully be called to account, and proceeded against by the censures of the Church, and by the power of the civil magistrate.[50]

When compared to the *Savoy Declaration* (1658), although much of what is written about "liberty of conscience" is retained, the accountability to

46. Calvin, *Institutes*, 3.19.15.
47. Zachman, *Assurance of Faith*, 2.
48. Bradbury, "Non-conformist Conscience?," 35.
49. Calvin, *Institutes*, 4.9.13; Bradbury, "Non-conformist Conscience?," 35.
50. England Parliament, *Confession of Faith*, 20.2, 20.4.

the church was removed.⁵¹ The *Savoy Declaration* was based on the Westminster Assembly's *Confession of Faith* and drafted by six divines led by Thomas Goodwin (1600–1680), who was one of the divines who participated in the Westminster Assembly, and John Owen (1616–83), a renown Puritan divine who had been an aide to Oliver Cromwell. However, the Savoy Assembly (which met for approximately 12 days in October 1658 and the declaration being its primary outcome) brought together mainly lay-people from the growing number of Independent churches in England. Therefore, the view of where authority lay in the church and, consequently, how church discipleship should be exercised differed from most of those gathered for the Westminster Assembly. For the Independents, authority was located in the local, gathered congregation of converted and covenanted Christians. This accounts for the difference between the two confessions and why with its declaration, the Savoy Assembly published their own description of church government entitled *Institution of Churches and Order in them appointed by Jesus Christ* (1658). The difference in the place of the church between Presbyterians and Independents can be observed in William Ames's (1576–1633) discourse, *Conscience with the Power and Cases Thereof* (1630, with the first English translation published in 1639). Ames followed Calvin's general train of thought with conscience relating to God's judgement and requiring the illumination of Scripture.⁵² However, Ames discussed the church from the point of view of the believer.⁵³ This understanding was also demonstrated by John Milton (1608–74) who insisted that "no man, synod, session of men, though called the church, can judge definitively the sense of scripture to another man's conscience."⁵⁴

Another change to the perception in conscience was the ascription of it to a natural, moral principal or natural habit, as suggested by Ames.⁵⁵ This can be seen in Ames's discussion of the giving of alms:

> Not only the will of God revealed in the Scriptures doth require this, but also the law of humane nature. For nothing is more natural then that wee should doe so to another, as wee would bee

---

51. Matthews, *Savoy Declaration*, 102–3.
52. Bradbury, "Non-conformist Conscience?," 36.
53. Bradbury, "Non-conformist Conscience?," 37.
54. Andrew, *Conscience and Its Critics*, 54.
55. Ames, *Conscience*, 6.

done to ourselves. And nothing is more humane, than to help the necessity of man.[56]

This individualistic and subjective shift by Ames offers some explanation as to what comes to be a rhetoric for freedom of conscience, particularly amongst Independents, in the later seventeenth century. The political liberty gained in the first Civil War accompanied a narrative in the church which was the liberty to worship and govern itself as it believed was right and fitting for God and the gathered community.[57] Although this view could be argued scripturally, it is far removed from Calvin's understanding of conscience being rooted in Scripture. What comes to be in the Independent churches of the late seventeenth century and eighteenth century is what the church historian Geoffrey Nuttall referred to as the principle of "voluntarism." Voluntarism is the idea that local churches are free gatherings of Christians who covenant with each other to seek the spiritual and moral good of that community and deny the right of government or magistrate to impose religious forms on the people. Although God is understood to be the primary "gatherer" of those people, "their response was a free and voluntary response given with a willing mind."[58] It was not, however, just voluntarism at work; there was also the practice of the requirement that prospective members of a community of believers should be able to demonstrate their conversion and thus also their belonging to the elect.

As the eighteenth century was about to dawn, the nature of the church had significantly changed. John Locke (1632–1704) observed:

> A church appears to me to be a free association of people coming together of their own accord to offer public worship to God in a manner which they believe will be acceptable to the Deity for the salvation of their souls.[59]

From this definition, the church was no longer primarily a divine institution, it was the product of individual consciences gathered together.[60] Those consciences, when influenced by the divine—interpreted from Scripture under the guidance of the Holy Spirit—would have been influenced by

---

56. Ames, *Conscience*, 258.
57. Jordon, "Early Independents and the Visible Church," 303.
58. Nuttall, *Visible Saints*, 108; Bradbury, "Non-conformist Conscience?," 38.
59. Bradbury, "Non-conformist Conscience?," 41.
60. Bradbury, "Non-conformist Conscience?," 41.

morals. These developed from experience and the environment, and would have wanted to see the gathered people living together and flourishing.[61]

Freedom of the Spirit

Of the Holy Spirit, William Dell (1607–69) wrote:

> Where we learn that the things of the Gospel and of the Kingdom of God, are not known at all, nor discerned in the least measure, but by Gods Spirit. Which Spirit is given to all that believe, and this Spirit alone is sufficient, both to enable us to know clearly and certainly the things of God, and also to publish them unto others, and nothing of Man or the Creature can add to it.[62]

Dell made the case that all who are in receipt of the Holy Spirit can be ministers of the Gospel, as foretold by the prophet Joel and in Jesus's instruction to the disciples (plain men of ordinary employment, as Dell described them) to stay in Jerusalem until they receive the Holy Spirit, and then to go and teach.[63] In doing so he emphasized the role of the Holy Spirit in all things, particularly human understanding of and response to God, which is demonstrated in how collectively the church worships. Dell believed, as did others, in the teaching in John's gospel that worship should be in the Spirit, therefore the Holy Spirit was to be understood as having a controlling influence in public worship.[64] Stephen Charnock (1628–80) suggested that it was the Holy Spirit that kindled worship in the heart.[65] Baxter went so far as to say that worship is only sufficient when aided by the Holy Spirit.[66] This widely held view among Puritans was reflected in the shaping of the Westminster Assembly's *Directory for the Public Worship of God*. In practice, how the freedom of the Holy Spirit was interpreted varied and this is demonstrated in the approaches and attitudes taken in regard to the illumination of the Word of God, preaching and prayer in public worship.

---

61. Andrew, *Conscience and its Critics*, 84; Thomas, *In Pursuit*, 346.
62. Dell, *Stumbling-Stone*, 25.
63. Joel 2:28; Luke 24:49; Dell, *Stumbling-Stone*, 24.
64. John 4:24; Dell, *Stumbling-Stone*, 19; Charnock, *Works*, 87.
65. Charnock, *Works*, 69.
66. Baxter, "Christian Ecclesiastics," 17.

Illuminating the Word of God

John Milton's acknowledgment of the importance of the Holy Spirit in understanding Scripture is evident in the formulations of the Westminster Assembly's *Confession of Faith* and later in the *Savoy Declaration*. Both confessions stated the necessity for the inward illumination of the Holy Spirit to understand what is revealed in Scripture as the Word of God.[67] Given the Calvinist base of Puritanism, it is not surprising that this idea followed Calvin's teaching on the Holy Spirit and its witness to the Scriptures in the human heart.[68] The Westminster Assembly's *Confession of Faith* clearly stated a belief in Scripture as the Word of God:

> The authority of the Holy Scripture, for which it ought to be believed, and obeyed, depends not upon the testimony of any man, or Church; but wholly upon God (who is truth itself) the author thereof: and therefore it is to be received, because it is the Word of God.[69]

The *Savoy Declaration*, although not denying this understanding of Scripture, concentrated on affirming the work of the Spirit:

> Our full perswasion and assurance of the infallible Truth and Divine Authority thereof, is from the inward work of the holy Spirit, bearing witness by and with the Word in our heart.[70]

It was the Holy Spirit that inspired the writers of Scripture and enlightened its hearers or readers.[71] For most Puritans at this time, dissociation of the Spirit's action from Scripture in bringing forth the Word of God was impossible. If worship could not be grounded or found to have authority within Scripture it was believed to be "will-worship" and the product of corrupt human invention and idolatrous.[72] Yet, as John Howe (1630–1705) demonstrated it was not inconceivable that in extraordinary circumstances the Spirit could speak without the written word:

> We speak not here of what God can do, but what he doth. Who can doubt but as God can, if he please, imprint on the mind the whole

---

67. England Parliament, *Confession of Faith*, 1.6; Matthews, *Savoy Declaration*, 77.
68. Calvin, *Institutes*, 1.7.4.
69. England Parliament, *Confession of Faith*, 1.6.
70. Matthews, *Savoy Declaration*, 76–77.
71. Nuttall, *Holy Spirit*, 22.
72. Ryrie, *Being Protestant*, 319.

> system of necessary truth, and on the heart the entire frame of holiness, without the help of an external revelation; so he can imprint this particular persuasion also without any outward means? Nor do we speak of what he more rarely doth, but of what he doth ordinarily; or what his more usual course and way of procedure is, in dealing with the spirits of men. The supreme power binds not its own hands. We may be sure, the inward testimony of the Spirit never is opposite to the outward testimony of his gospel (which is the Spirit's testimony also); and therefore it never says to an unholy man, an enemy to God, thou art in a reconciled and pardoned state. But we cannot be sure he never speaks or suggests things to the spirits of men but by the external testimony so as to make use of that as the means of informing them with what he hath to impart; nay, we know he sometimes hath imparted things (as to prophets and the sacred pen-men) without any external means, and (no doubt) excited suitable affections in them, to the import of the things imparted and made known.[73]

This strong doctrine of the Holy Spirit did not mean that moderate Puritans, those who are now described as Presbyterians or Independents, dissociated Spirit and Scripture; the Spirit always spoke according to Scripture or "upon some scriptural consideration."[74] This is shown by what Howe went on to say:

> Nor do I believe it can ever be proved, that he never doth immediately testify his own special love to holy souls without the intervention of some part of his external word, made use of as a present instrument to that purpose, or that he always doth it, in the way of methodical reasoning there from.[75]

Over the two centuries, as nonconformity established itself, understanding developed of the Holy Spirit's freedom to illuminate the Word of God in Scripture and away from. This is shown in the confession of faith written for the Independent Meeting House in Bury St. Edmunds in 1655 which stated:

> We does believe yt the holy spirit of God dwelleth in all the children of God, to teach, leade and guide them in ye way everlasting, to leade them into all truth.[76]

---

73. Howe, "Delighting in God," 64.
74. Nuttall, *Holy Spirit*, 33.
75. Howe, "Delighting in God," 64.
76. Bury St. Edmunds Independent Church, *Church Book*, "Confession of Faith, 1655."

This was a perspective shared by more radical Puritans. Nuttall wrote:

> In his farewell address, John Robinson is reported to have said, "The Lord has more truth and light yet to break forth out of his holy word"; and those who looked eagerly for more light were in some cases prepared to look for it not only out of but without "his holy word." Oliver Cromwell, for instance, a keen believer in "more light," says, God "speaks without the written word sometimes, yet according to it."[77]

In corporate worship this was most prominently observed through the development of preaching as exposition and application of the Word and in how the sermon became established as the central part of the service.

Preaching

The Westminster Assembly's *Confession of Faith* and the *Savoy Declaration* made the reading of Scripture, preaching and the hearing of God's Word equally important in public worship.[78] Although these statements could be understood as God's Word being heard separately through the ordinances of reading Scripture and preaching, it was through these ordinances together that God's Word was heard. This came from an emphasis on how the communication of God with humanity was oral. In time, though, the reading of Scripture for hearing God's Word became less important than preaching. Historian Arnold Hunt argued that this was because of the culture of the late sixteenth century, where the voice was associated "with self-presence, truth, authenticity and an immediate and transparent movement of meaning" which was not found in the written word even when spoken aloud.[79] A reason for this can be found in the works of Thomas Goodwin (1600–1680). Goodwin suggested that Scripture expounded rather than read was preferable. His argument was based on the general lack of understanding by the people of what they heard in the Scriptures as demonstrated by Philip's encounter with the eunuch, the inference that the gift of the Holy Spirit when Jesus ascended meant the gift of preaching, and the concept that preaching reveals the spiritual meaning of God's Word.[80] This

---

77. Nuttall, *Holy Spirit*, 24.

78. England Parliament, *Confession of Faith*, 21.5; Matthews, *Savoy Declaration*, 104–5.

79. Hunt, *Art of Hearing*, 21.

80. Goodwin, *Works*, 363–64. The story of Philip and the eunuch is in Acts 8:26–39, and the gift of preaching discussed in Acts 2:6–9 and Col 3:12–17.

change from the Word of God in Scripture and proclaimed to solely be the Word of God through preaching meant the perception of means of grace altered: salvation came from the Word of God preached.[81] From this interpretation of the apostle Paul's theology came the belief that the preaching of God's Word was the great ordinance that could not be neglected in worship. Faith came through hearing and the ordinance of preaching was the means by which spiritual good could be conveyed to those who attended to what was spoken.[82] Hunt developed this argument by demonstrating how the early modern sermon was more an aural than an oral phenomenon.[83] The sermon was not an act of speaking, rather an act of hearing due to the importance of the response of the audience, which followed Calvin's view of the sermons being God speaking through the mouths of the preacher.[84] This was an argument many Puritans also made in their theological works.

The Westminster Assembly's *Directory for the Public Worship of God* recommended to the minister that, if it was deemed necessary, the expounding of Scripture should occur after the reading of Scripture was ended and not to be made an essential part of the sermon. At the heart of the sermon there was to be doctrine and its application to edify the heart in what God's Word was teaching so that all who heard might be saved.[85] This occurring in corporate worship is demonstrated in the diary of Peter Walkden, who wrote that on the 11th March 1733:

> Went into Chappel, and prayed, and read ye 90th psalm and part of ye 15th of ye 1st to Corinthians, and Annalized on it, then we sang 5 verses of ye 90th psalm, and I prayed, then preached Richd Parkers funeral, from ye 73rd psalm 25th and 26th verses.[86]

Similarly, on the 18th March 1733, Walkden wrote:

> Being come to chapel, I went in and prayed for a Blessing and read a psalm, and 12th of ye 2nd to Corinths and Annalized on a few verses: then we sang part of a psalm, and I prayed, then preached, from ye 2nd to Corinths 13th 5th Know ye nor your own selves.[87]

---

81. Hambrick-Stowe, "Practical Divinity and Spirituality," 195; Hunt, *Art of Hearing*, 21; Nichols, *Corporate Worship*, 101–2.
82. Burroughs, *Gospel-Worship*, 201–2.
83. Hunt, *Art of Hearing*, 59.
84. DeVries, "Calvin's Preaching," 109; Selderhuis, *Calvin Handbook*, 412.
85. Scotland Parliament, *Directory of Publick Worship*, 33–39.
86. Walkden, *Diary*, 56.
87. Walkden, *Diary*, 63.

This separation of exegesis from the main sermon established the concept of a double sermon and merged two traditions. The first tradition was that of the European Reformers and the expounding of chapters of Scripture, which can be traced back to the Patristic Age and possibly even to the synagogue.[88] The second was the preaching order of the High Middle Ages where texts were analytically divided and applied to different doctrinal and moral questions.[89] It is not clear how and why this double sermon concept came to be but it is reminiscent of the method detailed in the preaching manual of William Perkins (1558–1602), *The Arte of Prophesying* (1592). Scholars have shown that *The Arte of Prophesying* was influential in the method of preaching until at least the 1660s and possibly beyond.[90] Perkins's method described a pattern based on Scripture-doctrine-application whilst making public prayer a key part of the experience. Preaching for Perkins had to come from the heart, hence the importance of prayer and an insistence that sermons should be extempore.[91]

The extempore sermon gave some concern in the mid-to-late-seventeenth century as what began to count was the earnest dependence on the Holy Spirit rather than education.[92] This was, in part, out of response to the discouragement of the reading of homilies in the church, which subsequently led to the development in some preachers of "an allergy to reading [one's] own sermons."[93] Richard Baxter (1615–91) in his pamphlet *One Sheet for the Ministry against the Malignants of All Sorts* (1657) responded to the accusation "you read your sermons out of paper; therefore have not the Spirit," thus:

> A strong Argument! I pray you take seven years time to prove the consequence. As wisely do the Quakers argue, that because we use spectacles, or hour-glasses and Pulpits, we have not the Spirit. It is not want of your abilities that makes Ministers use Notes: but it's a regard to the work and good of the hearers. I use notes as much as any man, when I take pains: and as little as any man when I am lazy, or busie, and have not leisure to prepare. It's easier to us to preach three Sermons without Notes, then one with them. He is a simple preacher that is not able to preach all day without

88. Old, *Reading and Preaching*, 5:29.
89. Old, *Reading and Preaching*, 5:29.
90. Schaeffer, "Topical Latitude," 457; Appleby, *Black Bartholomew Day*, 63.
91. Perkins, *Art of Prophesying*, 67.
92. Nuttall, *Holy Spirit*, 101.
93. van Dixhoorn, *God's Ambassadors*, 168.

preparation, if his strength would serve: especially if he preach at your rates.[94]

Sermons led by the Holy Spirit were not sermons that were not learned or without preparation. Theologian and historian Chad van Dixhoorn observed that the preaching of a solid sermon in the eyes of the Westminster Divines required "a commitment to prayerful dependence on the Spirit who would, in turn, bless the preacher's work at his writing desk and preaching desk—whatever his method of delivery."[95]

John Howe (1630–1705) and Matthew Henry (1662–1714) both championed systematic doctrinal preaching to teach the congregation.[96] Howe's argument was based on the concept that God's very nature was that of teacher so making teaching the essence of apostolic ministry. The commentator Hughes Oliphant Old summarized Howe's thinking as meaning "learning of God and his ways [was] an important dimension of the service God [had] asked of his people."[97] This was rooted in the general ideas that were developing in the academy of the rational nature of human beings, reason, and logic. Howe developed the thought that if human beings were by nature thinking creatures, this was even more true of God if humanity was created in the image of God.[98] It was in his doctrine of regeneration, which was based on his understanding of Johannine Wisdom theology, that Howe made the distinct connection between teaching and worship.

> Christian worship takes place when we are regenerated, and as children of God reflect the nature of our Father. This glorifies God. When the divine truth is both proclaimed and received by God's people, then God is glorified.[99]

Learned and doctrinal preaching did not mean that sermons could not be extempore. The Holy Spirit still needed the freedom to act on both the heart of the preacher and the hearer. This became more evident in the approach taken to preaching in the eighteenth century as science and religion were allied in the age of reason and logic. Not all doctrine in the Christian faith could be argued through reason and logic. John Jennings

---

94. Baxter, *Ministry against the Malignants*, 13–14.
95. van Dixhoorn, *God's Ambassadors*, 169.
96. Old, *Reading and Preaching*, 5:14, 34.
97. Old, *Reading and Preaching*, 5:15.
98. Gen 1:27.
99. Old, *Reading and Preaching*, 5:15.

(1687–1723), in his discourses on preaching, suggested that in maintaining a regard for Christ, divine revelation remained possible.[100] Both Jennings and Isaac Watts (1674–1748) concluded that this revelation was the work of the Holy Spirit. Graham Beynon, in his commentary on reason and passion in the theology of Watts, stated that Watts "believed that the use of reason and the work of the Spirit went hand in hand," and so dependence on the Holy Spirit was essential for preaching.[101] Regarding the preparation and composing of a sermon, Watts wrote:

> Seek the direction and assistance of the Spirit of God, for inclining your thoughts to proper subjects, for guiding you to proper scriptures, and framing your whole sermon both as to the matter and manner, that it may attain the divine and sacred ends proposed.[102]

Philip Doddridge (1702–51) also supported this view. Preaching, with the aid of the Holy Spirit, was the means by which God awakened people's hearts and consciences.[103] To allow for clear, well-reasoned sermons that engaged and taught congregations, preachers had to prepare as instructed in the Westminster Assembly's *Directory for the Public Worship of God*. Also, it was argued that notes should be followed despite the leaning in nonconformist churches toward extempore sermons. Jennings noted that the preacher's notes would always be imperfect, yet it was the Holy Spirit that would make them applicable to the hearer.[104] Similarly, Watts relied "on the Spirit for effective preaching that [would] reach the heart."[105] Watts recommended, therefore, the preparation of headings but speaking extempore, to inform and arouse the "listeners for the spiritual good."[106] Doddridge encouraged his students to preach from notes which were more than just a set of brief notes, whilst discouraging them from using fully prepared text.[107] In using detailed notes, Doddridge counselled his students to master them before delivering the sermon:

---

100. Rivers, *Reason, Grace, and Sentiment*, 1:186.
101. Beynon, *Isaac Watts*, 133.
102. Watts, "Humble Attempt," 595.
103. Clifford, *Good Doctor*, 159.
104. Jennings, "Two Discourses," 65.
105. Beynon, *Isaac Watts*, 138.
106. Beynon, *Isaac Watts*, 130.
107. Deconinck-Brossard, "Art of Preaching," 121.

Write your notes neatly and distinctly—Rule your paper, with a large margin—Let the heads be written apart, and the enlargement divided into various paragraphs, and each distinct sentence properly pointed, if in long hand—Let the scriptures be referred to in the margin, which will give an opportunity of recollecting much of the discourse, by a transient view,—especially if you write . . . not only those you professedly design to quote, but others whose phrases you borrow, or to which you only allude. Read over your notes attentively once or more, to fix your sermon in your memory, and to prevent the shame of frequently hesitating.[108]

Prayer

By the eighteenth century, the focal point of corporate worship in nonconformity had become the sermon, with all other aspects of worship building up to it.[109] This did not mean that prayer was thought insignificant. Matthew Henry (1662–1714) described prayer as being a principal part of religious worship as it was the means for solemn and devout offerings to God that both acknowledge God's glory and share the desire that God may bless.[110] The significant role of prayer was evident in the liturgies of the established church from which nonconformists distanced themselves, as well as in the Westminster Assembly's *Directory for the Public Worship of God*. In the *Directory for the Public Worship of God* prayer was a means of preparation and response for the congregation.

Prayer was not confined to corporate worship; it was perceived to be an important part of the Christian life as a whole. This led to a number of manuals on prayer being written that encouraged personal, as well as public or corporate prayer. These included *A Method for Prayer* (1710) by Henry and *A Guide to Prayer* (1715) by Watts. The importance of personal prayer was deduced from Scripture. Watts wrote:

> Prayer is a part of divine worship that is required of all men. . . . It is commanded to single persons in their private retirements . . . and, in the midst of the businesses of life. . . . It belongs also to the communities of men, whether they be natural, as families, or civil, as corporations, parliaments, courts, or societies for trade and business; and to religious communities, as when persons meet

---

108. Doddridge, *Works*, 5:465.
109. Watson, *English Hymn*, 55.
110. Henry, "Method of Prayer," 143.

> on any pious design, they should seek their God in the house of prayer.[111]

Henry shared this perspective. He wrote that prayer must

> run through the web of the whole Christian life; we must be frequently addressing ourselves to God in short and sudden ejaculations, by which we must keep up our communion with God in providences and common actions, as well as in ordinances and religious services.[112]

Therefore, along with the frequent reading of Scripture, prayer was encouraged in nonconformity to be a regular practice of both families and individuals to sustain their communion with God. Doddridge urged those whom he taught to carefully put time aside for private devotion and "make a serious business of secret and family prayer."[113] Watts urged Christians to pray always.[114] It was within this wider context that nonconformist divines of the eighteenth century discussed the content and practice of prayer.

The importance of prayer in corporate worship may not have differed much between the established and nonconformist churches, but the method adopted while praying did. By the beginning of the eighteenth century, extempore prayer was the accepted and most popular method of prayer in nonconformist worship.[115] This was a shift from what would have been the experience of prayer in corporate worship in the mid-seventeenth century, where there would have been a mixture of set forms of prayers read or recited alongside extempore prayer.[116] This is demonstrated from within the pages of the Westminster Assembly's *Directory for the Public Worship of God* where ministers were encouraged to pray in such a way that would stir up the congregation's emotions to compel evidence of the Holy Spirit and of God's grace:

> The minister who is to preach, is to endeavour to get his own and his hearers hearts to be rightly affected with their sins, that they,

---

111. Watts, *Guide to Prayer*, 10.
112. Henry, "Method of Prayer," 143.
113. Doddridge, *Works*, 5:467.
114. Watts, *Guide to Prayer*, 148.
115. Branch, *Rituals of Spontaneity*, 40.
116. Ryrie, *Being Protestants*, 214–15.

> may all mourn in sense thereof before the Lord, and hunger and thirst after the grace of God in Jesus Christ.[117]

> All which he is to endeavour to perform with suitable affections, answerable to such as holy action, and to stir up the like in the people.[118]

The *Book of Common Prayer* was perceived to stifle genuine, emotional responses and did not let the matters of the heart be brought before and be inspired by God.[119] This was true, literature scholar Lori Branch suggested, for all liturgical prayer. True prayer was that which had an "emotional authenticity and sincerity" only testified to in "spontaneous, unwritten and unpremeditated verbal prayer."[120] Watts wrote:

> The thoughts and affections of the heart that are truly pious and sincere, are wrought in us by the Spirit of God; and, if we deny them utterance, because they are not found in Prayer-books, we run the danger of resisting the Holy Ghost, quenching the Holy Spirit, and fighting again the kind designs of God towards us.[121]

Extempore or spontaneous prayer was, for the nonconformist divines of the seventeenth and eighteenth century, only true prayer when spoken through the power of the Holy Spirit. Jeremiah Burroughs (1600–1646) wrote:

> Thus God's name will be sanctified when we put forth the graces of the Spirit in us and the Spirit comes and helps. And what comes from us now comes from the breathing of the Holy Spirit in us, and then God, who knows the meaning of the Spirit, will know the meaning of our sins and groans. Therefore, when you are going to prayer, you are to eye the Spirit of God. You are, by the eye of faith, to look upon the Spirit of God and to cast your soul upon the assistance of the Spirit of God. You are to look upon the Holy Ghost as appointed by the Father and the Son to that office to be a helper to His poor servants in the duties of worship, and especially in that great duty of prayer.[122]

---

117. Scotland Parliament, *Directory for Publick Worship*, 25.
118. Scotland Parliament, *Directory for Publick Worship*, 50.
119. Branch, *Rituals of Spontaneity*, 46.
120. Branch, *Rituals of Spontaneity*, 43.
121. Watts, *Guide to Prayer*, 43.
122. Burroughs, *Gospel-Worship*, 388–89.

In a discourse on Romans 7:26 and the nature of prayer, John Owen (1616-83) spoke in very similar terms. He expressed the view that humanity could not pray as it ought without the assistance of the Holy Spirit.[123] Owen acknowledged that Scripture had its part in what was prayed, but it was only the Holy Spirit that could turn those words into prayer:

> It is true, that whatever we ought to pray for is declared in the Scripture . . . but it is one thing to have what we ought to pray for in the book, another thing to have it in our minds and hearts,—without which it will never be unto us the due matter of prayer. It is out of the "abundance of the heart" that the mouth must speak in this matter, Matt. xii. 34. There is, therefore, in us a threefold defect with respect unto the matter of prayer, which is supplied by the Holy Spirit, and can be so no other way nor by any other means; and therein is he unto us a Spirit of supplication according to promise. For,—1. We know not our own wants; 2. We know not the plies of them that are expressed in the promises of God; and, 3. We know not the end whereunto what we pray for is to be directed, which I add unto the former. Without the knowledge and understanding of all these, no man can pray as he ought; and we can no way know them but by the aid and assistance of the Spirit of grace. And if these things be manifest, it will be evident how in this first instance we are enabled to pray by the Holy Ghost.[124]

These sentiments were reiterated by Doddridge when he reminded his students it was not the words of others but the office of the Holy Spirit that would help them pray:

> Engage in it . . . in dependence upon [the Spirit of God]; and maintain a continual dependence on the intercession and influence of Christ.[125]

Interestingly, Watts cautioned against over and under relying on the Holy Spirit:

> It is evident . . . that there is such a thing as the assistance of the Spirit of God in the work of prayer; but how far this assistance extends, is a farther subject of enquiry; and it is very necessary to have a just notion of the nature and bounds of this divine influence,

---

123. Owen, *Pneumatologia*, 646.
124. Owen, *Pneumatologia*, 646–47.
125. Doddridge, *Works*, 5:468.

that we may not expect more than God has promised, nor sit down negligently contented, without such degrees as may be attained.[126]

From his study of Scripture, he believed that the Holy Spirit assisted in particular ways encouraging and enabling prayer but was not the sole source of a person's prayers. He wrote in his *Guide to Prayer*:

> In our prayers, the Spirit of God leaves us a great deal to ourselves, to mingle many weaknesses and defects with our duties, in the matter, and in the manner, and in the words; so that we cannot say of one whole sentence, that it is the perfect or the pure work of the Spirit of God.[127]

This did not mean that Watts believed that the Holy Spirit did not provide an individual with the matter and method of prayer.[128] Neither did he believe that at times the Holy Spirit did not provide apt and proper expression.[129] But more often the work of the Holy Spirit in prayer was more subtle: enabling understanding, judgement, confidence, blessing diligence in study, meditation, and attempts at prayer while inclining the heart to pray.[130]

When it came to corporate prayer, both Doddridge and Watts championed conceived rather than extempore prayer. Extempore prayer, as Watts and Doddridge defined it, was observed as prayer without forethought or consideration to matter and expression. Conceived prayer came from consideration and meditation on issues prior to the time of prayer, although no prayer was committed to paper such that it was repeated.[131] This was not a new concept, something very similar had been called for by Philip Nye (1595-1672) in the discussion of the *Directory for the Public Worship of God* at the Westminster Assembly. Conceived or studied prayer did not eliminate the work of the Holy Spirit or the passion that the Puritans believed the Holy Spirit gave to extempore prayer.[132] In Watts's and Doddridge's approach there was a refinement which encapsulated the logic and reason of the Enlightenment movement. A more reasoned approach to

126. Watts, *Guide to Prayer*, 148.
127. Watts, *Guide to Prayer*, 150.
128. Watts, *Guide to Prayer*, 153.
129. Watts, *Guide to Prayer*, 154.
130. Watts, *Guide to Prayer*, 150-51.
131. Beynon, *Isaac Watts*, 176-77.
132. Beynon, *Isaac Watts*, 181.

corporate prayer ensured that those gathered could understand and follow what was being prayed. Lengthy and obscure sentences were avoided and natural connection between petitions attempted to ensure a flowing transition.[133] Henry and Doddridge also encouraged the use of Scripture within prayer. It was believed by both that it aided expression and took away the unexpected, which was one of the concerns over extempore prayer. Doddridge wrote:

> Use many scripture expressions in prayer. They are peculiarly affecting and very proper; and the hearers also from the beginning of them will know what they are to expect; and thus one great objection against extempore prayer will be removed.[134]

The evidence shows that prayer was believed to be influenced by the Holy Spirit, but reliance should be restrained. The Holy Spirit would assist; but extempore prayer did not mean that the content and expression of prayers came solely from the Holy Spirit. Extempore prayer was, for the Puritans, as much about passion and freedom of expression as the work of the Holy Spirit, and this was a view that was maintained into the eighteenth century. In addition, Scripture, Henry observed, describes prayer as a drawing near to God, the lifting up of souls and the pouring out of hearts.[135] Therefore, in public prayer at least, with reference to Scripture, a more reasoned, informed, and prepared approach was favored to aid all that were gathered in worship.

Order

The freedom to worship as one's conscience dictated or in response to the Holy Spirit did not mean that worship was without order. There was a distrust in fixed liturgy and the over reliance on written material, but this did not prevent corporate worship taking an implicit liturgical order. This was centered on the Word of God, originating from the European Reformation's emphasis on the authority of Scripture and the need for the church to reform its worship in its light. By the eighteenth century when nonconformist Meeting Houses were being established, a typical order for

---

133. Doddridge, *Works*, 5:469; Beynon, *Isaac Watts*, 178.
134. Doddridge, *Works*, 5:470.
135. Henry, "Method of Prayer," 143.

a morning service on the Lord's Day, as recorded in an entry for 1723 in the Church Book of Bury Street Meeting House, St. Mary Axe, was:

> Begin with singing a psalm, then a short prayer follows to desire the Divine Presence in all the following parts of worship; after that, about half an hour is spent in the exposition of some portion of scripture, which is succeeded by singing a psalm or hymn. After this the minister prays more at large, for all variety of blessings, spiritual and temporal, for the whole congregation, with confession of sins, and thanksgiving for mercies; petitions also are offered up for the whole world, for the churches of Christ, for the nation in which we dwell, for all our rulers and governors, together with any particular cases which are represented. Then a sermon is preached, and the . . . worship is concluded with a short prayer and the benediction.[136]

This basic order is also shown to have been used in meetings other than Sunday worship. Jonathan Adams, minister of Scotts Lane Independent Chapel, Salisbury, recorded in his diary of 1784 that at a ministers' meeting the order their worship together took was a prayer and reading, followed by intercessory prayer and a sermon, and concluded with another prayer.[137]

What came to be the pattern of worship in nonconformist Meeting Houses, although influenced by the sixteenth century European Reformation, had its roots in some of the Puritan debates of the seventeenth century. Nonconformist ministers did not dismiss all liturgical material, and some of the early nonconformist ministers would have been well versed in the *Book of Common Prayer*. Yet, the orders recorded in the church records of Bury Street Church and the diary of Jonathan Adams are consistent with the directory authored by the Westminster Divines as they looked to reshape the English church. Given the publication of the *Directory for the Public Worship of God* during the first English Civil War, and the fact that it was never enforced by Parliament in the way that the *Book of Common Prayer* was, there is little evidence to suggest that it was widely adopted. Nevertheless, what was achieved in the *Directory for the Public Worship of God* has had a long-lasting influence on nonconformist worship, as well as being the standard from which worship in Presbyterian churches developed.

---

136. Anonymous, "Bury Street Church Records," 334; Cornick, *Under God's Good Hand*, 85.

137. Adams, *Diary*, March 17, 1784.

The Westminster Assembly's Directory for the Public Worship of God (1644)

The breadth within Puritanism in England meant that there was a broad spectrum of views on how public worship should be conducted. Although there was agreement that it should be based on Scripture and ruled by the Word of God, its form was a matter of debate. At one end of the scale there were those who conceived pure worship as definable by a prayer book. At the other end, there were those who understood worship as Spirit-inspired and therefore more spontaneous.[138] Consequently, when official reform of the English church began in the Westminster Assembly, a substantial part of the divines' work was the determination of how a uniform approach to public worship could be achieved across a diverse church. The Westminster Assembly, having identified the church in England and Scotland as reformed, saw its main concern as defining church governance and corporate worship.[139] Throughout the meetings of the Westminster Assembly in 1644, following the work of a small sub-committee,[140] the *Directory for the Public Worship of God* was drafted as a liturgical standard for the church. Some heralded the achievement as a triumph because it conceived a "mode of worship compatible with the Word of God," whilst others believed it "burdensome at best, and repugnant to scripture at worst."[141] It demonstrated "how reform of liturgy could be profoundly unitive because it was faithfully Biblical."[142] Yet, the *Directory for the Public Worship of God* was a book of compromise, going too far for some and not far enough for others in its instruction of the worship of the church. Robert Baillie (1602–62) one of the Scottish commissioners to the Westminster Assembly, in a report on discussions of the preface to the *Directory for the Public Worship of God*, demonstrated the breadth of views on its purpose:

> One party purposing by the preface to turn the Directorie to a straight Liturgie; the other to make it so loose and free, that it

---

138. Davies, *English Puritans*, 127; McNally, "Westminster Directory," 8.

139. Warfield, *Westminster Assembly*, 16.

140. The sub-committee consisted of Stephen Marshall (1584–1655) (chair), Herbert Palmer (1601–47), Thomas Goodwin (1600–1680), Thomas Young (1587–1655), Charles Herle (1598–1659), and the Scottish Commissioners (Davies, *English Puritans*, 128). Goodwin was the only member of the committee who could have been described as being on the independent end of the Puritan spectrum.

141. McNally, "Westminster Directory," 1.

142. Breward, *Westminster Directory*, 3.

should serve for little use: but God helped us to get both these rocks eschewed.[143]

The shared conviction of the Westminster Assembly was that the "acceptable way of worshipping the true God is instituted by himself, and so limited by his own revealed will, that he may not be worshipped according to the imaginations and devices of men, or the suggestion of Satan, under any visible representation or any other way not prescribed in the Holy Scriptures."[144] Although this was a response primarily made to the liturgy of the Roman Catholic Church, it also sets out why the Puritans sought to remove the formal ritual of the *Book of Common Prayer* and therefore this from the worship of the English church. In addition, the constraints of set prayers were believed to be devices that made and increased "an idle and unedifying ministry," suppressing the exercise of the gift of prayer given by Christ to those called to the office of minister.[145] George Gillespie (1613–48), another of the Scottish Commissioners to the Westminster Assembly, raised the point that "a man does better to stir up his own gifts than use set forms."[146]

To ensure that worship was sound in doctrine and prayer, and uniform across the church, ministers at least needed to be directed in the administration of the ordinances required of the church by God. Therefore, what was aimed for was a rubric that took the "merits of a prayer book without its attendant disadvantages."[147] The *Directory for the Public Worship of God* was intended to be scriptural, comprehensive and, most importantly, orderly. What the Westminster Divines achieved was an order of directives, some of which were suggestions, while others were commands: the minister "may do" something at times and then at other times "shall do." Chad van Dixhoorn and David Wright, in their transcription of the minutes of the Westminster Assembly, noted that "practices are variously termed 'necessary' or 'requisite,' but also 'expedient,' 'convenient' or 'sufficient.'"[148] There was also terminology such as "is to," "to this effect" and "shall judge it necessary." The "shall do" elements were related to the general order, the

---

143. Baillie, *Letters and Journals*, 242.
144. England Parliament, *Confession of Faith*, 21.1.
145. Scotland Parliament, *Directory for Publick Worship*, 18; Davies, *English Puritans*, 128.
146. Westminster Assembly, *Minutes and Papers*, 3:438.
147. Davies, *English Puritans*, 129.
148. Westminster Assembly, *Minutes and Papers*, 1:28.

practice of reading Scripture and the aspects of the administration of the sacraments. For example, when baptizing a child, the *Directory for the Public Worship of God* stated that the minister was to say, "I baptize thee in the name of the Father, and of the Son and of the Holy Ghost."[149] The "may do" elements related primarily to content. Where prayers were given, they were accompanied with the direction "to this effect." This suggested that the minister had a freedom of choice over the words used as long as the prayer kept to the purpose described. The expounding of Scriptures away from the preaching of the Word was also at the discretion of the minister, although the Westminster Divines did recommend the choice to do so should not be taken without regard to the rest of worship:

> When the minister who readeth shall judge it necessary to expound any part of what is read, let it not be done until the whole chapter or psalm be ended; and regard is always to be had unto the time, that neither preaching, nor other ordinances be straitened, or rendered tedious.[150]

The *Directory for the Public Worship of God* may have felt like a compromise for the Westminster Divines, not offering an act of corporate worship any of divines could own as fully representative of their position on worship and its practices. It provided a middle way: the combination "of spontaneity of free prayer with the advantages of an ordered context or framework for worship."[151] It avoided, as Horton Davies wrote, the "deadening effect of reiterated liturgy as also the pitfall of extempore prayer—the disorderly meanderings of the minister."[152] It also allowed for prayers that were not only extempore. Philip Nye (1595–1672), in the discussion over the content of the *Directory for the Public Worship of God*, argued the case for "conceived" or, as he called them, "studied" prayers:

> I plead for neither, but for studied prayers. Those are either such as are made once for all as some men, others attend to suite their prayers to occasions, but studied and premeditated. If you speake nothing here in way of prevention, I know noe reason if any man thinke upon a studied forme. I should advise such men rather take of[f] this than any of[f] their owne.[153]

---

149. Scotland Parliament, *Directory for Publick Worship*, 45.
150. Scotland Parliament, *Directory for Publick Worship*, 24.
151. Davies, *English Puritans*, 141.
152. Davies, *English Puritans*, 141.
153. Westminster Assembly, *Minutes and Papers*, 3:438.

This put the *Directory for the Public Worship of God* in the lineage of Geneva and the Calvinist liturgies by recognizing that the church was not claiming the liberty to worship God as it pleased, rather to worship God according to how God desired to be worshipped as revealed in Scripture.[154]

Participation

Puritan worship was "above all to be worship of the congregation, and therefore in the mother tongue and in contemporary language."[155] This reform of the worship of the church, which began in the sixteenth century with the European Reformers, was one that the Puritans ensured would be the case in the English church and beyond: "the right of common people to join in the praise of God."[156] The vernacular not only permitted a congregation to utter words of praise that might glorify God, it allowed them to be fully part of the communion with God that worship intends while enabling the congregation to make responses to God. This in turn solidified the concept of nonconformist churches being communions of saints who tried to make the true church of Christ visible in the world.

Communion with God and of the Saints

In the late sixteenth century and early seventeenth century, one of the areas the Puritans were at odds over was the nature of the true church. Those who were deeply rooted in the theology of John Calvin stated:

> Because a small and contemptible number are hidden in a huge multitude and a few grains of wheat are covered by a pile of chaff, we must leave to God alone the knowledge of his church, whose foundation is his secret election. It is not sufficient, indeed, for us to comprehend in mind and thought the multitude of the elect.[157]

Essentially, this made the true church invisible. Nevertheless, through the visible church the true church could be made manifest particularly where the Word of God was "purely preached and heard and the sacraments

---

154. Davies, *English Puritans*, 141–42.
155. Wakefield, *Puritan Devotion*, 64–65.
156. Davies, *English Puritans*, 162.
157. Calvin, *Institutes*, 4.1.2.

administered according to Christ's institution."[158] This meant that, for Calvin, salvation could not occur outside the visible church, but being a member of the visible church did not automatically mean one was saved. However, logically some among the elect might well be part of the visible church if the sovereignty of God is upheld fully, as Calvin would insist.[159] But there were those Puritans who saw the true church as being visible. This meant the church had to be separate from the world, governed only by Christ, the true head of the church. The tensions these different perspectives caused were primarily about governance and discipline within the church, not worship. Yet full participation in worship came from the understanding of being the church of God.

The middle ground achieved by the Westminster Assembly was:

> Saints, by profession, are bound to maintain an holy fellowship and communion in the worship of God, and in performing such other spiritual services as tend to their mutual edification; as also in relieving each other in outward things, according to their several abilities and necessities. Which communion, as God offereth opportunity, is to be extended unto all those who in every place call upon the name of Jesus Christ.[160]

The church as a communion of professed saints, those who demonstrated they were converted and properly belonged to the elect, was one that was visible and therefore bound to one another. In nonconformity, particularly in the Independent and then Congregational churches, this was underwritten by individuals covenanting to a way of being the church together in a particular place. Importantly, entering into such a covenant by individuals was voluntary, although it required new members to convince the church meeting that they were fully converted. This is key to why the communion of saints in this setting was understood as the true church visible. Historian Dorothea Jordon suggested that the word "voluntary" was understood in terms of religious liberty or freedom.[161] Religious freedom was initially understood in terms of knowledge of oneself being bound within the knowledge and judgement of God. Therefore, that communion with the saints related to being in communion with God, which in part was seen as an aim of worship. The concept of local congregations being governed by local

---

158. Calvin, *Institutes*, 4.1.9.
159. Bradbury, *Perpetually Reforming*, 42.
160. England Parliament, *Confession of Faith*, 26.2.
161. Jordon, "Early Independents and the Visible Church," 262.

covenants was not envisioned by the Westminster Divines for the English church. To be a part of a local congregation, an individual was to make a profession of faith. Discipline of that congregation, however, was governed by a scheme for the whole national church with reference to what should happen in local congregations.[162]

John Owen (1616–83), when addressing the role of the Holy Spirit in public worship in his sermon on Ephesians 2:18, tied together the communion of saints and the communion with God in worship by means of the Holy Spirit. Owen in the *Nature and Beauty of Gospel Worship* reiterated how the Holy Spirit illuminates Scripture, assists and gives the necessary gifts for prayer and preaching.[163] This is not all that the Holy Spirit does in public worship. According to Owen, "whenever the church gathers for worship, there the Spirit meets her and ushers her into the Father's presence through the Son."[164] Owen highlighted the "church gathered" because in Ephesians 2:21–22 this was the apostle Paul's message to the church in Ephesus: through Christ the church is built into the spiritual dwelling place of God.[165] Owen does not dismiss God's presence with the individual, but as David Clarkson (1622–86), a contemporary and colleague of Owen, wrote:

> You will say, Is not the Lord present with his servants when they worship him in private? It is true; but so much of his presence is not vouchsafed, nor ordinarily enjoyed, in private as in public. If the experience of any find it otherwise, they have cause to fear the Lord is angry, they have given him some distaste, some offence; if they find him not most, where ordinarily he is most to be found, and this is in public ordinances, for the Lord is most there where he is most engaged to be, but he has engaged himself to be most there where most of his people are. The Lord has engaged to be with every particular saint, but when the particulars are joined in public worship, there are all the engagements united together. The Lord engages himself to let forth as it were, a stream of his comfortable, quickening presence to every particular person that fears him, but when many of these particulars join together to worship God, then these several streams are united and meet in one. So that the presence of God, which, enjoyed in private, is but a stream, in public becomes a river, a river that makes glad

162. Westminster Assembly, *Church-Government and Ordination*, 6–9; Zakai, "Religious Toleration," 9.

163. McGraw, *Heavenly Directory*, 76–77.

164. McGraw, *Heavenly Directory*, 79.

165. Owen, "Nature and Beauty," vi.2.3.

the city of God. The Lord has a dish for every particular soul that truly serves him; but when many particulars meet together, there is a variety, a confluence, a multitude of dishes. The presence of the Lord in public worship makes it a spiritual feast, and so it is expressed, Isa. xxv. 6. There is, you see, more of God's presence in public worship.[166]

Therefore, corporate worship for Owen and Clarkson revealed the true church to the world and what being part of the church was about—part of the one body, Christ's—which was central to the definition of the church in both the Westminster Assembly's *Confession of Faith* and the *Savoy Declaration*.[167] How much these ideas translated into the eighteenth century is unclear, however, from the Church Book of Bury St. Edmunds Independent Church some of this can be observed in the words of their covenant. When renewing the covenant in 1700, and while speaking of the relationship between themselves at that time, their agreement with a confession of faith written for the church in 1655 was confirmed. In this confession of faith, when discussing the church, allusion was made to Calvin's visible-invisible distinction.[168] Yet, they did believe themselves a true visible church of Christ, which as a communion of saints waited on God through the ordinances brought together in public worship:

> We doe believe yt this particular visible church wch spiritually is called sion, is founded and built upon Christ Jesus the spirituall rock, and yt no stones may be laid in this building but such as are living and spirituall stones, visible saints and faithful in Xt Jesus, according to the promise of the father made unto the gospel and spirituall sion. . . . We doe believe yt this particular visible church consisting of visible saints and of such only, acknowledgeth no other Lord but Jesus Xt and that she lives, moves and acts in all things by influence of life, life and grace from him without whom she can doe nothing: And that she acteth according to his laws and institutions and them only rejecting all the prudential decress, Canons, Laws. Constitutions and inventions of men in the matters of worship and discipline as abominable and vile, seeing Gods alter is polluted if mans toole be lifted up upon it. . . . We doe believe yt communion of saints, prayer, hearing the word preached and singing of psalms are ordinances and appointments of It for

166. Clarkson, "Public Worship."

167. England Parliament, *Confession of Faith*, 25; Matthews, *Savoy Declaration*, 111–12.

168. Bury St. Edmunds Independent Church, *Church Book*, December 12, 1700.

conversion and edification of souls and for the worship and service of God.[169]

Response and Praise

Participation in the expression of the visible church may have been one way the congregation participated when coming to an act of corporate worship, but it was not all that came to be required of a congregation as a communion of saints. The Westminster Assembly's *Larger* and *Shorter Catechisms* began with the statement that the chief and highest end of humanity "is to glorify God and enjoy him forever."[170] This pertained to the necessity of response and praise in corporate worship. In the seventeenth and eighteenth centuries, how these were approached and developed can be seen in further examination of preaching of the time and discussion over the use of psalmody and later hymnody in public worship.

PREACHING

If the sermon was an act of hearing rather than an act of speaking, it must have included an element of application to allow, if not ensure, the response of the hearer. Historian Charles Hambrick-Stowe concluded:

> The Puritan movement called for exegetical and evangelistic sermons painstakingly prepared for each service of worship by preachers trained in biblical scholarship and delivered in plain language that would connect with the daily lives of ordinary people.[171]

The basic idea of the sermon was to divide it into doctrine, reason, and application. This was to help the listener understand that theology has been actively involved in the practice of faith. Hambrick-Stowe went on to say how "sermons aimed to engage listeners in the biblical redemption narrative and, by the work of the Holy Spirit, empower them for obedient

---

169. Bury St. Edmunds Independent Church, *Church Book*, January 1, 1655.
170. Westminster Assembly, *Larger Catechism*, 3; Westminster Assembly, *Shorter Catechism*, 3.
171. Hambrick-Stowe, "Practical Divinity and Spirituality," 195.

living."[172] This is demonstrated in the instructions in the *Directory for the Public Worship of God*:

> In raising doctrines from the text, his care ought to be, First, that the matter be the truth of God. Secondly, that it be a truth contained in, or grounded on, that text that the hearer may discern how God teacheth it from thence. Thirdly, that he chiefly insist upon those doctrines which are principally intended, and make most from the edification of his hearer.[173]

For the Word of God to be heard in the sermon, the preacher could only do so much: the hearer too had their part to play. John Newman (1677–1741) in his Eastcheap lecture *On the Nature of Hearing the Word* (1713) said to those that would be hearers of sermons:

> It is possible that persons may so far attend as to hear every word in a sermon, and yet, through the ignorance and darkness of their own minds, they may understand little or nothing of the heavenly doctrine couched in those words. . . . [Y]ou must be very sensible of the ignorance and blindness of your own minds; your very great proneness to fall into mistakes and errors, and of how much you stand in need of the special illuminations and teachings of the Holy Ghost.[174]

Therefore, it was not only the preacher who was to depend on the Holy Spirit, the ability of the congregation adequately to attend and participate in public worship involved the Holy Spirit. Jeremiah Burroughs (1600–1646) encouraged congregations themselves to pray for the aid of the Holy Spirit as they came to listen: "Pray beforehand that God would open your eyes and open your heart and accompany His Word."[175]

---

172. Hambrick-Stowe, "Practical Divinity and Spirituality," 196.

173. Scotland Parliament, *Directory for Publick Worship*, 34.

174. Newman, "Nature of Hearing," 23–24. The Eastcheap Lectures were a set of lectures endowed by prosperous dissenting merchants to promote an interest in psalmody and worship (Kaye, *King's Weigh House Church*, 26; see David L. Wykes, "Reynolds, Thomas [c. 1667–1727]," in Cannadine et al., *Oxford Dictionary of National Biography*). They began in 1708 with a series on the duty of singing but covered other subjects such as the Christian duties of prayer, praise, hearing the Word and reading the Scriptures. As well as Thomas Reynolds speaking at the lectures, other notable dissenting ministers and divines of the time were invited to give lectures including Benjamin Grosvenor (1676–1758), Thomas Bradbury (1677–1759), Jabez Earle (1676–1768), William Harris (1675–1740), and John Newman (1677–1741).

175. Burroughs, *Gospel-Worship*, 208.

Burroughs, in emphasizing the importance of the congregation's hearing God's Word in the sermon, also emphasized that from hearing the Word the people needed to live out God's will. He wrote:

> When you come to hear the Word, come with a resolution to yield whatever God shall reveal to be His mind. "I am not going to hear Your Word, O Lord, to wait upon You, to know what You have to say to me, And You who are the Searcher of all hearts, You know that I go with such a resolution to yield up myself to every truth of Yours."[176]

Hearing of God's Word should cause a response in the congregation. Primarily, this was in the way they lived their lives outside that gathering for public worship, but on occasions it would cause a response to be vocalized by members of the congregation within corporate worship.

For those churches that would have identified themselves as Independent in the late-seventeenth and the eighteenth centuries, to become a member of a particular church required an individual to make a testimony, either spoken or written. This relates back to the idea of the church being the visible communion of saints, and therefore was made a condition of a church's polity within the *Savoy Declaration*:

> The Members of these Churches are Saints by Calling, visible manifesting and evidencing (in and by their profession and walking) their obedience unto the Call of Christ, who being further known to each other by their confession of Faith wrought in them by the power of God, declared by themselves or otherwise manifested, do willing consent to walk together according to the appointment of Christ, giving up themselves to the Lord, and to one another by the will of God in professed subjection to the Ordinances of the Gospel.[177]

These testimonies were often related to how hearing the Word of God in a sermon had caused an individual to come to God. Joseph Hussey (1660–1726) recorded a number of such testimonies in the Church Book for the Great Meeting in Cambridge. In 1694, Hussey recorded Goody Lofts as having declared "God's work on her soul" and Mr. Blackly's daughter, who was "a great influence of Free Grace," admitted by "confession of the mouth."[178] There are also examples throughout the Church Book for the

---

176. Burroughs, *Gospel-Worship*, 206.

177. Matthews, *Savoy Declaration*, 122.

178. Taken from the photo archive of Joseph Hussey's Church Book, which covered his ministry at the Great Meeting, Cambridge, 1691–1791.

Independent Meeting House in Bury St. Edmunds. The pastor, John Beart, on February 24, 1712, recorded:

> John Adams single man related the dealings of God with his soul, how he was let to see his condition by Nature under Mr Rawlins ministry from Rom. 6 last and was wonderfully comforted by a sermon preach'd by ye Pastor, also at Bansfield-Hall from Gal. 3.13 of Christs redeeming from ye Curse of ye Law. He tho't he saw his miserable Condition by Nature & ye Love of Christ in laying down his Life. And was comforted by a sermon of Mr. Doughty from John 3.14, 15. As also very much from that Text 1 Joh. 1.7 etc.[179]

And on the 2nd May 1713:

> Henry Last of Chevington a poor Cripple from the Womb, having related how he was convinced of a lost Estate without Repentance with He knew not how to attain & tempted to think He was too old to repent & encouraged by ye Parable Matth. 20.1-7, & from ye Parable of ye Prodigal expounded by Mr Doughty, & a sermon preach'd by ye Pastor from Psalm 66.16 & how Christ was previous to him etc. & was encouraged to leave the World & follow ye Dissenters from Joh. 15.18, 19 wth some other Particulars was read with good satisfaction & sat down with us.[180]

Hymns

Psalmody was another part of corporate worship that was seen as essential for the praise of God, although not always practiced because of the persecution in the late seventeenth century, when singing could have alerted government spies and informers to the whereabouts of congregations.[181] Not to sing psalms would have gone against the authority of Scripture and there was the belief that the only proper words for worship were biblical words. Despite this, in the eighteenth century, theologians such as Isaac Watts (1674-1748) and Philip Doddridge (1702-51) raised the issue of the relevance of the Psalms to the church and although the Puritans argued that the Psalms were scriptural songs, Scripture did not restrict the church to just the singing of Psalms. Doddridge in his hymn writing believed that he was acting in accordance with scriptural teachings, highlighting that the

---

179. Bury St. Edmunds Independent Church, *Church Book*, February 12, 1712.
180. Bury St. Edmunds Independent Church, *Church Book*, May 2, 1713.
181. Kaye, *King's Weigh House Church*, 26.

apostle Paul urged the early church to praise God with hymns and spiritual songs and not just psalms.[182] Doddridge interpreted the apostle Paul to be saying that in public worship, along with the Davidic Psalms, other evangelical hymns composed under the influence of the Holy Spirit should be sung.[183] Watts, although taking a very scriptural approach to his hymn writing, argued the need for hymns from the perspective of doctrine. English professor J. R. Watson, in his discussion of Watts's hymnody, wrote that:

> Watts was so concerned about the absence of specifically Christian doctrine in the psalms that he felt it necessary to add some wherever possible, to give what he called "an evangelic turn to the Hebrew sense," and "to accommodate the book of Psalms to Christian worship."[184]

This need for songs that were meaningful to the church was a further interpretation of the apostle Paul's letter to the early church, particularly to the church in Colossae. Not only was the church to sing psalms, hymns and sacred songs, their purpose was both to glorify God and educate the church.[185] To that end, it was important that what the church was singing was understood by those assembled and had meaning in the context of their Christian faith, or as Jabez Earle (1676–1768) put it in one of his Eastcheap lectures:

> A man must understand and actually consider what he says, when he sings the Praises of God. . . . Otherwise what he does is no more an Act of Worship or Devotion, than the Noise of a musical Instrument.[186]

Therefore, by the late eighteenth century, singing in nonconformist worship had gained a high reputation and significant collections of hymns were being published.[187] Watts was one of the leading figures in this, but others such as Doddridge and Benjamin Beddome (1717–95) were writing hymns that enabled congregations to make collective responses of praise

---

182. Clifford, *Good Doctor*, 195.
183. Clifford, *Good Doctor*, 195.
184. Watson, *English Hymn*, 153.
185. Col 3:16. The King James version interprets this verse as: "Let the word of Christ dwell in you richly in all wisdom; teaching and admonishing one another in psalms and hymns and spiritual songs, singing with grace in your hearts to the Lord."
186. Earle, "Nature of Singing," 6–7.
187. Temperley, "Music of Dissent," 210.

and thanksgiving to God, as well as providing an additional tool to preaching for edification.

As with aspects of prayer in the worship of the church, the singing of hymns and psalms concerned making worship ultimately about the glorification of God. Congregational singing was another aspect of worship which emphasizes that idea of covenant in worship: in this instance, the covenant between God and humanity that all participate in through communion with God. Earle stated that the glory of God was the ultimate aim of Christians and their actions and that it is only by praising God that God is acknowledged and proclaimed.[188] For Watts there was more at stake than just the acknowledgment of God. It was in singing praise that the worship of the church achieved its nearest imitation of the worship of heaven.[189] To achieve this, praise had to come from worshippers speaking to God from their hearts.[190] This inference of the aim of singing to be the glorification of God demonstrated a subtle shift in the practice of worship in the eighteenth-century, which some suggest is linked to the rise of reason and the age of enlightenment.[191] This also returns to the ideas of the Westminster Divines contained in the *Larger* and *Shorter Catechisms* that the chief aim of human beings is to glorify God.[192] One way the divines believed this was done was through God's praises being uttered in worship.[193] So although the Puritan focus for worship had been the downward movement of God through word and sacrament, singing and hymnody reversed this and worship became again an upward movement from the people to God.[194] Therefore, praise had to be about more than just singing the words of Scripture in the Psalm; what was sung had to be about the personal experience of God whilst making a response, as Watts put it, as "a redeemed community."[195] In this we have participation as the community of saints in God brought together with an expression of participation in corporate worship. The singing of hymns enabling a corporate, ordered response.

188. Earle, "Nature of Singing," 9–10.
189. Watts, *Hymns*, iii.
190. Beynon, *Issac Watts*, 155.
191. Watson, *English Hymn*, 138; Beynon, *Isaac Watts*, 151–55.
192. Westminster Assembly, *Larger Catechism*, 3; Westminster Assembly, *Shorter Catechism*, 3.
193. Vincent, *Explicatory Catechism*, 12.
194. Beynon, *Isaac Watts*, 146.
195. Beynon, *Isaac Watts*, 156.

It was the need for personal experience and communal response to be reflected in the church's singing that led to Watts's hymns. Although based on Scripture, they were representative of the thoughts and feelings of those who were engaged with the philosophical and religious ideas of the age.[196] In the preface to his collection of *Hymns and Spiritual Songs*, Watts wrote:

> The most frequent Tempers and Changes of our Spirit, and Conditions of our Life are here copied, and the Breathings of our Piety exprest according to the variety of our Passions, our Love, our Fear, our Hope, our Desire, our Sorrow, our Wonder and our Joy, as they are refin'd into Devotion, and act under the Influence and Conduct of the Blessed Spirit; all conversing with God the Father by the new and living Way of Access to the Throne, even the Person and the Mediation of our Lord *Jesus Christ*. To him also . . . I have address'd many a Song; for thus doth the holy Scripture instruct and teach us to worship, in the various short Patterns of Christian Psalmodie described in Revelations. I have avoided the more obscure and controverted Points of Christianity that we might all obey the Direction of the Word of God, and *sing his Praises with Understanding*, Psal. 47.7.[197]

To that end, the shift from psalmody to hymnody became about the education of the congregation in the truths of the gospel and the glorification of God.

During the twentieth century, Erik Routley suggested that hymns are not a good source of doctrine, but they provide rhetorical presentations of aspects of faith.[198] Theologian Alan Clifford, in his discussion of Doddridge's life and work, shared a similar view saying that rather than theological documents, hymns are "visions in verse."[199] While this might be true, the hymns of Watts and Doddridge cannot be described as devoid of doctrine or to be without influence on the theology of the church's understanding of worship. Watts's first reform to the singing of the church was to recast the Psalms in Christian language and teaching.[200] The hymns of Watts, Doddridge, and others, did not just turn Scripture into words congregations could use collectively as a response to their faith in a way that was understandable to them. Their hymns spoke of the nature of God,

196. Watson, *English Hymn*, 133.
197. Watts, *Hymns*, vii.
198. Routley, *I'll Praise My Maker*, 66.
199. Clifford, *Good Doctor*, 195.
200. Watts, *Psalms of David*, preface; Watson, *English Hymn*, 153.

of Christ and of the church. Historian Bernard Lord Manning found within many of Watts's hymns a survey of nature and the central role of a crucified and dying creator within it.[201] Watson explained this finding by stating that Watts's hymnody was "based on a system of belief which he drew from his study of natural philosophy and theology" that insisted on the importance of a "revealed religion and the saving grace of Jesus Christ."[202] Routley found examples that spoke of the connection between grace and the providence of God in the hymns of Doddridge to help expound some of the mysteries of faith.[203] Routley suggested that this not only made the hymns poignant to the collective teaching of the church but also offered a tool for private meditation.[204]

The doctrinal themes that were evident in the hymns of the eighteenth century were very closely tied to the themes that were being preached from the pulpits. Watts to some extent, but Doddridge and Beddome particularly wrote hymns that versified and emphasized what had been taught in the sermon. The idea behind this, Watson explained, was to "make the sermon more memorable and help send the congregation out with the Bible message explained and elucidated and with spiritual inspiration and intellectual food for the coming week."[205] This connection with preaching also allowed for the application of personal feeling and testimony, as the hymn writers applied similar rules to those they used for writing sermons.[206] So, although hymns were designed mainly for congregational singing, as in preaching, the personal, Watson observed, gave an authenticity, which allowed the words of the hymns to be owned by the congregation.[207]

Conclusion

The understanding of freedom and participation by the end of the eighteenth century was significant in how nonconformists approached corporate worship. Participation was concerned with the formation and fellowship of church communities in worship, rather than actions

---

201. Manning, *Wesley and Watts*, 83; Cousland, "Significance of Isaac Watts," 295.
202. Watson, *English Hymn*, 135–36.
203. Routley, *I'll Praise My Maker*, 25.
204. Routley, *I'll Praise My Maker*, 27.
205. Watson, *English Hymn*, 58.
206. Watson, *English Hymn*, 57.
207. Watson, *English Hymn*, 58.

undertaken by the congregation in worship. This did not mean such elements were non-existent. Hymn and psalm singing was encouraged but spoken congregational responses were largely dismissed by Puritans as they believed it caused chaos and babble. Freedom in worship developed as an expression of freedom of conscience and thought, whilst also being an action of the Holy Spirit. In combination with the political tension over the governance of the church, fixed and prescribed liturgies for worship came to be disregarded, if not thought of as suspicious. Despite this, worship had an inherent order in which freedom and participation acted to enable the glorification of God and the edification of the people. This interrelationship between freedom, order and participation was the foundation from which Congregational and Presbyterian worship in England developed.

3

Worship in Congregationalism

ERNEST PRICE, A PRINCIPAL of Yorkshire United Independent College, Bradford, wrote that Congregationalists cherish freedom "because it makes for spiritual progress."[1] Through their belief that Christ leads the church in the way of truth, Price asserted that Congregationalists claim the freedom "to act in accordance with [Christ's] will," and "to shape Christian policy and program to meet the challenge" of the day and generation.[2] This was the premise of freedom established by the Puritans and early nonconformists in England. Yet, Price's assertion shows that freedom works with and in the spheres of order and participation, those conjoined elements that enable and provide a fuller description of corporate worship in the church. Therefore, corporate worship whilst couched in the language of freedom was not for Congregationalists only an action of freedom. It was a blending of order and freedom that enabled churches to worship God with reverence and encouraged the fullest possible participation.[3]

A Brief History of English-Speaking Congregationalism in England and Wales

Congregationalism in England took on the shape of a denomination from the second quarter of the nineteenth century.[4] Being recognized as Congre-

---

1. Price, *Handbook*, 37.

2. Price, *Handbook*, 37.

3. Congregational Union of England and Wales, *Yearbook, 1936*, 9; Congregational Church in England and Wales, *Order of Public Worship*, vii.

4. Congregational churches as part of the Congregational Union of England and

gational was not a new identification, there are instances of people defining themselves as such dating back at least to 1658. However, for the purposes of this book, this terminology is only going to be applied to the union of churches that established itself formally in the 1830s, acknowledging that much had changed in the meantime in self-understanding and in definition of identity and mission. They continued this development of their ecclesiological understanding up until the formation of the United Reformed Church in 1972.

Communication and fellowship between local Independent churches was not uncommon from their emergence in England.[5] They would gather for ordinations, inductions, funerals, "special days of fasting and humiliation or of thanksgiving," and in some areas for lecture series.[6] There was no common organization among them until the success of the Evangelical Revival which gave rise to radical alteration in Congregationalists' view of the church.[7] At this point it was perceived that the local gathered church of the saved was "no longer a spiritually self-sufficient unit," it needed its neighbors to feel stronger.[8] Therefore, Independent churches began to cooperate with other like-minded churches to make the mission of the

---

Wales would not have recognized themselves to be part of a denomination in the first instance. This terminology is relatively new and used in the discussion of modern ecclesiology. A denomination is a subgroup within a religion that operates under a common name, tradition and identity. It may not have a hierarchical organizational structure, but it will have a governing polity.

5. Independent churches were the nonconformist churches that advocated local congregational control of religious and church matters without a perceived need for wider ecclesiastical hierarchy. As gathered churches, their roots can be traced back to Robert Browne "who in 1581 gathered in Norwich a church of like-minded believers, bound to God and each other by mutual covenant" (Pope, *Nonconformity*, 579). This also led to the Separatist movement. Independent churches grew in number on the principle of working for reform of the church in England, and they set out a faith and order in the *Savoy Declaration* (1658). In England, a number of Congregational churches were founded as Independent churches between 1643 and 1660. However, there were also a number that were a result of the Great Ejectment in 1662 when approximately 2500 clergy lost or left their livings because of dissent to or concerns over the demands and constraints placed on clergy by the *Act of Uniformity* (Cornick, *Under God's Good Hand*, 61).

6. Browne, *Congregationalism*, 187; Wadsworth, *Yorkshire Congregational Union*, 13.

7. Evangelical Revival was a movement in the eighteenth century that emphasized the biblical faith, personal conversion, and piety. It was primarily a movement of the Anglican tradition, but the ideas of evangelism, social welfare and mission influenced the nonconformist churches.

8. Routley, *Congregationalism*, 63–64.

church successful in cities and countryside.⁹ This led initially to the establishment of County Unions or District Associations, where collectively the Independent churches in an area set out their purpose of association. For example, the aim of the Wiltshire and East Somerset Association (formed in 1796) was "to promote mutual edification by Christian and ministerial intercourse, and to diffuse plans for the spread of the Gospel."¹⁰ In general terms, what the Wiltshire and East Somerset Association set out as its purpose was the same for all the County Unions. This can be seen in the constitution of the Yorkshire Congregational Union (established in 1872). The premise of the Wiltshire and East Somerset Association aim is behind the more detailed and ordered objectives of the Yorkshire Union:

> To cultivate Christian communion among the churches, to promote co-operation among the associated churches, to . . . promote the formation of Congregational Churches, to give pecuniary aid to small or new churches and support evangelists, to promote Evangelical religion, to collect and disseminate information, to . . . prevent the alienation of trust property, to obtain and maintain the civil and religious rights of Protestant Nonconformists.¹¹

Similarly, the Surrey Union described its purpose as being "to promote the union and efficiency of the churches, and the spread of evangelical religion; to advance the principles of Nonconformity; and to uphold and enlarge civil and religious freedom."¹²

As the churches began to discover the strength that was derived from these County Unions, and more were being formalized across the country in England, the argument was made for a national confederation.¹³ The proposal for a national union was first made in 1806 by the London Board of Congregational ministers. Congregational minister R. W. Dale observed that the proposal met resistance because of the fear that churches would lose their autonomy.¹⁴ In the formation of the County Unions it was clearly recognized that all the associated churches maintained their independence to manage their own affairs.¹⁵ Inevitably, as the idea of a large, central

---

9. Peel, *English Congregationalism*, 70.
10. Peel, *English Congregationalism*, 70; Routley, *Congregationalism*, 69.
11. Wadsworth, *Yorkshire Congregational Union*, 15.
12. Cleal and Crippen, *Congregationalism in Surrey*, xiii.
13. Dale, *English Congregationalism*, 686.
14. Dale, *English Congregationalism*, 687.
15. In the constitution of the Yorkshire Congregational Union it states the principle

organization developed, questions of polity arose, particularly concerning the principle of freedom and how much of it could be maintained by affiliated churches.[16] There was also the view held by some that one of the positive features of Independency was that it was not a denomination.[17] Despite the vociferous arguments against a national Union, the need for such a Union became apparent as the number of churches grew, as did practical problems which were difficult to solve in isolation, (e.g., the provision, maintenance, and training of pastors). The promotion of publications like the *Congregational Magazine* among the churches began to instill a denominational consciousness.[18] Alongside this, Congregationalists in England believed that the organization and management of the church should be separate from the government of the state and wanted this principle to be evident in the lives of their churches. This was best achieved by organization and structures that allowed the collation of statistical information and brought ecclesiastical principles together for effective public assertion.[19] Erik Routley also observed from an article in the *Eclectic Review* published at the time, that a national union was "a more public recognition of the unity of the Body," which suggests that to make an impact Congregationalists needed to appear and act as a united community.[20] Consequently, organizational structures became essential.[21] Therefore, twenty-five years after first being tabled, a constitution was finally negotiated and approved by twenty-six of the thirty-four existing County Unions/District Associations establishing a Union of Congregational Churches and Ministers throughout England and Wales.[22] The inaugural meeting was held in 1832 when the decisive motion "that the Union be now established" was made and the Congregational

---

that there was to be "the clear recognition of the Scriptural right of every Church to maintain Independence in the management of its own affairs" (Wadsworth, *Yorkshire Congregational Union*, 15).

16. Peel, *English Congregationalism*, 70.
17. Peel, *English Congregationalism*, 70.
18. Peel, *English Congregationalism*, 71.
19. Dale, *English Congregationalism*, 691; Peel, *English Congregationalism*, 72–73.
20. Routley, *Congregationalism*, 75.
21. Brownell, "Voluntary Saints," 7.
22. Those County Unions and District Associations that withheld their support remained independent of the Congregational Union of England and Wales. However, some of those Unions and Associations did come to change their minds. Routley recorded that within twenty-five years the Congregational Union of England and Wales consisted of all but a small number of Congregational churches (Routley, *Congregationalism*, 79).

Union of England and Wales came into being.[23] Initially the Union was to consist only of the County Unions and District Associations. On formation, however, it was agreed that the membership would be "extended to include ministers and churches recognized by the Associations."[24]

The general Union, like the County Unions, was founded on the principle that every church that joined would maintain independence in government and administration. Despite this, during the same meeting in which the Union was inaugurated, a declaration on the principles of faith and order for the body was presented. It was deemed pertinent to ascertain whether the Union should have a public statement that declared the leading articles of its faith and order.[25] The meeting agreed that a document to communicate information to the public on the doctrines generally held and maintained by Congregationalists would be prepared by a committee.[26] Therefore, within a year the *Declaration of the Faith, Church Order, and Discipline of the Congregational or Independent Dissenters* was written, agreed and adopted. R. W. Dale (1829–95) commented on the remarkable speed with which this document passed through the Assembly in 1833 given the number of subjects he identified as controversial. Dale's explanation for this was:

> It was not a creed to be subscribed to by ministers and Churches as a condition of membership of the Union. It was not even a confession of the belief of the ministers and delegates who adopted it. It was simply a statement, "for general information," of "what is commonly believed" among Congregationalists.[27]

As implied by Dale, the *Declaration* (1833) was a list of general statements offering no proofs, reasons, or arguments to the doctrines presented. In the preliminary notes that prefaced the declaration there was the recognition that there would be differences in opinion held over certain doctrines and practices and each member of the Union had the "right to form an unbiased judgement of the Word of God."[28] In this statement was the basis of the understanding of "freedom" central to the practice of Congregationalists in regard to polity and worship. Interestingly, the preliminary notes also

23. Routley, *Congregationalism*, 77.
24. Dale, *English Congregationalism*, 696; Jones, *Congregationalism*, 243.
25. Dale, *English Congregationalism*, 700.
26. Dale, *English Congregationalism*, 700.
27. Dale, *English Congregationalism*, 701.
28. Congregational Union of England and Wales, *Declaration*, Preliminary Note 6.

asserted that "no minister, and no church among them . . . would deny the substance of any one of the [stated] doctrines of religion."[29] The root of this assumption is not clear in the motions made to the 1832 Assembly recorded by Dale, other than the statement implied there was a looking back to similar statements and declarations of faith and order made by previous generations, for example the *Savoy Declaration* (1658).[30] Nevertheless, this could be related to the voluntary principle which Congregationalists had begun to perceive as foundational to the identity of congregations: they were voluntary gathered communities of saints. John Pye Smith (1774–1851) is reported to have said true Congregational voluntarism came from members joining through "their own deliberate and free choice; and that they continue[d] in membership and in the exercise of their duties with the same freedom."[31] All this, Smith stated, rested "upon the absolute necessity of inward personal godliness."[32] This suggests that there was thought to be a spiritual characteristic to the voluntarism exercised in the churches, which is important to remember when considering freedom in worship.

The production of the *Declaration* in 1833 along with the objectives agreed at its formation gave the general Union its foundation from which an organized institution emerged. A central fund was created to which all member churches contributed in order to encourage growth and expansion of the activities of Congregationalism. With this ordering of church polity came a tension between the principles of freedom and fellowship. Historian Albert Peel observed that much of the first hundred years of Union could be discussed in terms of the interplay between the "independence of the individual churches and cooperation among them" and finding a balance.[33] Despite the authorship of statements relating to faith and order,[34] the principle that was central to Congregationalism was that the "church [was] a free, independent, and legitimate association in spiritual fellowship of those who were 'in Christ,' deriving its validity and its function from the presence

---

29. Congregational Union of England and Wales, *Declaration*, Preliminary Note 7.
30. Dale, *English Congregationalism*, 699–700.
31. Brownell, "Voluntary Saints," 91.
32. Brownell, "Voluntary Saints," 91.
33. Peel, *English Congregationalism*, 78.
34. There were two statements published in the life of the Congregational Union of England and Wales/Congregational Church in England and Wales: *Declaration of Faith, Church Order, and Discipline of the Congregational or Independent Dissenters*, 1833 and *A Declaration of Faith*, 1964 (revised 1967).

of Christ with the society."[35] Theologian Cecil Cadoux remarked that the "real differentia of the Congregational polity [was] a passionate trust in the Christian's freedom from external control and in the guidance of the Holy Spirit in all matters of religion, both for the individual and the group."[36] Maintaining this ethos became the challenge as circumstances changed in the local churches and there was the need to "increase efficiency," Peel stated, "in denominational machinery."[37]

Alongside this was a sense that Congregationalism had to develop as society changed. Historian Benjamin Millard stated that "Congregationalism [was] a living thing and wherever there [was] life there must be adjustment to the environment."[38] Histories of Congregationalism written during the twentieth century showed that adaptation to changing circumstances was achieved and that in certain areas of society, e.g., education of children, Congregationalists were pioneers. In the late nineteenth and early twentieth century Congregational churches were busy places as they were hives of all types of social activity. Historian R. Tudur Jones noted that this gave rise to the idea that a busy church was a successful church.[39] Routley wrote:

> No church order imposes on its individual members more athletic demands; none lives more openly "in the world"; none lives more dangerously; none is farther from the principle of shutting all doors in order to keep the devotional air. Through the open windows the east wind blows now and again, slamming doors and knocking precious ornaments off the mantelpiece. Not all the furniture is in good repair and here and there a light switch is found to be inoperative. But with all that, it is a happy, harum-scarum house, and those who love it best are often heard to say that they do so because it looks more like a church acting in this world and doing the Lord's work here and now than any other institution more powerful, more efficient, more consistent, that they know.[40]

Was this busyness of the Church at the cost of churchmanship? The biblical ethos that the church should be in the world was clearly a strength of

---

35. Milliard, *Congregationalism*, 55.
36. Cadoux, *Pilgrim's Further Progress*, 149.
37. Peel, *English Congregationalism*, 80.
38. Milliard, *Congregationalism*, 53.
39. Jones, *Congregationalism*, 297.
40. Routley, *Congregationalism*, 102.

Congregationalism.[41] But churches being places for socializing and leisure activity may have been spiritually costly. The gathering of the church was more of a social occasion than a time when spiritual enrichment was encouraged. The sacramentality and solemnity of worship was being lost to "chit-chat" and "communication of domestic intelligence," which was observed in the church as a whole, but more profoundly in groups such as the woman's fellowship where their reason for meeting became more about being a place where women could come together and support one another than spiritual teaching. This was something spoken out against in the 1835 Manual for Carrs Lane Congregational Church, Birmingham.[42] The rise of the church as a social venue caused a tension in Congregational churches between their role as covenanted communities of believers meeting for worship, instruction, and mutual education, and being a social club open to all. This may be the natural result of exploring and developing mission in a locality which opens up church buildings as places for wider communities to gather. Yet over a hundred years later, in 1939, in a call for reform drafted by Bernard Manning (1892–1941), John Whale (1896–1997), and Nathaniel Micklem (1888–1976), and signed by five other Congregational leaders, the state of the churches in the Union because of this was a real concern:

> The condition of our churches, as they actually exist today, in great cities, in country towns and in villages, is itself often almost desperate. . . . We are short of [people] and money, but this is not our most serious need, for God is able to take the weak things of the world to confound the strong. Our dreadful weakness is religious. We are not declaring the Gospel with power to a dispirited and disillusioned age; we are not living in the discipline of Gospel fellowship; only in a very imperfect degree are our churches God's resting place and holy habitation.[43]

This weakness in the churches of the Union was by some perceived to relate to the tradition of freedom in Congregationalism.[44] The answer was not to limit freedom, rather to draw on theology in exploring church order and discipline.

---

41. Routley, *Congregationalism*, 90.

42. Cashdollar, *Spiritual Home*, 37.

43. See Sydney Cave et al., "Call to Reformation, 1939," in Routley, *Congregationalism*, 165–66.

44. Routley, *Congregationalism*, 94.

The Congregational Union of England and Wales, from the period of the Second World War onwards, acknowledged that it was suffering decline. Commentator on Congregationalism Alan Argent stated that in "1949 the General Purposes Committee reported Congregational churches had declined by over 100,000 members in twenty years," and that this committee sensed "Congregationalism as a specific and identifiable church order [was] fast disappearing."[45] A number of initiatives tried to bring about growth while policies were explored that considered denominational unity on the local and national level. At the Union meeting of 1959, a program of commissions was affirmed to inform the policies of the Congregational Union of England and Wales for what was called the "Next Ten Years." One of the commissions reflected on the status of the relationship between the individual churches of the Union. The outcome of discussions was to urge the Congregational churches to enter into a covenantal relationship "for the purpose of their distinctive Churchmanship and to express in some corporate form their 'belonging together' which [was] a fact of their experience."[46] This became reality in 1966, with the Church's *Declaration of Faith and A Short Affirmation of Faith*, being approved at the assembly of 1967.[47] It was also at the 1967 meeting that the basis of the union with the Presbyterian Church of England was presented and the vision for wider unity gained support.

The importance of congregational freedom was maintained in managing the proposed union with the Presbyterian Church of England. In 1972 when the churches voted for the scheme of union that would bring about the formation of the United Reformed Church, 465 of the 2,133 congregations of the Congregational Church in England and Wales voted not to join.[48] The Congregational churches outside the United Reformed Church did not unify as one body. Some affiliated to the Congregational Federation, others to an Evangelical Fellowship of Congregational Churches, while still others reverted to independency.[49]

---

45. Argent, *Transformation of Congregationalism*, 436.
46. Argent, *Transformation of Congregationalism*, 457–58.
47. Argent, *Transformation of Congregationalism*, 476.
48. Argent, *Transformation of Congregationalism*, 482.
49. Argent, *Transformation of Congregationalism*, 495.

Freedom in Worship

As the Congregational Union of England and Wales was established, Congregationalists would likely have framed freedom in worship in terms of the Holy Spirit. Through the leading of the Holy Spirit the will of God through Christ came to be known in the worship of the church and God was glorified in that worship. For Congregationalists, though, freedom was not just this; it was also a response to the recollection of the suffering endured by previous generations. Therefore, worship was to be conducted without the constraint of a prayer book. As the denomination grew, the understanding of freedom in worship developed with the freedom the Congregationalists inhabited through the voluntary principle that became central to their polity, finances, and missional activities.

Freedom and the Holy Spirit

The notion of worship having to be free so that the Holy Spirit is free to act came from the idea that worship is only true when it is of the Holy Spirit. In 1957, theologian Raymond Abba wrote:

> Worship, like saving faith, is "[humanity's] response to the nature and action of God." But the response of worship, like the response of faith, is itself the gift of God. It is evoked. . . . No representation of God's saving acts will in fact draw forth the response of real worship unless their truth "comes home" to men and women; and that can only happen through . . . "the inward testimony of the Holy Spirit."[50]

In other words, all worship is dependent on God—it comes from God and returns to God through the people. This is enabled by the Holy Spirit and only feasible if the Holy Spirit is free to act. Therefore, freedom in worship is bound by obedience to the will of God made known by the Holy Spirit. As stated by theologian Daniel Jenkins: "freedom which the Church knows is the reflection of the divine freedom and it is known only through obedience to the will of God."[51] Perfect freedom is then secured by the Holy Spirit creating "reverential awe, peaceful trust, the fervor of love and the exultation of hope."[52] This has the effect of taking human freedom out of the

---

50. Abba, *Principles of Christian Worship*, 7.
51. Jenkins, *Congregationalism*, 68.
52. Dale, *Holy Spirit*, 34.

equation. In worship, neither the one leading worship nor the congregation are free to do as they please or act according to personal taste. Instead, each person worships in that essential freedom which comes from God's willingness to act and to make God's will known. There is no freedom to ignore or to change that. The thoughts and words of the Scriptures have a controlling influence in what is known, yet this knowledge and the church's comprehension of Christ comes only through the guidance of the Holy Spirit, and the Holy Spirit's inspiration of the Scriptures.[53] Abba wrote:

> The written Word not only testifies to the Word made flesh; it mediates to [humanity] His presence and His saving love. Worship, therefore, if it be dependent upon revelation, must have the Bible at its centre. It is through the reading of Holy Scripture from pulpit or lectern that the assembled Church is confronted anew with the biblical revelation, in response to which alone it can offer worship in Spirit and in truth.[54]

Although spoken of as freedom, the church is captive to the Holy Spirit in every aspect of its life and worship. This was brought into the understanding of the church by nonconformist theologians in explorations of nonconformity (for example in P. T. Forsyth's *Charter of the Church* [1896] and Daniel Jenkins's *Congregationalism: A Restatement* [1954]), yet not likely understood or observed in the worship of the local church. In practice, worship was emotive. Nevertheless, the principle of the Word of God inspired by the Holy Spirit was central. As Dale stated:

> It is [the Spirit] who creates in the heart a thirst for communion with God. By [the Spirit] "we have access to the Father." [The Spirit] reveals to [humanity] what "eye hath not seen, nor ear heard"—the wisdom, strength, and joy "which God hath prepared for them that love him"—and kindles a vehement desire for all spirit blessing.[55]

There would also have been a somewhat naïve belief that sincerity and spontaneity were an expression of the movement of the Holy Spirit in worship.[56] These understandings are evident in how preaching and prayer was approached in corporate worship.

---

53. Jenkins, *Congregationalism*, 68; Abba, *Principles of Christian Worship*, 60.
54. Abba, *Principles of Christian Worship*, 47.
55. Dale, *Holy Spirit*, 38.
56. Jenkins, *Congregationalism*, 90.

Worship in Congregationalism

The Sermon

Congregationalism inherited the expectation that central to a corporate act of worship was the sermon. The Word of God was made fully known through preaching—proclamation and explanation of the Word—and the reading of Scripture. The good news of the grace of God had to be declared as well as heard.[57] This meant that the sermon was how the Word of God was to be made known while edifying the people in the content of the Scriptures, Christian doctrine, and right living. This entwinement of proclamation and edification shaped corporate worship and influenced how the congregation participated in worship. The centrality of the sermon in the corporate worship of Congregationalists led to preaching being a significant topic in discourses on worship. A number of single volumes on preaching were written as well as being included in works on worship in Congregationalism. Later examples include: P. T. Forsyth's *Positive Preaching and the Modern Mind* (1907), G. Campbell Morgan's *Preaching* (1937) and E. Shillito's chapter on *The Preaching of the Word* in Nathaniel Micklem's collection of essays, *Christian Worship* (1936). There was a distinct approach to preaching discussed within these texts that came from defining freedom in worship being the Holy Spirit's.

In the nineteenth century, it was common for preachers to enter the pulpit of Independent/Congregational churches without a script or any notes for the sermon. This was because of the belief that the revelation of the Word of God was the operation of the Holy Spirit. The preacher, therefore, had to be free of anything that might impede the work of the Holy Spirit. This was not to say that if a preacher did use notes instead of preaching extemporaneously that their words were any less inspired by the Holy Spirit. In the Lyman Beecher Lectures that Dale delivered on preaching at Yale University in 1877, he said:

> Is it fair to say that those who read their sermons show a distrust of the aid of the Holy Spirit. Our self-distrust, our dependence upon Divine teaching and aid, may be just as perfect when we are writing as when we are speaking. I do not accept the superstition which implies that the Spirit of God is with [the preacher] in the pulpit and not in the study.[58]

---

57. Abba, *Principles of Christian Worship*, 62.
58. Dale, *Nine Lectures*, 157–58.

In the same lecture, Dale confessed that he lacked courage at times to enter the pulpit without notes and would on occasion "read every sentence from the first to the last."[59] The important advantage Dale highlighted for the extemporary preacher was having the ability to watch the faces of the congregation so that statements that might seem perfectly clear to the preacher could be repeated, illustrated or expounded when they were obviously unclear to those listening.[60] There was more flexibility to be direct and have an ease in speaking which was lost when sermons were read. According to Dale, this did come at the cost of accuracy.[61]

Dale's view of the Holy Spirit being at work in both the pulpit and the study finds support in Joseph Parker's (1830–1902) discussion of the inspiration of the Holy Spirit in preparation and utterance. Parker argued that these were separate operations of the Holy Spirit and could not occur simultaneously. Interpretation to allow the Scriptures to be expounded upon took time and diligence on the part of the preacher. To enter the pulpit with the expectation that the Holy Spirit would inspire the understanding of the word of Scripture allowing the preacher to give the sermon was, in Parker's view, impious and limited the "Holy One of Israel under pretense of magnifying His power."[62] Parker believed that the trust placed in the Holy Spirit in the pulpit was "for the gift of suitable and efficient utterance."[63] T. T. James, a moderator of the Lancashire Congregational Union, drew this together in stating that if the minister comes to the congregation from "communion with God, carrying with [them] something of the mystical presence, [the minister's words] will do their work and achieve their end."[64]

The freedom of the Holy Spirit in worship was not perceived only to impact on the words of the preacher. The Holy Spirit was also understood to be at work in the congregation, if the Word of God was to be heard.[65] William Taylor (1829–95) wrote:

> God prepares preacher and hearer for meeting each other, and by the providence of His Spirit gives the one a message for the other,

---

59. Dale, *Nine Lectures*, 151.
60. Dale, *Nine Lectures*, 165.
61. Dale, *Nine Lectures*, 165.
62. Parker, *Paraclete*, 88–89.
63. Parker, *Paraclete*, 91.
64. James, *Work and Administration*, 51.
65. Taylor, *Ministry of the Word*, 108; Abba, *Principles of Christian Worship*, 65.

there would be in them both a devout sense of reverence towards God in the exercise of delivering and listening to a sermon.[66]

The expansion and clarification of thought on how the Holy Spirit related to preaching and the hearing of the Word of God in corporate worship was influential in the attempt to reform the worship of Congregational churches during the life of the Congregational Union of England and Wales.

Free or Extemporary Prayer

The correlation between freedom and the spontaneous nature of the Holy Spirit in corporate worship, as well as the worship of the individual, was discussed most frequently by Congregationalists in association with extemporary or free prayer. The conviction was held that sincerity in prayer was only achieved when speaking to God in the "freedom and intimacy of the Holy Spirit."[67] Free prayer was believed to give the one leading worship the full liberty to respond to the prompting of the Holy Spirit relating it to the particular needs and conditions of the worshippers.[68] Prayer arose out of the moment.[69] James described "free and spontaneous prayer" as being in the "blood of Congregational churches."[70] This suggests that free prayer is more than a response to the leading of the Holy Spirit, it is the way by which a people's communion with Jesus Christ through the Holy Spirit is affirmed and expressed. Dale wrote:

> The Congregational polity is rooted in the belief that the Lord Jesus Christ is personally present with those who are gathered together in His name. He is present, not merely to be the Object of their worship, but to be the foundation of their faith, their devotion, and their joy in God. They are penetrated by His Spirit; they are controlled by His will. Their petitions for themselves and their intercession for others are His as well as theirs. The minister and the people are one in Him. Free prayer seems necessary to the realisation of this great conception. For those who hold this faith it is natural to believe that when a church meets for worship, and

---

66. Taylor, *Ministry of the Word*, 207–8.
67. Davies, *Worship and Theology*, 5:350.
68. Abba, *Principles of Christian Worship*, 111–12.
69. See K. L. Parry, "Prayer and Praise," in Micklem, *Christian Worship*, 235.
70. James, *Work and Administration*, 50.

realises its unity in Christ, it will receive, direct from Him, the light and life it needs for acts of worship and prayer."[71]

Understanding free prayer as an outworking of a people's communion with God is a concept supported by K. Parry, a Congregational minister.[72] Parry highlighted that this understanding could fall short in practice depending on the relative emphasis "given to the content of the prayer and the act of communion with God."[73]

In the same way as the sermon could be a mouthpiece for a particular view held by the preacher, so could times of prayer.[74] There was every potential that a local church could find the content of extemporary prayer addressed to them rather than God.[75] John McClure (1860–1922), Chairman of the Congregational Union of England and Wales in 1919, noted in his Spring address that some of the free prayer experienced in the churches could be better described as "preaching with eyes shut."[76] Raymond Abba observed that prayer at times could "be more concerned with edification than with adoration."[77] This was because these prayers could be born out of the communion between the minister and the congregation—the pastoral relationship. The freedom to pray extempore meant that the minister could gather up and express the feelings of or about the congregation as were discerned in the moment.[78] This was a flaw with free prayer in corporate worship that was recognized by John Spencer Pearsall in his address to the meeting of the Union in 1866. The spontaneity of free prayer, whether it

---

71. Dale, *Manual*, 164. What Dale meant by "free prayer" in this quotation is not entirely clear. Dale may be defining 'Free Prayer' in this context as prayers not restricted by a set liturgy rather than as extemporaneous prayer. However, even if Dale does mean "conceived prayer"—prayers prepared in the study for an act of worship—this quotation still demonstrated the direct link between the communion of the people with Christ and the Spirit's inspiration of their prayers.

72. See Parry, "Prayer and Praise," in Micklem, *Christian Worship*, 225–42.

73. See Parry, "Prayer and Praise," in Micklem, *Christian Worship*, 235.

74. It should be noted that this would never have been the expectation of the sermon or prayers, nor would it have been what ministerial educators would have taught.

75. See Parry, "Prayer and Praise," in Micklem, *Christian Worship*, 235; Abba, *Principles of Christian Worship*, 112.

76. See Sir John D. McClure, "The Public Worship of God," in Congregational Union of England and Wales, *Yearbook, 1920*, 55.

77. Abba, *Principles of Christian Worship*, 112.

78. See Parry, "Prayer and Praise," in Micklem, *Christian Worship*, 235; Abba, *Principles of Christian Worship*, 112.

was believed to be conceived through the Holy Spirit or not, meant there was no preparation. Pearsall suggested that public prayer should be prepared in some way, like sermons. He wrote:

> The extent of preparation for public prayer we venture not to prescribe. Some ministers will, by devout meditation, seek the spirit of prayer; others will not only *feel*, but *think out*, the burden of their supplications; others will make brief notes; others will occasionally write out a prayer, not to be read, but as discipline for the mind in attaining and preserving the style of composition suitable for *public* prayer; all will, if true ministers, try to pray *from the heart*, and rely on the *prompting of the Spirit*.[79]

This led to Pearsall calling for a shift in the approach taken to prayer in corporate worship.

Freedom from the Prescribed

As previously demonstrated, the argument for spontaneity in the worship of the Church was rooted in a theology of the Holy Spirit and the principle of the rule of Jesus Christ in the Church. Routley wrote:

> A "free" form of worship—with nothing prescribed—implies a conviction that in worship the human imperative has no place. It implies that [humanity] are walking with God as friends, and can speak to [God] without formality or ceremony.[80]

Yet, although there is a sense of this in the understanding of freedom in worship in Congregational churches, it was not the only governing factor. There was a historical element which specifically related to the prescription of a set liturgy. From early in the seventeenth century, as demonstrated in the debates about worship at the Westminster Assembly, there was an aversion to fixed liturgy that filtered into what became nonconformist churches and was subsequently *de rigueur* throughout the life of the Congregational Union of England and Wales.[81]

In any discussion on the public worship of Congregationalism, the Church was reminded of its heritage. The Annual Report to the

---

79. Pearsall, *Public Worship*, 14–15.

80. Routley, *Into a Far Country*, 104.

81. In this instance "liturgy" should be understood as ordered public worship with set words and prayers.

Congregational Union of England and Wales in 1863, while reflecting on the bicentenary of 1662, reminded those gathered of the "right of free, open speech on platform and in pulpits" which came as the result of the stance by nonconformists in 1662.[82] The reasons for the events of 1662 were not as simple as freedom of speech, freedom of religion, or even freedom of worship.[83] Despite this, it was within this view of history that reform of corporate worship in Congregationalism was argued and this led to questions of liturgy.

On the matter of liturgy Dale wrote:

> Discussions about the mere arrangement and order of our services may be very necessary; it is inconsistent with our faith in the living presence of the Spirit of God in the church to regard with distrust and resentment every departure from the customs of our fathers.[84]

McClure in his 1919 Spring Address also said:

> I realize that there are many objections to the use of a liturgy. What was best for the sixteenth century may not be best for the twentieth; and yet it is hard to change forms which are hallowed by so many sacred associations. There is a very real danger lest we cling too closely to the past, and forget that the Church must satisfy the spiritual needs of the present. We ought not to seek to pledge our descendants either as to forms of worship or articles of faith. Revelation has not come to an end: for "the Lord hath more light and truth yet, to break forth out of His holy Word."[85]

Despite being tackled by figures such as Dale and McClure, the historically rooted suspicion of fixed liturgy continued to affect discourse on corporate worship and liturgy well into the twentieth century. John Huxtable, John Marsh, Romilly Micklem, and James Todd wrote in the preface to their *Book of Public Worship* (1948):

> Congregationalists . . . although they love freedom . . . are not liturgical anarchists . . . their ancestors were convinced that "standards of worship could not be fixed by the State; they had been determined by the Gospel."[86]

---

82. See Congregational Union of England and Wales, "Proceedings of the 32nd Annual Meeting," in *Yearbook, 1863*, 30.

83. Thompson, "Remembering 1662," 169–70.

84. Dale, *Holy Spirit*, 36.

85. See McClure, "Public Worship of God," 55–56.

86. Huxtable et al., *Book of Public Worship*, vii; Davies, *Worship and Theology*, 5:373.

The historical concern over liturgy did not mean Congregational worship was without liturgy. It is evident from early in their history that the churches that became Congregational held a loose but nonetheless discernible liturgy to their worship. There were common, expected elements in corporate worship although the order may have differed from church to church. While these were developed during the eighteenth century, they were rooted in the perception that how the church should worship collectively was prescribed in the Scriptures. The Common Close Congregational Church in Warminster published a "manual" in 1865 which stated:

> In Divine Service, scripture prescribes the parts, as praise, prayer, lessons from God's Word, and preaching the Gospel, but leaves the order and the hour of Public Worship undetermined.[87]

For a church that had a strong belief in freedom this is interesting as it demonstrates that there were boundaries to that freedom. How this affects the understanding of freedom in worship can only be fully realized by considering how the Congregational churches engaged with the concepts of order and participation in worship.

Development of Public Worship in Congregationalism: The Question of Order and Participation

In exploring how Congregationalists understood freedom in worship, it is evident that inadvertently the individual could become central: members of the congregation feeling individually moved by an act of worship; worship being so minister-centric that it appeared as if the congregation were looking on instead of participating. This was not the intention. The whole gathered congregation was to be led in worship, as described by William Taylor in a lecture he delivered to theological students on the subject of conducting corporate worship in the nineteenth century:

> Public prayer should be common, and not minutely individual. The preacher should not obtrude his own personal experiences and necessities, and ignore the great general wants of the congregation as a whole. His prayers should not be a pious soliloquy which he simply permits his people to overhear. Neither should it be a highly-wrought rhapsody in which the imagination of the speaker soars to such a height that the average worshipper cannot

---

87. Common Close Congregational Church, *Minute Book*, "Manual, 1865."

> accompany him. He must lead the people to the throne of grace, and give utterance for them there to the desires which in them are yearning for expression.[88]

As demonstrated by Taylor, in advice offered by theologians and ministerial educators suggestions were made for how corporate worship could be developed to ensure participation of the whole gathered congregation. In the nineteenth century, though, it was the singing of psalms and hymns that was the common feature in worship of the churches which came to make up the Congregational Union of England and Wales, that encouraged most corporate engagement. Although, this was not always perceived as fulfilling the concept that worship was the communion of people with God.[89]

The models of corporate worship exercised in church were not thought "sufficient for the spiritual life of the Church."[90] Without dismissing the importance of freedom and the unease with fixed or prescribed liturgy dictating corporate worship, what was understood by liturgy and how it was approached and used was reexamined. Through the expansion of the place of order and participation in worship, change was brought about through exploring liturgy in its simplest form—ordered corporate worship—to the offering of fully scripted acts of worship including prayers and congregational responses.

Order

The inherited suspicion among Congregationalists of prescribed liturgy and the conflict that can arise in considering corporate worship as having both order and freedom was summed up by G. S. Barrett in his paper on "Congregational Worship," presented to the Union meeting of 1896: "Form, it is said, is nothing in the worship of God, but spirit is everything, and attention to form is sure to degenerate, sooner or later, into formal worship."[91] By its very nature corporate worship has to have a form—some ordered structure—to enable it to be corporate and collective. Congregationalists knew this and did have an order to their public worship or at least a sense of what should be included. The fear was that overemphasis of order could lead

---

88. Taylor, *Ministry of the Word*, 245.

89. Thomas, *Ministry and the Church*, 9.

90. See G. S. Barrett, "Congregational Worship," in Congregational Union of England and Wales, *Yearbook, 1897*, 83.

91. See Barrett, "Congregational Worship," 84.

to a fixed liturgy that would suppress the worship of a church, particularly its prayer. Thomas Binney (1798–1874) noted this concern in his imagined conversation in the Milton Club entitled "Touching the Question: 'Are Dissenters to Have a Liturgy?'" which was included as an appendix to the volume he edited of the American Presbyterian minister and historian Charles Baird's *A Chapter on Liturgies*.[92] In the conversation, one of the participants stated the opinion: "the effect of a Liturgy is to quench and restrain—to depress and deaden the spirit of prayer."[93] The resonance of this uneasiness around liturgy in Congregational churches in the mid-to-late-nineteenth century is evident in an exchange recorded in the church meeting minutes of Sanford Street Congregational Church, Swindon. In the January and February church meetings in 1884 there was a discussion about the use of set prayers after it was found that such prayers were being read in the Sunday School. After considerable discussion across two church meetings, the resolution was unanimously passed "that no set forms of prayer, taken from a liturgy, be publicly used in either . . . chapel or school without first being approved by a church meeting."[94] In the February church meeting, having agreed this resolution, the prayer which had sparked the debate was then read to the meeting. The following outcome was recorded:

> Mr Thompson then moved, and Mr Williamson seconded, "That the form of Prayer which had just been read to the meeting, and which has recently been in use in the children's morning service be not permitted in the conduct of our Sunday School."
>
> Mr George Stone moved and Mr Longman seconded, as an amendment, "That the use of said form of prayer be permitted in our School, and that the Church hereby expresses its full confidence in the Superintendent and teachers of the School."
>
> A long and exhaustive discussion followed, a resolution moved and seconded, that the vote be taken by ballot, was lost. The chairman then put the amendment, which was carried by 13 to 9; and the original motion, was lost by 9 to 15.[95]

Although the congregation was clearly of the mind that it should be consulted on the use of set prayers in its worshipping life, it appears that the majority did not oppose their use. If appropriate and used in the right

92. Baird and Binney, *Chapter on Liturgies*, 285–328.

93. Baird and Binney, *Chapter on Liturgies*, 305.

94. Sanford Street Congregational Church, *Minutes*, January 30, 1884, and February 27, 1884.

95. Sanford Street Congregational Church, *Minutes*, February 27, 1884.

manner, set or liturgical prayers had the potential to enhance worship especially in the corporate setting. This sentiment finds support in the writings of Binney and others, such as David Thomas (1813–94) who explained in the introduction to his *Biblical Liturgy*, a work in which he sought to improve the quality of worship, that he did not see liturgy as superseding free prayer, instead considered it to be a means to stimulate and direct the prayers of the people.[96] Liturgy as a way of ordering and providing content for worship, as it was accepted and/or explored by Congregationalists, came to offer a method of ensuring corporate worship was a true expression of the congregation. It was a means of moderating the situation that has already been described as having taken place in corporate worship where it was the congregation addressed by the minister in prayers not God. Nathaniel Micklem (1888–1976) made the case for liturgical forms which would "rescue both ministers and congregations from being at the mercy of ministerial moods."[97]

The shift in parts of Congregationalism over the nineteenth and in the twentieth century towards corporate worship using liturgical forms was not solely about its corporate nature. It also related to aesthetics and enlivening those gathered in their worship of God. Barrett, in his paper, reminded Congregationalists that the "only worship acceptable to God is worship in spirit and truth."[98] This Scripture-based concept was not just about the freedom of the Holy Spirit in worship, it concerned the attitude of worshippers. Barrett spoke of the reverence of the worshippers and how form, be it a full liturgy or worship that had an order, played its part:

> Form counts for something even in relation to the spirit of worship. It helps to preserve and sometimes to intensify that spirit, for it is not more true to say that undevoutness of spirit often leads to irreverence of manner than it is to say irreverence of manner frequently lead to undevoutness of spirit.[99]

This perspective was supported by Christopher Newman Hall (1816–1902) and John Hunter (1849–1917). In the preface to the *Free Church Service Book* (1866), Newman Hall wrote:

---

96. Thomas, *Biblical Liturgy*, ii.
97. Davies, *Worship and Theology*, 5:355.
98. See Barrett, "Congregational Worship," 83.
99. See Barrett, "Congregational Worship," 84.

> It is often urged in opposition to form that *worship should be spiritual*. But the spirituality of worship depends on the state of the heart, on the style of its expression. There may be true worship with forms, and more formality with none.[100]

Hunter, acknowledged how liturgy can cultivate "reverent habits" and "form may be the vehicle and helper of the spirit."[101]

Worship that was aesthetically more pleasing and that emotionally moved the congregation developed across the ecclesiological landscape. The Oxford Movement in the mid-nineteenth century sought to reinvigorate, in a very particular way, the spirituality and religion of the Church of England through returning to the Church Fathers and recovering the Church's catholic and apostolic inheritance.[102] Although it was a movement that was intended to challenge ecclesiology and theology, its ideas and views impacted approaches taken to worship and liturgical innovation.[103] Following this, while not directly connected, in the early twentieth century the Liturgical Movement emerged from the Roman Catholic Church. This was a movement that was concerned with the "decline of interest in institutional religion, the tendency to minimize supernatural religion as a religion of grace and to lay the whole emphasis on the practical expression of Christianity in its bearing on the problems of the day."[104] Its main influence was on corporate worship, drawing the devotional life of the individual into what the church does corporately when it comes to worship God. These movements might have begun in certain church traditions, but their theories and ideas crossed denominational boundaries. This is shown through the influence of the Liturgical Movement in the Ecumenical Movement,[105] and is evident in Congregationalism from papers on worship that were presented at annual meetings of the Union over its lifetime, as well as in the writings and use of books of prayer and liturgy in corporate worship.[106] However,

---

100. Hall, *Free Church Service Book*, v.
101. Hunter, *Devotional Services*, 325.
102. Brown et al., *Oxford Movement*, 1.
103. Brown et al., *Oxford Movement*, 3.
104. Srawley, *Liturgical Movement*, 7.

105. The Ecumenical Movement began in the nineteenth century seeking to reunite the body of Christ through theological dialogue, collaborative mission and other expression of ecumenical life. It sought to bring about renewal and transformation of the church universal by bringing together common priorities for the life and worship of the church.

106. See Septimus March, "Sensuousness in Worship," in Congregational Union

it should be noted that nonconformists were universally suspicious of the Oxford Movement.

Not all the responses to the changing patterns of worship in Congregationalism, because of these various movements, were positive. To the 1873 annual meeting of the Union Septimus March gave a paper that warned against the rise of sensuousness in worship, making the case for aspects of Congregationalism that should not be ignored when considering its corporate worship. He wrote:

> Under colour of the modern cant phrase of "keeping abreast of the age," it is now and then urged that, if our youth is to be retained amongst us we must go as far as may be toward increasing sensuousness and symbolism in our worship. The chapel must be Gothic and cruciform, regardless of comfort and acoustic properties; a chancel is indispensable; the pulpit must be put on one side, to give a good view of the coloured window and the table draped like an altar; the prayer, if still extemporaneous, must be mainly composed of memoriter repetitions from the Church of England liturgy; and choral must supplant congregational singing. This sort of thing is consistent with High Church doctrine and sacramentarianism, but is absurd, meaningless and dishonest in connection with the tenets of Evangelical Nonconformity.[107]

March did not discount all that was happening in the worship of Congregational churches regarding ordered worship. For him, the Holy Spirit was still the primary agent for engaging a church in worship:

> But let us bear in mind that spirituality is the true converse and counteractive of sensuousness, and if this does not accompany the simplicity of our service it is poor indeed. If in our sanctuaries the Scriptures are languidly read; if the prayers are theological discourses, . . . if our preaching is only a Biblical dissertation, lacking all religious fervour; the people may well leave us for Ritualistic celebrations. But if there be the indescribable glow pervading all that comes from the presence of God's Spirit; if men and women with aching hearts, and many cares, and longings after something this world cannot give, hear one speak who has come from communion with Christ, who feels that heaven and hell are real as day

---

of England and Wales, *Yearbook, 1874*; see J. P. Allen, "The Work of the Churches in Preaching and Otherwise Promoting the Gospel," in Congregational Union of England and Wales, *Yearbook, 1876*; see Barrett, "Congregational Worship"; see McClure, "Public Worship of God."

107. See March, "Sensuousness in Worship," 116–17.

and night, who really does plead and pray for those he seeks to
save, the attractions of scenic display and richest music will be all
outdone.[108]

As Congregational churches shifted to embrace liturgy more in corporate worship and to have worship, which historian Charles Cashdollar described as being about head and heart, and eye and ear, then a delicate balance between order and freedom had to be observed.[109] This was especially important if worship was to be in and of the Holy Spirit. Dale wrote:

> The problem solved by those who are interested in the aesthetics of public worship is singularly delicate. They have to consider how they can secure perfect freedom for the highest activities of our spiritual nature; but they must not attempt to stimulate and intensify these activities. Reverential awe, peaceful trust, the fervour of love, the exultation of hope, can be created only by the Holy Ghost; all that Art can do is to provide for these supernatural affections a just and adequate expression. It may provide the instrument for the Divine hand, but must not attempt itself to strike the chords.[110]

Dale went on to express the view that there could never be one liturgical order to fit all times and context. He also believed that the simpler the order the more likely it would bring worshippers to a point of true worship of God.[111] Given the number of books of liturgies and prayers published by individual Congregational churches and the Congregational Union, and approaches taken to their use, these principles of Dale's rang true.[112] Order and freedom married in Congregational worship through the development of liturgies which responded to schools of thought in the Free Churches and movements of the church universal.

Worship Books

The worship of Congregational churches was never without order. William Hale White (1831–1914), writing under his pseudonym Mark Rutherford, remembered in his childhood a service consisted of "a hymn, a Bible reading, another hymn, a prayer, the sermon, a third hymn, and a short final

---

108. See March, "Sensuousness in Worship," 117–18.
109. Cashdollar, *Spiritual Home*, 36.
110. Dale, *Holy Spirit*, 34.
111. Dale, *Holy Spirit*, 34.
112. Colechin, "Worship of the United Reformed Church," 321–28.

prayer."[113] The use of that order to enhance corporate worship and develop its corporate nature gained impetus in the lifetime of the Congregational Union of England and Wales. Yet, the order as described by White remained relatively unchanged. This is shown in table 1 which compares the orders for a service of the Word detailed in three of the four service books that were published by the Congregational Union of England and Wales. The most significant difference is with the order from *An Order of Public Worship* (1970) where there is no provision for a "children's address" and "Intercessions" come after the sermon. Although in the notes on the order children were still expected to be present in the early part of the service, there is no evidence to suggest why this element was removed.[114] The relocation of the "Intercessions" made these prayers part of the congregation's response to God's Word, rather than as part of the preparation to hear God's Word. The reason for this shift could have been the influence of the Liturgical and Ecumenical Movements. However, the same shift happened in the order of corporate worship outlined by the Presbyterian Church of England at a similar time coinciding with when the Congregationalists and Presbyterians were in conversation about possible union and were working more closely on the question of worship of the church. Therefore, it is also possible that the two denominations may have influenced each other as they moved towards a union which would be supported by corporate worship.

TABLE 1. *Comparison of rubrics for a service of the Word in the services books of the Congregational Union in England and Wales*

Book of Congregational Worship (1920)	A Book of Services and Prayers (1959)	An Order of Public Worship (1970)
Sanctus/Hymn of adoration		
	Call to worship Scripture sentences	Call to worship Scripture sentences
Prayer of approach (and confession)	Prayer of adoration and invocation	

---

113. Rutherford, *Autobiography*, 7; Spinks, *Freedom or Order*, 87.
114. Congregational Church in England and Wales, *Order of Public Worship*, 29.

Book of Congregational Worship (1920)	A Book of Services and Prayers (1959)	An Order of Public Worship (1970)
Canticles (or just a hymn and the canticles can come after 2nd reading or children's address)	Hymn	Hymn/Psalm
	Confession of sin Assurance of Pardon (Prayer for grace)	Prayer of approach Confession of sin Assurance of Pardon
		Prayer for grace
Scripture reading	Old Testament reading	Old Testament reading
Psalm or other passage of Scripture (chanted or read responsively)	Psalm/Canticle	Psalm/Canticle/Hymn
Scripture reading or Children's address	New Testament reading	New Testament readings (Epistle and Gospel)
	Children's address	
Hymn	Hymn (suitable for children)	Hymn
Prayer and Lord's prayer	Prayers of thanksgiving and intercession, and Lord's prayer	
	Notices	
Hymn	Hymn	
Sermon	Sermon	Sermon (followed by collect or doxology)
	Offering	
	Prayer of thanksgiving for the Word of God, with supplication for grace and remembrance of the church of Christ (and dedication of offering taken beforehand, the Lord's prayer might come here too)	Intercessions (could be followed by Lord's prayer)
Offering		Offering
Hymn	Hymn	Hymn/Doxology
Benediction	Blessing	Dismissal

A Historical Theology of Worship

A survey of resources written by Congregationalists or commissioned by Congregational churches identified twenty-two volumes dedicated to providing liturgies or prayers for use in worship.[115] Theologian Bryan Spinks in his work on eucharistic liturgies used in Congregationalism, also identified a number of liturgies used by churches which were based on the Church of England's *Book of Common Prayer*.[116] Neither of these lists were thought to be exhaustive and, therefore, significant to how freedom in corporate worship had come to be understood. As only four volumes were commissioned by the Congregational Union of England and Wales, and the rest by individuals or local congregations, freedom can still be concluded as an important principle. Christopher Newman Hall (1816–1902) observed that the promotion of form did not limit freedom, but instead extended it.[117] The foreword to the liturgies compiled for use at Derby Street Congregational Church, Bolton, expressed the view that "the spirit of the devout and intelligent worshippers is greatly helped when a clear understanding obtains as to the plan and sequence of the service."[118] Most of the books identified stated that there was a place for extemporaneous or free prayer within the written services. Others talked of the liturgies and orders being aids for the preparation of worship and not intended to be used verbatim. This all built freedom into worship while constraining but not limiting it by order. Horton Davies observed that using liturgy as an aid provided "a theological structure for worship with an abundance of alternative prayers so that familiarity cannot breed contempt, nor capriciousness lead to congregational confusion."[119]

In demonstrating an understanding and embracement of liturgical order in worship, the extensive number of service and liturgy books illustrate how liturgy came to be seen as a way of reaffirming the corporate nature of public worship in Congregationalism. Many of the liturgies encouraged participation of the congregation through audible response. W. E. Orchard (1877–1955) stated that as well as securing "comprehension and order in our prayers," liturgy "enables the congregation to follow with greater ease" and through "frequent audible response" make "the prayers their own."[120]

---

115. Colechin, "Worship of the United Reformed Church," 321–28.
116. Spinks, *Freedom or Order*, 91–105.
117. Hall, *Free Church Service Book*, ii.
118. Jones, *Church Meets for Worship*, 3.
119. Davies, *Worship and Theology*, 5:374.
120. Orchard, *Divine Service*, 4.

The Liturgical Movement encouraged churches to address the issue that congregations were being perceived by some as audiences, an argument also made repeatedly by Thomas Binney.[121] Worship was not there to entertain people, rather people should be "actively engaged in the corporate worship of God."[122]

Participation

John McClure, in his Chairman's address to the Union in 1919, observed that public worship was the seeking of communion with God and with fellow-worshippers and "neither communion can be fully realized without the other."[123] This translates into the concept that worship should be the responsibility of all those in attendance and not rest simply with the minister. James explained this as worship being the "conscious and deliberate cooperation of all," and illustrated it as follows:

> The service of praise belongs not only to the choir, but to all God's people. The prayer made in the pulpit will find prevailing power as it is backed by the earnest and passionate sympathy and petition of those who occupy the pews. The sermon has been made in the study, but it will be re-made by a [minister's] people if they meet with the keen desire to see it fashioned into an instrument of divine energy.[124]

This might have come to be the view of some Congregationalists by the 1920s. But as has been demonstrated throughout this chapter, this shared responsibility was not the lived experience of all at corporate worship. Given one of the aims of the final order of service published by the Congregational Church in England and Wales in 1970 was "to encourage the fullest possible congregational participation," attitudes, at least at a denominational level, did appear to have changed.[125]

Early in the life of the Congregational Union of England and Wales, there were two schools of thought on corporate worship and the role of the congregation. Joseph Parker wrote in a sermon on Isaiah that, "worship

---

121. Baird and Binney, *Chapter on Liturgies*, 292; Morgan, "Spirituality, Worship, and Congregational Life," 513.
122. Jones, *Church Meets for Worship*, 3.
123. See McClure, "Public Worship of God," 45.
124. James, *Work and Administration*, 52.
125. Congregational Church in England and Wales, *Order of Public Worship*, vii.

is an experience of entering into the refining, purifying presence of God. Worship is communion with God."[126] However, the communion of the people with God, David Thomas observed, was solely the responsibility of the minister.[127] By the mid-to-late-nineteenth century, there was a sense that the lived reality of Congregational churches, when they came to worship, was not something that always brought congregations into the presence of God. Ministers and educators such as Thomas Binney, David Thomas, and William Taylor recognized that the role of the minister in worship needed to change subtly, even if there was not a revolutionary reimagining of worship itself in Congregationalism. Ministers needed to be reminded that they should be acting with the people and not for them.[128]

A governing principle within Congregationalism is the "priesthood of all believers." The apostle Paul spoke of the Holy Spirit giving gifts to the whole church to be used in the church's discipleship and mission.[129] Although published not long before the union with the Presbyterian Church of England, the Congregational Church in England and Wales reflected on what this means in the life of the Church in its *Declaration of Faith* (1967):

> Men and women, called in Christian discipleship to share the corporate life of God's faithful people, receive power, each according to [their] need and opportunity: power to love God in response to his own loving, power to obey him, power to learn from him and hold fast to his ways despite external and internal dissuasives. There is power for each as all participate in the worship of the Church and in its local and world-wide life and mission.[130]

Therefore, worship being minster-centric feels at odds with this principle of Congregational polity. What appears evident from studying what was written on corporate worship in the late nineteenth century and early twentieth century was an awakening of Congregationalists to the principle of the "priesthood of all believers" being more fully emphasized in worship. This was thought out in the writings of leading Congregationalists from early on, yet what this meant in practice for local congregations took longer to discern and varied from place to place.

---

126. Old, *Reading and Preaching*, 6:422.
127. Thomas, *Ministry and the Church*, 9.
128. Binney, *Service of Song*, 72.
129. Eph 4:11–13.
130. Congregational Church in England and Wales, *Declaration of Faith*, 46.

Worship in Congregationalism

The minister-centricity of worship in Congregational churches was in part due to the central place of preaching in public worship inherited from previous generations. McClure observed that this took away from worship what should have made worship a common act. He wrote:

> For whatever preaching may do to exhort, rebuke, direct, enlighten, edify, or inspire, it should do so through the feelings awakened in the congregation by their acts of common worship. Only as it speaks to souls uplifted and purified can it exercise its true function, and fulfil its purpose; only thus can it become what it is meant to be—an act of worship for all and by all. Because we have failed to realize this, our assemblies for worship are too often looked upon as mere public meetings, and our churches as the lecture-rooms of popular speakers.[131]

The redressing of this came through changing a congregation's perspective on prayer and praise. Worship in Congregationalism was not devoid of elements that encouraged the people corporately to praise God; the singing of psalms and hymns was practiced. The content and use of hymns became a focal point for participation, especially as the organ and choir came to be used to enhance the musicality of hymnody. Henry Allon (1818–92) wrote that "church song is the only congregational act," and was, therefore, cautious over how choirs were being used:

> We do not sing when we merely listen to a choir, any more that we preach when we merely listen to a sermon: the song or the sermon may affect us, but it is the act of another, and not our own. God cannot be worshipped vicariously.[132]

In the annual report to the thirty-second Annual Meeting of the Congregational Union of England and Wales, it was noted that while the human spirit sings "it can soar up into the beatific vision of the pure in heart who see God," and such "communion in spiritual song is true worship."[133] As Allon wrote, "poetic song is the natural expression of praise, the spontaneous form of adoration, thanksgiving, and joy."[134] Hymnody in Congregationalism did develop into corporate expressions of adoration, confession,

---

131. See McClure, "Public Worship of God," 53.
132. Allon, *Church Song*, 11.
133. Congregational Union of England and Wales, *Yearbook, 1863*, 61.
134. Allon, *Church Song*, 8.

thanksgiving and intercessions.[135] Therefore, hymns became the primary vehicle for Congregationalists to participate in worship. In the preface to *A Book of Public Worship*, the compilers acknowledged the importance of psalms and hymns in public worship and how they can be the only means of the congregation vocally entering into the service and recommended that these considerations be kept in mind when choosing a psalm or a hymn, including "its place in the service, the capacities of the choir and congregation, familiarity of words and tunes, [and] the subject of the sermon."[136] Given this emphasis it is no surprise that Daniel Jenkins observed that the aspect of worship Congregationalists took an "active interest in" and had greatest "understanding of" was their hymnody.[137] Therefore, it is of note that in the life of the Congregational Union of England and Wales, five hymn books were compiled and published: *Congregational Hymn Book* (1836), *New Congregational Hymn Book* (1859), *Congregational Church Hymnal* (1887), *Congregational Hymnary* (1916), and *Congregational Praise* (1951).

Bernard Lord Manning made the claim that the hymn book was the liturgy of Congregationalists, Jenkins, however, stated that this remark "displays a misleading conception of the nature of liturgy and probably exaggerates the influence" of hymns.[138] Liturgy was not only used to order Congregational worship; it was used to encourage participation and enable congregations to make prayer as well as praise common. The skepticism of past generations was never lost, but, as McClure noted, the advantages of a liturgy came to outweigh its potential defects. By "enabling all to join more heartily and more intelligently in common worship, [written liturgy] provides a much needed means of grace for both minister and congregation."[139] In some churches, this was shown to be true. In the foreword of the revised edition of the *Rodbourgh Bede Book* it stated that the first edition was found to enable the "congregation to participate vocally in the worship."[140] Despite this, the widespread use of responsive liturgies in Congregational churches cannot be assumed, especially as it was not until the publication of *An Order of Public Worship* (1970) that a service book was published by the denomination that included prayers with congregational responses. All the

135. Morgan, "Spirituality, Worship, and Congregational Life," 519.
136. Huxtable et al., *Book of Public Worship*, xv.
137. Jenkins, *Congregationalism*, 92.
138. Jenkins, *Congregationalism*, 91.
139. See McClure, "Public Worship of God," 56.
140. Chapman, *Rodborough Bede Book*, Foreword.

other service books published by the Congregational Union of England and Wales were designed as directories and the prayers offered were examples for use by the minister or worship leader in preparing to lead a congregation in prayer not to be prayed with direct congregational participation.

Horton Davies saw the silence of the congregation in public prayer as restricting full participation, but the absence of responsive prayers could also suggest that congregations may not have felt participation required audible response beyond the singing of hymns.[141] This is demonstrated by the early attitudes taken by churches to praying the Lord's prayer in unison and ending prayers with a collective "Amen." Although neither of these actions were remarkable in Congregational worship by the mid-twentieth century, these easy ways of encouraging congregational participation in prayer and making prayer corporate did meet resistance, particularly in the late nineteenth century.[142] Barrett observed:

> Any change that tends to make our worship unministeral and more congregational would be gladly welcomed by our people, but it is a curious anomaly that the very churches most fiercely intolerant of sacerdotalism in this country should be so unwilling for any voice to be heard in public prayers other than that of the minister who leads those prayers.[143]

Examples of this were found in the church meeting minutes of Fisherton Street Congregational Church, Salisbury, where in 1873 and again in 1875, the pastor proposed that the people responded with "Amen" at the close of prayers and said the Lord's Prayer in unison with him during worship. On both occasions the church meeting was divided, so the pastor withdrew his proposal.[144] When presenting the case for repetition of the Lord's Prayer and the saying of "Amen" by the people for the second time, the pastor reassured those present at the church meeting that "these changes were perfectly consistent with . . . nonconformist principles, maintaining that the real question was whether or not the adoption of these two . . . alterations were conducive to more or less spirituality in worship."[145] Around the same time, similar discussion occurred in the church meeting of Emmanuel

---

141. Davies, *Worship and Theology*, 5:377.
142. Cashdollar, *Spiritual Home*, 41.
143. See Barrett, "Congregational Worship," 87.
144. Fisherton Congregational Church, *Church Book*, October 2, 1873, and January 5, 1875.
145. Fisherton Congregational Church, *Church Book*, January 5, 1875.

Congregational Church, Cambridge. The Church was divided over the audible reciting of the Lord's prayer in worship. The minutes of the church meeting held in October 1874 masterfully resolved:

> The right of every member of the congregation to repeat the Lord's Prayer with the minister if [they] be so inclined.[146]

Although this resolution received unanimous approval, when asked if "the Church desired members to exercise this liberty," no consensus was reached.[147]

The influence of the Liturgical Movement was the perception of worship as the communion of all with God and with each other through the inclusion of audible, common responses as part of liturgy in which all actively participate. However, if a congregation is led in a way that is about the fellowship worshipping God, then even an "Amen" may not be necessary. Although written by Taylor in the late nineteenth century, participation in worship in Congregationalism could be described in this way throughout the twentieth century too:

> It is alleged . . . by many that we who have no formal liturgy, exalt the sermon at the expense of the worship. But they who speak in such a fashion, forget that preaching and hearing from the Word of God, when they are engaged in by the pastor and people out of love to Christ, and with a desire to honour Him, are as really worship as praise and prayer.[148]

Freedom in worship is, therefore, the ability for people to participate freely in the communion with God and with each other as part of corporate worship. The one tension in this is the acknowledgement that not all people will want to make that participation in the same way. This is when the liturgy as described by a directory benefits public worship.

Conclusion

The principles of freedom, order, and participation in approaching corporate worship that were established by the end of the eighteenth century in nonconformity were upheld in how Congregationalists viewed corporate

---

146. Randall, "Emmanuel Congregational Church," 75.
147. Randall, "Emmanuel Congregational Church," 75.
148. Taylor, *Ministry of the Word*, 207.

worship. As might be expected, there was development of thought and different perspectives taken. In practice, freedom in worship, one of the most crucial principles for Congregationalists, became more about choice and a sense of upholding a historical convention. The Holy Spirit still played a role in why freedom was emphasized in the worship of the Congregationalists, but the work of the Holy Spirit was perceived to be inspiring and giving revelation primarily to the words of the minister. If worship was completely open to the action of the Holy Spirit, then worship cannot be understood as free in the human sense of the term. Worship free to action of the Holy Spirit would be entirely controlled by God. Although this ideal may have been believed in early Congregational worship, what has become evident is that human freedom—the right to choose and participate as one felt appropriate—was primarily how freedom in worship was interpreted. Divine inspiration may have been sought as part of that freedom but this was the limit of divine freedom.

With the elaboration of what freedom in worship actually meant for Congregationalists came the need to balance order and freedom in worship. This was to ensure that worship both glorified God and edified the congregation, which is an essential purpose of the church gathering for worship. Although, as with the worship of the seventeenth and eighteenth centuries, Congregational worship was never without order, what that order incorporated and what it meant to the overall action of corporate worship was more purposefully considered. Neither the Congregational Union of England and Wales nor the Congregational Church in England and Wales ever prescribed a set liturgy. But attempts were made by the denomination and individuals to suggest patterns and contents that would enhance the worship of the church. In the twentieth century this reflected what was happening in the wider church through the Liturgical and Ecumenical Movements.

The more active consideration of the interrelationship of freedom and order also developed the understanding of what it meant to participate. The introduction of written liturgies began to encourage the use of other verbal responses by congregations in addition to the singing of hymns and psalms. As identified in the exploration of worship in the earlier centuries, participation was not only about the outward action of the congregation within an act of corporate worship. In Congregationalism, participation began to be seen as the development of the communion of the congregation with God as well as with each other when they gathered for that corporate act of prayer, praise and listening. The important emphasis on the hearing of the Word of God, enabled by the Holy Spirit, was maintained in what it meant for the congregation to participate.

4

Worship in Presbyterianism

THE BASIS OF UNION, agreed by those who came together to form the Presbyterian Church of England in 1876, stated that "the Westminster Directory of Worship generally [exhibited] the order of public worship and of the ministration of the Sacraments in this Church."[1] It seems remarkable that after 231 years the Westminster Assembly's *Directory for the Public Worship of God* would be the document that the reemerged tradition of Presbyterianism in England would turn to for guiding the corporate worship of the Church. In the nineteenth century, as a tradition whose reemergence was due to primarily Scottish migrants, but added to by Irish and Welsh migrants, it might be expected that their worship would be predominantly influenced by the tradition these migrants brought with them. Nevertheless, it cannot be ignored that there continued to be deep-seated suspicions in English nonconformity of Catholic influence. Therefore, this prevented wider exploration of how corporate worship might be ordered and conducted. Horton Davies in his commentary on Presbyterian worship stated, the principle of "a form of worship which would combine the advantages of common order with the freedom of the Holy Spirit," established in the seventeenth century in the *Directory for the Public Worship of God*, was the natural anchor for the worship of the English Presbyterians.[2] This meant that from the outset corporate worship in English Presbyterianism was understood in terms of order and freedom, where order was the guiding hand that would ensure freedom did not lead to chaos. As found with the blending of freedom and order in the worship of the English

---

1. Presbyterian Church of England, *Memorial of the Union*, 181–82.
2. Davies, *Worship and Theology*, 3:91.

Congregationalists, the interrelationship of order and freedom enabled the participation of Presbyterian congregations in corporate worship. This was important for Presbyterians because the *Shorter* and *Longer Catechisms*, written by the Westminster Assembly, remained instrumental in the conduct of one's religious life and the first statement of both was "[Humanity's] chief end is to glorify God, and to enjoy him forever."[3]

Brief History of the Presbyterian Church of England

The Presbyterianism, formational in the United Reformed Church, has roots in migrant, dissenting Scottish traditions. During the first half of the eighteenth century much of what could be described as English Presbyterianism lost its Trinitarian moorings, adopting Arian and Socinian views as congregations migrated towards Unitarianism. This was not the case for all congregations who at the beginning of the eighteenth century identified themselves as Presbyterian. At this point in history two-thirds of nonconformists in England would have identified themselves thus, although it cannot be claimed that they all intended the same thing by the term.[4] Therefore, not everyone who described themselves as Presbyterian became Unitarian, but the title of Presbyterian generally fell into disuse. Small pockets of Presbyterians did survive in the north of England, around Newcastle and Northumberland, and in London. These congregations maintained doctrinal orthodoxy by securing ministers from Scotland.

The expansion of Presbyterianism in England gained momentum in the nineteenth century with Scottish migrants forming their own churches. The primary locations for these churches were Liverpool, Manchester, Newcastle, and London. Around Liverpool, in Lancashire, and in other pockets around England, there were also Irish influences on Presbyterianism due to the Irish migrants found in those areas of the country.[5] As the number of

---

3. Westminster Assembly, *Larger Catechism*, 3; Westminster Assembly, *Shorter Catechism*, 3.

4. Smith and Kemeny, *Presbyterianism*, 122. It is of note that at this point in Church History the term "Presbyterian" was almost synonymous with the terms "Puritan" and "Precisian." Although there were differences, they were to all intents and purpose nicknames. Presbyterianism was linked with a particular understanding of Church governance that was observed in the Reformed churches in Europe and hoped for in the English church (Drysdale, *Presbyterians in England*, 4–8).

5. Buick Knox in his paper on the links between Irish and English Presbyterianism gave examples of how both Irish migrants led to the planting of churches and became

churches grew, they organized themselves into presbyteries, foundational for Presbyterian governance. Presbyterian minister and historian Carnegie Simpson (1865–1945), in a lecture to the Presbyterian Historical Society of England given in 1936, said: "Presbyterianism is the form of church government which was adopted—or rather was reverted to—at the Reformation by churches which were free, in matters of polity, to follow what they believed to be New Testament direction."[6] In this definition, Simpson did not intend to suggest that "Presbyterianism was an exact replica of the system of the New Testament churches" but it followed a conciliar model of church government.[7] Conciliarity ran throughout the organization of the Church. To demonstrate this, Simpson said:

> It is government not by one man but by *brethren conferring and acting together*. The congregation is under, not an individual minister (or priest or rector), but a "session"; and ecclesiastical district is under, not a bishop but the "presbytery"; the church as a whole, in a national or other large area, is under, not a primate but a general "synod" or "assembly."[8]

These councils, although they imply a democratic ideal were essentially theocratic. Simpson stated:

> It is that the church is composed of the people of God; and this supernatural society governs itself in His Name. This . . . is agreeable to the New Testament, where the Apostles—whatever their special function in regard to ordination—acted with the body of the people in matters of church legislation and government. The Church of Christ is a self-governing society; and its members are not to be put under a ruling any more than under a sacerdotal

---

influential characters in English Presbyterian churches. In Plymouth, the influx comprised soldiers, sailors and shipwrights from Belfast suggesting the need for a Presbyterian church and through support from the Presbytery of Belfast, a church was founded in 1857 (Knox, "Irish and English Presbyterianism," 8). Although often observed as being a 'Scottish' church, two of the earliest elders of St. Columba's Church in Cambridge came from Irish Presbyterianism and subscriptions to raise money for the building of the church also came from a number of Irish contributors (Knox, "Irish and English Presbyterianism," 8–9). Knox also noted that when the Presbyterian Church in England lost ministers back to Scotland, ministers from Ireland came initially to fill the gaps in the ministry of the Church (Knox, "Irish and English Presbyterianism," 4).

6. Simpson, *Character of Presbytery*, 4.
7. Simpson, *Character of Presbytery*, 4–5.
8. Simpson, *Character of Presbytery*, 5.

order, but are—in New Testament language—"kings" as well as "priests unto God."[9]

The conciliarity of Presbyterianism was different from the polity of Congregationalism. Congregationalism was governed by the church meeting and, therefore, the focus was on single, local congregations even when they participated in wider unions. Presbyterianism understood the "visible church of Christ," being "more than the local congregation."[10] Consequently, as Presbyterian churches were founded in areas of England, it was important for their ecclesiology that they organize themselves into presbyteries and ultimately a synod.

Given the primarily Scottish core in the churches, individual presbyteries initially approached the Church of Scotland to establish a connection to a synod. All these applications were refused. Yet, in 1835, as recorded by Presbyterian commentator and historian S. W. Carruthers, the General Assembly of the Church of Scotland recommended to all the presbyteries in England that they "form one or more synods, and promised that [the Church of Scotland] would then enter into such a communion with them as may distinctly mark their recognition of them as a branch of the Church of Scotland."[11] In accordance with this advice, the presbyteries of Lancashire and the North-west of England formed a synod in 1836, adopting the "Westminster Standards in doctrine, discipline, government and worship."[12] The synod grew by incorporating the presbyteries of London and Newcastle in 1839, adopting the title of "the Presbyterian Synod in England in connection with the Church of Scotland."[13] However, this synod was never received into the Church of Scotland and it dropped the words "in connection with the Church of Scotland" from its title in 1844 as a result of the "Disruption" of the previous year.[14] In 1843, ten years of conflict in the Church of Scotland (hereafter referred to as the Kirk) came to a head. There were two factions in the Kirk: the Evangelicals who wanted the Kirk to be free of patronage and free to purify itself through mission and Bible circulation; and the Moderates who accepted oversight by the state and

---

9. Simpson, *Character of Presbytery*, 6.
10. Simpson, *Character of Presbytery*, 8.
11. Carruthers, *1844*, 4.
12. Presbyterian Church of England, *Memorial of the Union*, 23.
13. Carruthers, *1844*, 4; Smith and Kemeny, *Presbyterianism*, 127.
14. Carruthers, *1844*, 4.

found "missioning suspicious and vulgar."[15] As the Evangelicals became more influential in the Kirk's General Assembly and started to try to bring about changes in the relationship between the Kirk and the State, tensions with Parliament in Westminster increased. After drawing up a "Claim of Right" in 1842, leaders of the Kirk's General Assembly attempted to convince Parliament they did so as an act of integrity and on the principle that Jesus Christ, and not the State, was the head of the church.[16] However, their actions were seen as putting the Kirk above the law of the land. In protest of Parliament's rejection of the "Claim of Right," the retiring Moderator of the General Assembly walked out of the General Assembly in 1843 taking with him "over one-third of the Kirk's ministers to form the Free Church of Scotland."[17] With this split in the Kirk any aspirations held by the Presbyterians in England to be formally recognized as part of the Church of Scotland were lost, not only because of the political issues related to the Church of Scotland having churches south of the Tweed but also because predominantly the English Synod sympathies were with the Free Church of Scotland.[18] This did not prevent continued division among English Presbyterians on their identity as there were those who still considered themselves as "the scattered sheep of Scotland in the difficult pastures of the English cities," and those "charged with an English mission and in consequence wanted the [Presbyterian Church in England] to shed its Scottish clothing and glory in pure Presbyterianism."[19] But the Presbyterian Synod in England could not maintain a position that was not one or the other as "a steady flow of ministers left England for vacant parishes in the Kirk" between 1843 and 1844.[20] Therefore, in 1844 the meeting of the Presbyterian Synod in England declared independence from the Kirk and recognized its future lay as "part of English Dissent not as an alternative 'British' establishment."[21] By the end of the meeting, the Presbyterian Synod in England's organization had been established, a committee appointed to develop the *Book of Order*, and steps taken to create a theological college enabling the training

---

15. Wallace, *Scottish Presbyterianism*, 6.
16. General Assembly of the Church of Scotland, "Claim, Declaration, and Protest."
17. Wallace, *Scottish Presbyterianism*, 7.
18. Knox, "Irish and English Presbyterianism," 3; Sell, "Living in the Half Lights," 18.
19. Cornick, "Catch a Scotchman Becoming an Englishman," 203.
20. Cornick, "Disruption in London," 291.
21. Cornick, "Disruption in London," 292.

of ministers.[22] By 1847, there was a committee employed in the preparation of a hymn book.

The Presbyterian Church in England (as the Presbyterian Synod in England came to be known) was not the only Presbyterian church that established itself in the nineteenth century. This was recognized early on by the Presbyterian Church in England and a committee was appointed "to put themselves into communication with such presbyteries in [the] country as adhere to the Westminster standards, with the view of cultivating a [mutually supportive] spirit, which may at some future period issue in a union."[23] One of these such churches was the United Presbyterian Church of Scotland that came from schisms in the Church of Scotland which occurred in eighteenth century: the "Secession" in 1733 and the "Relief (from Patronage)" in 1752. It had planted churches in England from the middle of the 1800s and, by 1867, had formed an English Synod due to strong evidence that the churches in England needed to be treated separately.[24] On June 13, 1876, in Liverpool, the Synod of the Presbyterian Church in England and the English Synod of the United Presbyterian Church of Scotland, both met for the last time and via an act of public witness (both Synods leaving their places of meeting and marching through the streets of Liverpool to the Philharmonic Hall) united to form the Presbyterian Church of England.[25] Included in this union was also a single congregation from the Reformed Presbyterian Church of Scotland in England which met at Shaw Street, Liverpool.[26]

The mission of this newly formed church was not to convert England to Presbyterianism but instead to further the Kingdom of God in England by enabling people to come to a loyal and catholic Christianity. The Church intended to undertake this work, Carruthers wrote, by using the best elements of Presbyterianism and the spirit of revival and union which had brought about the Presbyterian Church of England.[27] This understanding of its mission raised the question of the Church's relationship with the

---

22. Carruthers, *1844*, 4; Cornick, "Disruption in London," 292; Sell, "Living in the Half Lights," 18.

23. Carruthers, *1844*, 9.

24. Carruthers, *Fifty Years*, 6; Cashdollar, *Spiritual Home*, 5.

25. Carruthers, *1844*, 9; Doodson, *Presbyterians in Liverpool*, 313; Sell, "Living in the Half Lights," 19; Smith and Kemeny, *Presbyterianism*, 129.

26. Doodson, *Presbyterians in Liverpool*, 313, 371.

27. Carruthers, *Fifty Years*, 7.

Westminster Assembly's *Confession of Faith*. Could this continue to be the doctrinal standard of Presbyterianism? This was a question that had already been asked within Scottish Presbyterianism as changes in theological thought and development in biblical criticism challenged points in the Confession.[28] Given the interconnection between the Presbyterians of the British Isles through the movement of people and ministers, it is unsurprising that in 1883, three presbyteries—Liverpool, London and Birmingham—sent overtures to Synod conveying the view that the Westminster Assembly's *Confession of Faith* was "no longer well suited in form and expression" to the condition and aspirations of the Church.[29] Carruthers recorded:

> By an extremely large majority a Committee was appointed with instructions to consider the possibility of (1) changes in existing formulas of subscription, and (2) an explanatory declaration.[30]

This led to the appointed committee suggesting to Synod in 1884 that subscription, tying oneself or a church to a doctrinal creed or confession, should not be "to the doctrine of the [Westminster Assembly's *Confession of Faith*]" but to "the system of doctrine contained in" that confession.[31] An explanatory statement was submitted to Synod in 1885 which dealt with doctrinal matters in the Westminster Assembly's *Confession of Faith* that were considered difficult at times. The statement, which was approved by all the presbyteries and many of the sessions, discussed the universal offer of salvation, the question of humanity's total depravity, the mercy of God to infants and those beyond the reach of ordinary means of salvation, and persecution.[32] Although not immediately, this led to the preparation of *Articles of Faith* that were "doctrinal, credal in form, and trinitarian in arrangement (i.e., on the lines of the Apostles' Creed)," which were appended to "all matters of polity, worship, and civil relations."[33] Carruthers noted that although this emphasized and strengthened the character of the Presbyterian Church of England, it was not intended to separate it from its

---

28. Murray, "Disruption to Union," 87.
29. Carruthers, *Fifty Years*, 18.
30. Carruthers, *Fifty Years*, 18.
31. Carruthers, *Fifty Years*, 18.
32. Carruthers, *Fifty Years*, 18.
33. Carruthers, *Fifty Years*, 18.

sister churches.³⁴ However, it did set them apart from their sister churches because the Articles satisfied both those in the Presbyterian Church of England "who want the substance of the faith defined" and those who wanted definitions that were not over burdensome.³⁵ This approach to the Articles was also visible in the direction taken by the Church in other aspects of its life including worship.

Order in Worship

Presbyterian minister J. T. Middlemiss, in his paper to the Newcastle Presbytery on Presbyterian worship in 1893 suggested that liturgy had nothing to do with Presbyterianism.³⁶ However, Donald Fraser (1826–92), three years before, in a paper to the Synod meeting of the Presbyterian Church of England had shown that it was a mistake to say this about Presbyterian worship. Both in terms of their shared Reformed heritage and historically as part of the church in England, liturgical services had their place in the corporate worship of English Presbyterians.³⁷ Yet, in making that statement Middlemiss was questioning liturgy as that which was prescribed and must be conducted as written down. Although not deemed necessary by Middlemiss, written liturgy that gave substance and structure to worship but did not bind the minister, allowed the "exercise of gifts and graces." This was thought expedient particularly in preserving order and giving the worship of a denomination a "measured uniformity."³⁸ Therefore, liturgy as something that gave good order to worship was important, especially at a time when the opinion was widely held that the corporate worship of many congregations was without shape or form. Middlemiss stated:

> Order and beauty should characterise our mode of worship. Order and beauty in worship, of necessity, be good since they are divine. . . . Order and beauty are of God, and are evident in all His works. What adorns the outer courts of God's temple cannot be from its nature inadmissible into the inner, but ought to be, from His nature, ever present.³⁹

---

34. Carruthers, *Fifty Years*, 19.
35. Statter, "Managing the Disruptions," 69.
36. Middlemiss, *Directory of Worship Necessary*, 1.
37. Fraser, *Presbyterian Church of England*, 9–10.
38. Middlemiss, *Directory of Worship Necessary*, 2.
39. Middlemiss, *Directory of Worship Necessary*, 3.

When corporate worship of the Presbyterian Church of England received serious consideration by Synod, it was concerned primarily to consider order. "Beauty" followed as directories of worship were revised and became service books during the life of the Church. As a church with a more formal organizational structure, the resourcing of worship was predominantly based at the center through committees of the Synod and later the General Assembly. This was shown in research where all but three worship-related publications connected to the Presbyterian Church were found to be compiled by committees of the Church.[40] This was very different to Congregationalism. Although the two traditions did unite and they have shared commonalities historically and theologically, their polities were poles apart. Therefore, the development of worship books in English Presbyterianism was chronicled in the records of Synod and General Assembly meetings. It was by committee rather than individuals that reforms of the worship of the Church came about. This was not the case in Congregationalism.

Worship Books and Their Development

The approach taken by the Presbyterian Church of England to corporate worship was not given serious consideration by Synod until 1885. Overtures, which were submitted questions or proposals by individuals or presbyteries to the Synod, had been brought in preceding years relating to specific acts of worship—marriage and burial services—due to changes in law over who may preside over these rites.[41] In spite of these, no action was taken until an overture proposing that the use of the Westminster Assembly *Directory for the Public Worship of God* and its content by the Church be reviewed. A committee to consider the possibility of drafting a new directory was appointed and they began by consulting the churches over their customs in worship. Two hundred answers were scrutinized by the Committee, finding that "printed forms of worship for the Lord's Supper, marriages, burials and the reception of new communicants" were generally used, of which there were twenty-four different forms.[42] The sources of these different forms were not identified, although the Committee noted one instance of a minister using the Westminster Assembly *Directory for*

---

40. Colechin, "Worship of the United Reformed Church," 329–34.

41. Davies, *Worship and Theology*, 3:108.

42. Presbyterian Church of England, "Synod Records 1887," in *Synod Records 1885–1898*, 507; Davies, *Worship and Theology*, 3:109.

the Public Worship of God in baptismal services.[43] In Horton Davies's analysis of the Committee's findings, he stated that for the conduct of regular Sunday services, the Committee found considerable diversity:

> All but 30 of the congregations had two Scripture lections in the morning service, but the practice was most uncommon in the evenings. One hundred and eighteen congregations only repeated the Lord's Prayer at either the morning or evening service, but none repeated the Apostles' Creed. Very few congregations repeated the Creed even in the Communion service.[44]

Given that the Committee could not ascertain any principle on which the order of worship in congregations was based and the great variety in practice,[45] their conclusion was brought in the recommendation below to the Synod of 1886:

> The Committee . . . are of the opinion that it is desirable to prepare . . . a Revised Directory of Public Worship, on the basis of the "Westminster Directory," which "exhibits generally the order of public worship, and of the administration of sacraments in the Church;" and that, along with this, forms of service should be provided for optional use on special occasions, as at marriages, burials, ordinations of office-bearers, reception of young communicants, and the like. They are agreed in thinking that in this way the Church may gain much in respect of the completeness, concord, and decorum of her services.[46]

The Committee was instructed to undertake the proposed revision and the first draft of the revised *Directory for Public Worship* was presented to Synod in 1889 with copies circulated for comment. This initial draft contained seven chapters that covered public, corporate worship, the administering of the sacraments, marriage, and funeral services. Donald Fraser, Convener of the Committee, stated that most of the content followed the plan of a directory and were not to be considered as liturgies. He asserted:

> The Committee had taken this course, understanding it to be the wish of the Church to afford guidance to the inexperienced, and to place some restraint on individuals or local idiosyncrasies, but

---

43. Presbyterian Church of England, "Synod Records 1887," 508.

44. Davies, *Worship and Theology*, 3:109.

45. Presbyterian Church of England, "Synod Records 1887," 507.

46. Presbyterian Church of England, "Synod Records 1886," in *Synod Records 1885–1898*, 209.

by no means to stereotype the public worship under rigid forms of words.[47]

There was the proposal that specimen services could be included to illustrate the directions, but none had been drafted when the draft version of the directory was shared with the Synod. Although complete liturgies for baptism, marriage, and burial services were included due to the nature of these rites. The reasons given for the inclusion of prescribed language in the baptismal service were:

> (i) persons who are called on to make a public profession of faith and a solemn promise, ought to know beforehand what will be required of them; (ii) the method and the very terms of the administration of this rite, as the gate of entrance into the Church, should not vary, but be the same for all.[48]

Despite the fullness of the liturgies in each of these services, there was scope for extempory or unprescribed prayer.

Care had been taken by the Committee to justify the different aspects of the directory, but there was reticence in the Synod as far as the publication of liturgically complete resources was concerned. Davies, from evidence of the debates held in the Synod in 1889, stated that "there was a clear and acute division of opinion."[49] Sources quoted by Davies suggested that there were those who expressed the view that the directory should contain more liturgical material and be akin to the worship of John Knox (1514–72) and Andrew Melville (1545–1622). There were also those in the Synod who believed the worship of the Church should be representative of the nonconformist practice of the day.[50] Davies's analysis did not define what was meant by this but given the address made by Middlemiss to the Newcastle Presbytery in 1893, it can be assumed that there were those who felt the directory should not impinge on the freedom that was advocated by the Independents when the Westminster Assembly's *Directory for the Public Worship of God* was discussed and written.[51]

---

47. Presbyterian Church of England, "Synod Records 1889," in *Synod Records 1885–1898*, 272.
48. Presbyterian Church of England, "Synod Records 1889," 272.
49. Davies, *Worship and Theology*, 4:109–10.
50. Davies, *Worship and Theology*, 4:110.
51. Middlemiss, *Directory of Worship Necessary*, 4.

Initially, this did not prevent continuation of the drafting process. Controversy over the content of the directory did come to hamper its progress and led to work halting for a couple of years as discussions were postponed in Synod due to insufficient time and detail for proper, intelligent discussion.[52] In the Committee's defense of its work given to the Synod in 1894 and in Middlemiss's paper that was written as a response to the delay in Synod of the directory's progress because of objections raised by individuals and presbyteries, it was clear that the question of freedom in worship was of greatest concern.[53] The diversity of views held by the Church's councils in the early years of the Church is of note, and how one committee tried to find a middle ground. It also reflects how the Church, at this point in its history, was still divided between Presbyterian migrants and those with the mission to make the Presbyterians part of the nonconformist contingent in the ecclesiological landscape of England. In trying to persuade the Newcastle Presbytery of the case for the *Directory for Public Worship*, Middlemiss attempted to bridge this gap. Although he spoke out against the influence of the Independents, he recognized that the disunity in the approach taken to worship could be ascribed to the different influences of Independency and Scottish Presbyterianism. He argued:

> Perhaps the strongest argument against a directory is the fact that we have allowed that which we already possess to fall into general disuse. Things have gone so well under the present method (or want of method) that the introduction of this proposed book of order is not required. There may be something in that, but that something is very little. If things have been good in the past it is legitimate to desire that they be made better. Our service can be made better. They can be made more helpful and more orderly—more helpful, it seems to me, because more orderly. They can be made both, by following the lines laid down by the most sainted and most learned of our forefathers. We may be sure that men like ALEXANDER HENDERSON, SAMUEL RUTHERFORD, ROBERT BAILLIE, and GEORGE GILLESPIE knew which were the best methods for divine services from the standpoint of presbytery. And their views find support from the writings and practices of JOHN CALVIN and JOHN KNOX, names not lightly esteemed

---

52. Presbyterian Church of England, "Synod Records 1892," in *Synod Records 1885–1898*, 44; Presbyterian Church of England, "Synod Records 1893," in *Synod Records 1885–1898*, 343.

53. Presbyterian Church of England, "Synod Records 1894," in *Synod Records 1885–1898*, 852; Middlemiss, *Directory of Worship Necessary*, 4.

in the succession to which we belong. I therefore, as an English Presbyterian, prefer to follow those names I have mentioned rather than take my lead from the Brownists or Independents in anything pertaining to the worship of the church, and in following them I am persuaded I shall not transgress the teaching of scripture.[54]

What difference this made to the Presbytery's view it is not possible to conclude. Such interjection at presbytery level may, however, have had an effect given what happened when Synod met in 1894.

At the Synod of 1894, although the Synod was still divided, work recommenced on the directory with additional members being elected to the Committee on Public Worship to give further perspective on the objections made by Synod on the insertion of the Apostles' Creed, liturgical forms, and other matters that had been raised which were not detailed in the Synod minutes.[55] After a further four years of work the draft brought before the Synod was received and authorized for publication. Nonetheless, although the resolution passed by Synod agreed it for use by the Church, it did so with the proviso that ministers and Sessions could "adopt it as far as they judge[d] this desirable and expedient."[56] This is interesting in terms of the polity of the Church because by doing so Synod were giving a level of autonomy to ministers and congregations over the use of the directory. This may have made official existing practice in regard to corporate worship, but it was a different approach to how other Synod decisions had been acted on across the denomination. As the Synod was made up of every minister and one elder from every congregation, a decision made by Synod, even when about the life of a congregation, was followed without question. This also meant Synod bypassed the need for agreement of the presbyteries with the directory, which had been another sticking point along the way in the drafting of the revised *Directory for Public Worship*.[57]

In his early defense of the *Directory for Public Worship*, Middlemiss observed that as a Presbyterian it was "not proper for each minister to have his own order of worship."[58] He believed the Church lost something of itself

---

54. Middlemiss, *Directory of Worship Necessary*, 5.

55. Presbyterian Church of England, "Synod Records 1894," 664.

56. Carruthers, *Fifty Years*, 19; Presbyterian Church of England, "Synod Records 1898," in *Synod Records 1885–1898*, 30.

57. Presbyterian Church of England, "Synod Records 1891," in *Synod Records 1885–1898*, 949; Presbyterian Church of England, "Synod Records 1892," in *Synod Records 1885–1898*, 216.

58. Middlemiss, *Directory of Worship Necessary*, 5.

when there was no common order. What was required was a directory of worship "suitable to the time in which [the Church lived] and in accordance with all that [was] best in the history of devotional practice of [the] Church."⁵⁹ The *Directory for Public Worship*, although divisive, did offer a common, if optional, norm for the worship of the Presbyterian Church of England.⁶⁰ Therefore, it is interesting to note Carruthers's observation that "even where [the *Directory for Public Worship* was] not used its influence . . . conduced to the greater regularity and reverence of services."⁶¹ In its non-use, as well as its use, the *Directory for Public Worship* appears to have encouraged the worship of the Church to be more orderly.

The question of the *Directory for Public Worship* did not return to Synod until 1913, when the Report by the Committee on the State of Religion and Public Morals suggested that it might be desirable to revise and supplement it. The report stated the opinion that, although the *Directory for Public Worship* was "of the nature of an experiment," it had been a useful book. Given this and the belief that there was the demand for a book that embodied more of the "treasures" of Presbyterian devotion and bringing the Presbyterian Church of England more into line with Presbyterian churches across the world in its worship, a resolution was put that a committee be formed to consider a work of revision of the *Directory for Public Worship*.⁶² In 1914 a special committee was convened.

The final draft of the revision initiated in 1914 was presented to Synod in 1920. Compared to the edition of the *Directory for Public Worship* published in 1898, this version was distinctly different. It was not a book of guidance on how worship should flow and what might be said at a given point, it was a book of liturgies. During the drafting process, this approach appears not to have been questioned by Synod even though approval of certain liturgies had been sought by the Committee from both presbyteries and Synod, (i.e., the services of ordination and induction). Interestingly, as a completed collection, the Committee sought its approval on the same terms as the *Directory for Public Worship* of 1898. Its adoption by a congregation, the Committee felt, should remain the choice of the minister and

---

59. Middlemiss, *Directory of Worship Necessary*, 8.

60. Davies, *Worship and Theology*, 4:111.

61. Carruthers, *Fifty Years*, 20.

62. Presbyterian Church of England, "Synod Records 1913," in *Synod Records 1913–1920*, 317.

Session.[63] In the resolutions that recommended and gave final authorization for the publication of the directory, this was not mentioned. Nevertheless, although emphasized in a different way, that sense of freedom and choice in how the directory was to be used was stated within the book's preface:

> The Forms of Service in this book are not intended to interfere with the freedom of our worship, or to be in any sense obligatory.[64]

A possible reason for the emphasis being placed on the content of the liturgies rather than the adoption of the directory was that with the 1921 edition of the *Directory for Public Worship* there were aspects of certain liturgies that Synod deemed must be used within certain acts of corporate worship held within the churches. Also, it would appear that Synod believed it was right that uniformity in aspects of corporate worship should be encouraged and therefore suggested the use of certain liturgies would be desirable. In the preface the Committee stated:

> The only exceptions are those portions of the Orders of Service for Ordination and Induction which the Synod has enjoined to be used as they stand; and certain words in the Marriage Service, which are prescribed by Act of Parliament, and are therefore essential to the validity of the marriage. It is most desirable, however, that, as far as possible, the procedure should be uniform throughout the Church in the Administration of the Sacraments, the Admission of Young Communicants, and the Dedication of Churches.[65]

The combination of this with elements within the liturgies being labelled as "if desirable" and "may be used" permitted and enabled ministers/worship leaders to use the book freely while developing a link between church order and worship. This is important, not only because this reflected the hierarchical structure of Presbyterianism but reemphasized the importance of good order in the whole life of the Church.

In the presentation of the full final draft of the 1921 edition of the *Directory for Public Worship* for review by both presbyteries and Synod, it was not surprising that criticisms were once again received relating to what

---

63. Presbyterian Church of England, "Synod Records 1920," in *Synod Records 1913–1920*, 544.

64. Presbyterian Church of England, "Synod Records 1920," 545; Presbyterian Church of England, *Directory of Public Worship for Use*, vii.

65. Presbyterian Church of England, "Synod Records 1920," 545; Presbyterian Church of England, *Directory of Public Worship for Use*, vii.

had or had not been included and concerns expressed over whether the directory was to be obligatory. Many of the criticisms were easily refuted and the Committee noted that they were all made out of the desire "to make the directory as useful and as worthy of [the] Church as it could be."[66] The Committee concluded their response to the comments with the hope that "the general outline of services [would] commend itself to the judgement of the Church" and through its adoption make corporate worship easier to follow "with intelligence and spiritual profit."[67] Carruthers expressed the view that the 1921 edition of the *Directory for Public Worship* did this because "it look[ed] at worship from an essentially Presbyterian standpoint, but expressed it in a fashion especially suited for England."[68] He went on to suggest that revision of the directory would not be for a long time to come.

It was after a gap of twenty-three years that the revision of the *Directory for Public Worship* returned to the floor of Synod, then called General Assembly. The Publications Committee brought the proposal in response to the stocks of the 1921 edition being exhausted. The suggestion was made that it might be appropriate to compile a service book that was common to all the British Presbyterian churches. A special committee was convened and made its first report to General Assembly in 1945, when it was confirmed that a joint service book would be written with the Presbyterian Church of Wales. Work proceeded with the service book without General Assembly seeing draft sections, countering the approach taken to develop the 1921 edition of the *Directory for Public Worship*. The proposed preface, table of contents and "a sample page indicating the form of printing" were presented to General Assembly in 1947, on which the publication was authorized with the condition that any portions relating to the law of the Church were checked by the Committee on Law and History prior to publication.[69] Therefore, in 1948 the *Presbyterian Service Book for use in the Presbyterian Churches of England and Wales* was published.

As with the 1921 edition of the *Directory for Public Worship*, the *Presbyterian Service Book* expanded the Church's liturgy. The Committee reported in 1947 that they had been unanimous in the belief that a

---

66. Presbyterian Church of England, "General Assembly Records 1921," in *General Assembly Records 1921–1923*, 888.

67. Presbyterian Church of England, "General Assembly Records 1921," 888.

68. Carruthers, *Fifty Years*, 20.

69. Presbyterian Church of England, "General Assembly Records 1947," in *General Assembly Records 1944–1949*, 54, 132.

"comprehensive set of services" were needed to act as "guides and suggestions for devotion" to "deepen reverent worship and enrich the inward life of ministers and people alike."[70] The Committee also felt that all the services included would find full acceptance by any that held to the traditions of the Reformed churches. These were bold statements to make when the book itself combined two traditions of worship: the simpler, freer form of worship that was akin to the worship of the Puritan tradition which was still strong in Wales and the more liturgical tradition that had come to be characteristic of Scottish and English worship.[71] It was substantively achieved by offering a number of alternative orders for Sunday worship and Holy Communion. There were three orders for Sunday public worship: one credal in character, one not, and the third arising from the Welsh tradition.[72] Similarly for the celebration of Holy Communion: there were two described as being different expressions of the Reformed tradition, one more aligned to the Welsh tradition and a fourth shorter order for use with the sick or in other circumstances where an abbreviated service might have been desirable.[73] As with the previous editions of the *Directory for Public Worship*, ministers and Sessions were not obliged to use the services within the book, other than those services where the General Assemblies had prescribed their use, (e.g., in the matter of ordinations and inductions and when the service included a legal requirement as found in the Marriage Service).

In the preface to the *Presbyterian Service Book*, the compilers stated that one of their objectives with the book was to "give a richer expression to the liturgical tradition of Church Catholic and Reformed."[74] Davies, in his analysis of the service book, suggested this was in part influenced by the founding and growth of the Iona Community and George MacLeod's theology and understanding of worship.[75] In his book on the Iona Community, *We Shall Re-build*, George MacLeod discussed the worship of the church in terms of the church catholic and reformed, and the need to recapture elements of this in the worship of the community.[76] Further evidence of

---

70. Presbyterian Church of England, "General Assembly Records 1947," in *General Assembly Records 1944–1949*, 55.

71. Davies, *Worship and Theology*, 5:377.

72. Presbyterian Churches of England and Wales, *Presbyterian Service Book*, 1948:2.

73. Presbyterian Churches of England and Wales, *Presbyterian Service Book*, 1948:2.

74. Presbyterian Churches of England and Wales, *Presbyterian Service Book*, 1948:1.

75. Davies, *Worship and Theology*, 5:378.

76. MacLeod, *We Shall Re-build*, 81–90.

MacLeod's potential influence is demonstrated by a statement at the end of the book's preface where the compilers wrote: "The book is sent forth with the earnest prayer that, by the blessing of God, it may foster a deeper spirit of worship in the hearts of the people and be for greater glory of His name."[77] This hints at the need for something that is truly corporate and that satisfies the souls of the people, which MacLeod emphasized in his discourse on worship.[78] Davies noted this potential influence because there were members of the drafting Committee for the *Presbyterian Service Book* who were members of a group known as the "Parkgate Group." This group were early English enthusiasts of the work of the Iona Community and also studied aspects of worship and had a zeal for its reform.[79]

The other potential influence was the publication of the Scottish *Book of Common Order* in 1940, which Davies suggested was taken up by many English Presbyterian ministers.[80] This claim is supported by the similarities in approach to content in the *Presbyterian Service Book* and the *Book of Common Order*, and that the "First Order" for Holy Communion in the *Presbyterian Service Book* is the same liturgy as the service of "The Lord's Supper or Holy Communion" printed in the *Book of Common Order*.[81]

Between 1956 and 1957, the Committee on Public Worship and Aids to Devotion took it upon themselves to discover how the *Presbyterian Service Book* was employed across the Church in response to the question from the Publications Committee on whether the book should be reprinted. From the initial 129 returns from ministers, it was found: seventy-five used the book regularly (forty-five used only this book and thirty used it with other service books); forty-one used the book occasionally; and twelve did not use the book at all.[82] Although these initial returns showed the book was being used, the Committee observed a general dissatisfaction with some of its content which suggested to them it was time to rewrite the service book.[83]

77. Presbyterian Churches of England and Wales, *Presbyterian Service Book*, 1948:2.
78. MacLeod, *We Shall Re-build*, 82–83.
79. Davies, *Worship and Theology*, 5:378–79.
80. Davies, *Worship and Theology*, 5:379.
81. Church of Scotland, *Book of Common Order*, 111–23; Presbyterian Churches of England and Wales, *Presbyterian Service Book*, 1948:50–59; Davies, *Worship and Theology*, 5:379.
82. Presbyterian Church of England, *Minutes of Committee on Public Worship and Aids of Devotion*, October 29, 1956.
83. Presbyterian Church of England, *Minutes of Committee on Public Worship and Aids of Devotion*, July 17, 1957; Presbyterian Church of England, "General Assembly Records 1957," in *General Assembly Records 1954–1972*, 254.

General Assembly in 1958 authorized the Committee to begin a piecemeal rewriting of services and publishing them as pamphlets. Revision was carried out in conjunction with the Presbyterian Church of Wales. During the process of redrafting, certain services were given permission to be used in the Church by General Assembly. These included the services for "Adult Baptism and Confirmation" and "Confirmation of Baptism and Admission to the Lord's Supper."[84] General Assembly in 1964 was presented with drafts for twelve services that were proposed for inclusion in the new edition of the service book with the hope that it would agree that the Church could experiment with the liturgies in its corporate worship. As with previous times when such resolutions were put, much discussion was generated on the floor of General Assembly and the resolution was amended. In the General Assembly minutes, the amendments put imply there were concerns over doctrine and polity expressed in some of the services. The resolution finally adopted was:

> The Assembly authorises for experimental use the draft services of Infant Baptism, Confirmation of Baptised Persons, Joint Service of Adult baptism and confirmation, Ordination of Ministers, Induction of an Ordained Minister, Licensing of Probationers, Ordination of Elders, Setting-Apart of Deacons, Recognition of Lay Preachers, Dedication of Teachers and Youth Leaders, A Morning Service and Services for the Ministry of Healing; instructs the Committees on Doctrine and on Law and History to examine them and communicate their comments on them to the Committee on Public Worship and Aids to Devotion before the 31st May, 1965; and invites others interested to send written comments to the Committee by the same date.[85]

From comments received in the allotted time schedule and in consultation with the Committees on Doctrine, and Law and History, these services were revised, and the remaining sections were drafted. Some additional services were presented in the Committee's report to General Assembly in 1966 for consideration, although the resolution for General Assembly to agree the Church's experimentation with them was withdrawn. The final table of contents was approved in 1967 and the Committee was instructed to proceed with publication. This took place in time for the meeting of

---

84. Presbyterian Church of England, "General Assembly Records 1961," in *General Assembly Records 1954–1972*, 482.

85. Presbyterian Church of England, "General Assembly Records 1964," in *General Assembly Records 1954–1972*, 510–11.

General Assembly in 1968 when the revised *Presbyterian Service Book* was commended "to the use of ministers and others responsible for leadership of Public Worship" in the Church.[86] This did not restrict the worship of the Church to the service book, but neither the resolution nor the preface make mention of "freedom" as emphasized in the editions of the *Directory for Public Worship* or the previous version of the service book. Through the consultation method used in the drafting of the book, the Committee offered the Church an ownership of the book's authoring, which could be interpreted as there being no need for such a statement as the contained liturgies were truly deemed reflective of the Church's corporate worship and it was written in a way that freedom could be inferred. This interpretation of the evidence is supported by the final statement made by the Committee in the preface:

> It is the hope of the Committee that, in the words of the Preface of the 1921 Directory, "this book may voice the present needs, the urgent desires and united hopes of the people of Christ in the language of orderly devotion so that the Public Services of Religion may be conducted to the glory of God and the edification of the worshippers."[87]

The Committee in its preface to this edition of the service book described it as reflecting the "thinking on public worship of the newer generation," which emphasized "the missionary nature of the Church and ministry of laity."[88] This was apparent in the choice of language and some of the subjects contained in the prayers. Yet, this was still a book designed for use by the worship leader and not to be in the hands of the whole congregation. At no point in the discussion on service books was the potential raised for congregation members to have their own copy of the service book, as would have been seen in the Church of England and the Methodist Church. Therefore, from the content of the service book, it appears that there was only limited innovation in the Church's worship. Previous influences of the Liturgical and Ecumenical Movements and the Church of Scotland are apparent in the construction of the liturgies through the use of particular terminology, phrases and responses. For example, the use of the term "intimations" for the giving of church notices was continued in some orders

---

86. Presbyterian Church of England, "General Assembly Records 1968," in *General Assembly Records 1954–1972*, 132.

87. Presbyterian Churches of England and Wales, *Presbyterian Service Book*, 1968:v.

88. Presbyterian Churches of England and Wales, *Presbyterian Service Book*, 1968:iv.

which came from the Church of Scotland. The continued influence of the Liturgical and Ecumenical Movements can be seen in one order of the Holy Communion including the *sursum corda*, the *sanctus* and the *agnus dei*, which had come to be seen as part of corporate worship in the universal church. These maintained the service book's character as a book of liturgies but it is difficult to describe them as a reflection of a "newer generation." The revolution may have been in the use and acceptance of the book within the Church—something which was never measured as this book was published in the midst of the conversations of the union of the Presbyterian Church of England with the Congregational Church in England and Wales to form the United Reformed Church. Despite this, it was reported to General Assembly in 1969 that 1,020 copies had been sold and that the service book had been well received.[89] It is not clear whether this number included sales in the Presbyterian Church of Wales, given that in 1969 there were only 334 churches in the Presbyterian Church of England with 279 ministers in charge (these were the numbers recorded on the 1 January 1969 and does not include all ministers on the roll).[90] This level of uptake, however, does support a high regard for this service book and it is difficult to avoid the conclusion that a small percentage of the members would have also owned a copy.

Liturgies in the 1948 edition of the *Presbyterian Service Book* were described as being Reformed. However, it was not until the 1968 edition that the order reflected that of practices in the churches of Zurich, Strasbourg and Geneva at the time of the European Reformation in the sixteenth century. Until this point, the sermon came at the end of the service, as it had done in the Westminster Assembly's *Directory for the Public Worship of God*. In the first order of morning worship in the 1968 service book an alternative position for the sermon was suggested:

> Beginning with the Little Entry with its stress that all worship is based upon the Word of God, of which the Minister is the servant, it proceeds to praise. After confession and pardon follow the reading of the Word and the exposition of the Word in the sermon. After the hearing of God's Word comes the response to the Word in thanksgiving, intercession and offering.[91]

---

89. Presbyterian Church of England, "General Assembly Records 1969," in *General Assembly Records 1954–1972*, 226.

90. Presbyterian Church of England, *Yearbook, 1970*, 410.

91. Presbyterian Churches of England and Wales, *Presbyterian Service Book*, 1968:iv.

This follows the order provided by John Calvin for use in the Reformed churches in Strasbourg and Geneva in the 1540s, where the people were encouraged to respond to having heard the Word of God through their prayers.[92] This was not an innovation in the worship of the church made by Calvin alone, it came from the development of the pattern for Reformed worship set out by Huldrych Zwingli (1484–1531) and progressed by Martin Bucer (1491–1551) and Guillaume Farel (1489–1565).[93]

Despite all the different influences on content of the directories and service books published by the Presbyterian Church of England, it is of note, that the overall order of corporate worship was consistent. This is shown in the table below comparing the orders for a Service of the Word from the five directories/service books published on behalf of the Presbyterian Church of England. As with Congregational worship, the only distinctive difference is the relationship of the sermon and "prayers of thanksgiving and intercession" in the 1968 edition of *The Presbyterian Service Book* compared with all other volumes. It should be recognized that there was an order of worship in the 1968 edition of *The Presbyterian Service Book* that did have the sermon coming after the prayers of thanksgiving and intercession, as in the 1948 edition, so this change in order cannot be concluded as universal in the worship of the Presbyterians.[94]

TABLE 2. *Comparison of rubrics for a service of the Word in the service books of the Presbyterian Church of England*

Directory for Public Worship (1889)	Directory for Public Worship (1898)	Directory for Public Worship (1921)	The Presbyterian Service Book (1948)	The Presbyterian Service Book (1968)
			Venite *(optional)*	
Call to worship Scripture sentences	Call to worship Scripture sentences	Call to worship Scripture sentences	Scripture sentences	Call to worship
Prayer of adoration and invocation	Prayer of invocation	Prayer of invocation	Prayer of approach	Prayer of invocation

92. Maag, *Lifting Hearts to the Lord*, 74–76.

93. Rice and Huffstutler, *Reformed Worship*, 30–33.

94. Presbyterian Churches of England and Wales, *Presbyterian Service Book*, 1968:11–17.

Directory for Public Worship (1889)	Directory for Public Worship (1898)	Directory for Public Worship (1921)	The Presbyterian Service Book (1948)	The Presbyterian Service Book (1968)
Hymn	Psalm/Hymn	Psalm/Hymn	Psalm (metrical)/Hymn	Psalm/Hymn
Confession of sin with petitions for absolution and cleansing	Prayer of adoration Confession of sin with petitions for forgiveness and cleansing	Prayer of adoration Confession of sin Petition for pardon Thanksgiving Supplication for grace	Confession of sin Petition for pardon Lord's prayer	Confession of sin Petition for pardon Lord's prayer
		Psalm (metrical)/Hymn		
Old Testament reading	Old Testament reading	Old Testament reading	Old Testament reading	Old Testament reading
Hymn *(optional)*	Hymn/Psalm	Psalm/Canticle/Hymn	Hymn/Canticle	Psalm *(metrical/prose)* or Children's address with hymn
New Testament reading	New Testament reading	New Testament reading	New Testament reading	New Testament reading
			Apostles' creed	Apostles' creed *(optional)*
Children's address	Children's address *(this could also come after the Old Testament reading)*	Children's address	Children's address and prayer	
Hymn *(suitable for children)*	Hymn *(suitable for children)*	Hymn *(suitable for children)*	Hymn	Hymn
Apostles' Creed	Apostles' Creed	Apostles' Creed		

Directory for Public Worship (1889)	Directory for Public Worship (1898)	Directory for Public Worship (1921)	The Presbyterian Service Book (1948)	The Presbyterian Service Book (1968)
Prayers of thanksgiving, supplication for grace and intercession, and Lord's prayer	Prayers of thanksgiving, supplication for grace and intercession, and Lord's prayer	Prayers of intercession, and Lord's prayer	Prayers of thanksgiving and intercessions	
		Notices	Notices	
		Offering *(and prayer of dedication)*	Offering *(and prayer of dedication)*	
Hymn	Psalm/Hymn	Hymn	Hymn	
Notices	*Notices*			
Prayer of illumination	Prayer of illumination	Prayer of illumination		
Sermon	Sermon	Sermon	Sermon	Sermon
Prayer	Prayer	Prayer	Doxology	Hymn
Offering	Offering			
				Prayer of thanksgiving and intercessions
				Notices
				Offering
Hymn	Hymn	Hymn/ Doxology	Hymn	Hymn
Apostolic Benediction	Apostolic Benediction	Apostolic Benediction	Prayer and Benediction	Dismissal and Blessing

Order with Freedom

Carnegie Simpson in his paper to the Presbyterian History Society on the *Character of the Presbytery* (1936) observed that the church ultimately should have spiritual freedom:

> The only true "high" idea of the Church is that the Church is Christ's Church, and therefore must be free, in those spiritual

matters—faith, morals, worship and discipline—on which He speaks to it, to listen and follow His voice alone.[95]

But the nature of the church is such that even in polities that emphasize freedom, such as Congregationalism and Presbyterianism, there are boundaries. There was an acceptance of this in how the Presbyterian Church of England approached corporate worship, although not always with great willingness. When the 1921 edition of the *Directory for Public Worship* went before Synod in 1920, the drafting Committee anticipated the concerns over freedom in worship the directory would again raise, and made the statement:

> Concerning the manner in which different Forms are to be profitably used, it is to be remembered that, while churches of Presbyterian order do not impose a Liturgy by authority, nor confine Ministers to set Forms of Prayer, they have always been careful to preserve the order, dignity and reverence of Public Worship, and to ensure that the several parts of the Service of the House of God maintained in due proportion, and that they should not be demeaned by irregular, irreverent or extravagant utterances.[96]

Therefore, despite high ideals, freedom in worship needed to be bound within order to ensure "a corporate response by the church to God's mighty act of redemption in Jesus Christ."[97]

In the controversy of the drafting of the first publication of the revised *Directory for Public Worship* in the 1880s and 1890s, the concern was that the publication would constrain the worship of the Church. Individuals did not want their liberty to be restricted or to be prevented from leading worship as they believed fitting for their congregations. Committee reports to Synod demonstrated that this was never the intention, although members of Synod evidently interpreted the process as such. It is interesting to note that, unlike in the conversation on public worship in Congregationalism at this time, the argument for freedom in worship was not related to the activity of the Holy Spirit. Although declared and established as an independent Presbyterian church, in the early years, the Presbyterian Church of England (as discussed in the history of the tradition) still grappled with what this meant in terms of the ecclesiological landscape in England and

---

95. Simpson, *Character of Presbytery*, 14.

96. Presbyterian Church of England, "Synod Records 1920," in *Synod Records 1913–1920*, 545.

97. Macleod, *Presbyterian Worship*, 9.

the culture inherent within the Church because of its people (i.e., migrants from other Presbyterian churches in the British Isles). Nonconformity in England was based on the concept of freedom, particularly from what had been prescribed in the context of worship. Yet, given the structure and order that was at the heart of Presbyterianism, uniformity in approach to worship would seem essential and that was why there was an initial call for a directory that would enable this in the 1880s. Freedom from prescribed liturgy and uniformity in the denomination's worship were not easy to reconcile, especially when views expressed both by individuals and presbyteries were polar opposites in Synod and the presbyteries themselves. As with the Westminster Assembly's *Directory for the Public Worship of God* in the seventeenth century, finally middle ground was found through a *Directory for Public Worship* which was a book of guidance on how public worship should flow, what ideally should be contained and how specific actions of the church might be undertaken. This attitude of freedom being about choice and conviction was carried forward into subsequent editions of the *Directory for Public Worship* and then the *Presbyterian Service Book*. It was distinctly reiterated in the preface in the revision of the *Directory for Public Worship* published in 1921.[98]

The emphasis of the liberty of choice in the understanding of freedom in worship rather than the actions of the Holy Spirit also reflects how Presbyterianism in England was very different from the other nonconformist traditions. In the Moderator's Committee report to Synod in 1922 on corporate worship, freedom in worship was talked about in the broadest sense. There was a focus on how this related to prayer and the use of extemporary, written, old and new prayers and responses:

> The freedom as to the form of worship, which is part of our precious heritage from the past, is freedom to use many varieties and methods of expression, freedom to use written or printed forms of prayer along with prayers that are extemporary, freedom to invite the congregation to say aloud certain prayers (such as the General Thanksgiving), to repeat responses which have come down from very ancient times, or to unite for a few minutes in that silent prayer which many find solemn and helpful.[99]

---

98. Presbyterian Church of England, *Directory for Public Worship for Use*, vii.

99. Presbyterian Church of England, "General Assembly Records 1922," in *General Assembly Records 1921–1923*, 194.

Regarding prayer, this was picked up later by James Todd, a Congregationalist, in a paper given at a "Symposium on Worship" organized by the Committee on Public Worship and Aids to Devotion of the Presbyterian Church of England immediately prior to the formation of the United Reformed Church.[100] Todd discussed the forms prayer can take in corporate worship. Although extemporization in his tradition of Congregationalism was perceived as the truest outworking of freedom in worship, he made the observation that prayer does not have to be only extemporary to be free:

> Because all true Christian prayer is not simply a human activity but is made possible through the work of the Holy Spirit it has often been supposed that the writing and reading of a prayer means a quenching of the Spirit. Today in our Reformed churches it is generally accepted and commonly expected that the prayers of the service will be carefully prepared and written, and probably read. Those who have suffered from long, rumbling and sometimes ungrammatical utterances are thankful for this and would not want to go back on it.[101]

This and the acknowledgement that other material was being used by ministers in the survey undertaken by the Committee of Public Worship and Aids to Devotion between 1956 and 1957, shows how ministers understood they were free to use other sources both for prayers and for liturgy. This, of course, is further supported by how the directories and the service books were only ever commended to the use of the Church. The very nature of the *Directory for Public Worship* made this clear, particularly in its earliest form when the service was a description of what should be done when and examples of prayer or liturgy were only given for the sacraments or ordinances when ministers would benefit from, or required, exact wording (e.g., the marriage service). In striving for a uniformity in the corporate worship of the Presbyterian Church of England, there was a sense that freedom should always be bound to the defined order that the directory or service book suggested. It was not until the 1968 edition of the *Presbyterian Service Book* that freedom in the actual order, and not just within the order, was acknowledged as a feasible interpretation of the relationship between

---

100. The Symposium on Worship included papers given by Congregationalists (e.g. James Todd). From early in the process of the discussions on union, there had been cooperation in matters of worship and devotion. In 1960 the two churches began to share devotional resources for Lent and Holy Week (Presbyterian Church of England, "General Assembly Records 1960," in *General Assembly Records 1954–1972*, 237).

101. Todd, "Spontaneity in Prayer," 1.

freedom and order. The possibility of this was expressed about the content of the book and there was open acceptance of the freedom to utilize worship material according to the needs of the congregation:

> The order for morning worship has a note appended giving the rationale of the order, and this order has been adopted, where applicable for the other services. There will, inevitably, be differences of opinion on this, but it is easy enough for those who wish to follow a different order, to utilise the material provided according to their taste.[102]

The concentration on freedom as an individual's or council's liberty when discussing in the first instance how freedom and order work together in the worship of the Presbyterian Church of England, did not mean that the freedom of the Holy Spirit within the worship was not important. Middlemiss made reference to the significant role of the Holy Spirit in his paper to the Newcastle presbytery in 1893. He outlined the negative response to the *Directory for Public Worship* as restricting the possibilities for the Holy Spirit to act:

> There have been those, and there be those still, who prefer that divine service should be conducted entirely as the Holy Spirit directs—who have no order of service, and who desire none.... Others again, without taking that position exactly, resent the imposition of a directory as an interference with spiritual liberty.[103]

As Middlemiss's paper was only presented to the Newcastle Presbytery and its intention was to gather support for the *Directory for Public Worship*, these comments were possibly never conveyed to the Committee on the Directory for Public Worship in Synod. Nonetheless, although the Committee never intentionally spoke about freedom of the Holy Spirit in worship, the preface of the *Directory for Public Worship* in 1898 referenced the original preface of the Westminster Assembly's *Directory for the Public Worship of God* and the statement that the directory was not intended to make the church "slothful and negligent in the stirring up the gifts of Christ in them."[104] Therefore, as came to be understood in the worship of the

---

102. Presbyterian Church of England, "General Assembly Records 1964," in *General Assembly Records 1954–1972*, 424.

103. Middlemiss, *Directory of Worship Necessary*, 4.

104. Presbyterian Church of England, *Directory for Public Worship of God*, iv.

Congregationalists, freedom in worship was two-fold in nature: a liberty of choice and the work of the Holy Spirit. It could be argued that the work of the Holy Spirit is revealed within the liberty of choice. Theologian Donald Macleod, in commentating on Presbyterian worship generally and from the perspective of a national identity, observed that for Presbyterian worship "to have meaning, shape, and unity" the downward movement of the Word of God must be recognized, "becoming real in Jesus Christ, and an upward movement of [the congregation's] response with the Holy Spirit bringing forth new creations for this tremendous encounter in the realm of grace and faith."[105] This observation by Macleod also makes the case for why freedom in worship had to be bound to order. Well-ordered worship ensured soundness in doctrine and prayer, as identified by the Westminster Divines as essential when they drafted the *Directory for the Public Worship of God* and this principle remained fundamental within Presbyterian worship.

Order and Participation

As Presbyterianism in England began to give due consideration to its worship there was a sense, as in Congregationalism, that there was something to put right. The concern for the Presbyterians, through the *Directory for Public Worship*, was ensuring worship had an order that was complete and reverent. Although the *Directory for Public Worship* and the development of it in the 1880s and 1890s does not specifically address this matter, order was observed to be essential for worship to be corporate. Donald Fraser commented on this in terms of participation by all those gathered to worship:

> The Presbyterian Church loves a sober and simple worship, rendered by the Christian people, as themselves a holy priesthood offering spiritual sacrifice through Jesus Christ.[106]

In worship, other than the singing of hymns and psalms, there was no evidence of what that meant for Fraser and other Presbyterians of his time. There was no suggestion in the *Directory for Public Worship* (1898) that the people should make responses in worship, other than when required in the sacrament of baptism and the ordinances of communion, ordination and induction. The use of congregational responses was first suggested in the 1921 edition. There was no reason given as to why this approach was

---

105. Macleod, *Presbyterian Worship*, 16.
106. Fraser, *Presbyterian Church of England*, 9.

adopted in the liturgies although the drafting of this directory coincided with the beginning of a movement of high churchmanship in English Presbyterianism and the formation of the Church Society in 1917. The Society was formed "with the object of developing the study of English Presbyterianism, particularly on the subject of ordination, church worship and similar questions."[107] However, the Society was short lived and there is no suggestion of a connection between it and the drafting committee. It was recorded that the Committee during drafting consulted other manuals of worship used within Reformed churches as well as considering the expression of prayer and praise in ancient and modern Christianity, and these may have been influential.[108]

Participation in worship is a natural outcome of liturgy that includes responses or order with congregational singing. Despite this, in a paper to the Committee on Public Worship and Aids to Devotion in 1968, J. E. Fenn observed how order alone can enhance participation in worship:

> Worship is not communing with one's self. Nor is it simply thinking about other people. . . . It presupposes a dynamic inter-change between God and us, with all that this implies and involves. The familiar progression in public worship from Recollection through Confession to hearing of the "Word," and Intercession represents a hitherto reliable discipline of mind and emotions through which the reality of God, and the realisation of our dependence upon him can issue in new dedication and service of brethren: but the heart of it is the reality of God.[109]

This paper was read when the influence of the Liturgical Movement was most significant in the approach churches were taking to corporate worship and there was a clear desire to emphasize the corporate in congregational worship. Therefore, suggesting participation can develop from the discipline of a familiar order without adding further elements that encouraged the congregation to participate with prescribed responses was counter intuitive, yet it made sense in the context of congregations' lived experience. This is supported by the comment made by Nella Ross in another of the papers given to the "Symposium on Worship" (1971). Ross stated:

> It would be nonsense to suggest that the congregation cannot participate in the traditional Presbyterian service: the history of

---

107. Murray, "High Church Presbyterianism," 227.
108. Presbyterian Church of England, *Directory for Public Worship for Use*, vii.
109. Fenn, "Worship in the Mid-Twentieth Century," 1.

Worship in Presbyterianism

> Presbyterianism is the history of a people who have found their services meaningful and worshipful—and even if there is a tendency for the sermon to dominate them, there is also a tendency to follow the sermon with an attentiveness which amounts to participation.[110]

Fenn did not expand the idea of order enabling participation. Interestingly, although not in response to Fenn's paper, Ross did offer more insight into lack of participation, suggesting that it may be due to services being badly conducted:

> If the prayers are too fast; or the pauses are in the wrong places; or there is too much verbiage and too little content, it is difficult for the congregation to enter into them. It is even more difficult if the prayers are sermons in disguise and are prayed at the congregation rather than with them. A greater concern of ministers to lead their congregations into corporate praying would increase participation.[111]

The aim of the revision of the Westminster Assembly's *Directory for the Public Worship of God* in the 1880s and 1890s was to improve the quality of services which, following Ross's argument, should have enhanced the participation of the congregation in corporate worship. Nonetheless, as wider influences impacted the Church and its perception of worship, good shape and flow to corporate worship were not seen as the means of participation. This was particularly evident in the 1960s when participation of the congregation was more of a concern. Then it was the more openly active approaches offered through responsive liturgies that were discussed in detail.

There was an understanding that responsive liturgies were not going to be effective in all congregational settings. This was demonstrated by how both editions of the *Presbyterian Service Book* used congregational responses minimally in the liturgies. When the 1968 edition was being drafted the committee observed that, in the context of Presbyterian worship, the congregation would not in general have a full order of service in their hands. Therefore, it was extremely difficult to encourage congregational participation in this way. Their resolution was the promotion of the congregational "Amen" at the end of prayers and breaking the intercessory prayers into

---

110. Ross, "Silence," 2.
111. Ross, "Silence," 2.

"a series of short prayers on specific subjects which would provide for the congregation to respond with the 'Amen' at the end of each prayer."[112]

The use of silence in worship was offered as another method for enabling participation of the congregation. The use of silence was not supported by Ross in her discussion on the topic in Presbyterian worship to the "Symposium on Worship" (1971), suggesting that it actually lessened participation because it was unfamiliar to congregations.[113] But Ross did go on to say that where silence had been experimented with it had fulfilled a need. The value was dependent on how congregations were led in this form of participation.[114]

In Presbyterian worship there was an argument that order and/or liturgy, in the sense of a fully scripted act of worship, had the ability to enable participation. Counter to this argument was one that suggested participation led to improved liturgy (worship content as well as order). This revolved around the importance of the "priesthood of all believers." If the Church owned this ideal then Donald McIlhagga, in his paper to the "Symposium on Worship" (1971) on experimental worship, suggested that worship would be the work of the whole people, both in terms of preparation and execution.[115] McIlhagga, when discussing the shape of "Family Church Worship" noted such worship might include "responses, corporate prayers, (creed), laymen reading one or two of the lessons, and a layman usually leading the intercessions (unless they are corporately prepared, or corporately extempore)."[116] This concept finds support in Donald Macleod's discussion of Presbyterian worship. He wrote, that in Presbyterian worship, liturgy was not the creation of any one person because it is the "form in which the congregation received God's word in word and sacrament, and in which it, at the same time, clothes its prayers, its praise and its confession of faith."[117] Therefore, it had to be the activity and product of the belief of the body of Christ. For Macleod this meant that if the people were engaged then worship was corporate and liturgical.[118]

---

112. Presbyterian Church of England, "General Assembly Records 1964," in *General Assembly Records 1954–1972*, 424.

113. Ross, "Silence," 2.

114. Ross, "Silence," 3.

115. McIlhagga, "Experimental Worship," 3, 5.

116. McIlhagga, "Experimental Worship," 5.

117. Macleod, *Presbyterian Worship*, 10–11.

118. Macleod, *Presbyterian Worship*, 14.

Conclusion

In the preface to the 1994 edition of the Church of Scotland's *Book of Common Order*, John Bell, convenor of the authoring committee, described how order, freedom and participation interrelate from the perspective of Presbyterian worship:

> In worship we engage as the Body of Christ in an encounter with almighty God. This engagement should never become a rambling incoherence of well-meaning phrases and gestures. It should exhibit that deliberate and historical patterning of sentiment and expression which befits the meeting of the sons and daughters of earth with the King of kings. Further, in public worship, as distinct from personal devotions, it is important the whole congregation sense a purpose and direction in their representation before God. They should never be placed in the position of being spectators at a performance which is entirely dependent on aesthetics, emotional, and spiritual whims of its leaders. This in no way precluded or denies the inspiration and direction of the Holy Spirit. The enemy of the Spirit is not form but anarchy.[119]

From the beginning of the Presbyterian Church of England's consideration of its corporate worship in the 1880s to the union with the Congregational Church in England and Wales in 1972, this has been at the core of discussions. Compared to the Congregationalists, the starting point was order as the Presbyterians believed that reverence came from good order. Nevertheless, in achieving good order, freedom was not precluded. Originally, as with the worship of the Congregationalists, there had to be order with freedom—prayers and liturgy were not to be prescribed—unless essential for legal or polity reasons, (e.g., set words in marriage and ordination services). That understanding organically shifted over time to freedom in order. It was not only the content of the order that could change, but when deemed right the order could too.

Good order in worship also enhanced participation in worship. Although not spoken of in these terms, this was recognized early on. In its development, the *Directory for Public Worship* did encourage more oral participation of the congregation in worship through the addition of responses. This came from wider influences including the Liturgical and Ecumenical Movements and the Church of Scotland. This was not in response to the belief that participation was lacking in the worship of the Church.

---

119. Panel on the Worship of the Church of Scotland, *Book of Common Order*, x.

This acknowledgement of the entwinement of order and participation early on in the development of the Church's worship is distinctly different to what was observed in the worship of Congregationalists, although they both related to how the people came together in the presence of God.

5

A Theology of Freedom, Order, and Participation

IN THE PREFACE TO the first book of services published by the United Reformed Church in 1980, John Huxtable emphasized the importance of freedom in worship. Huxtable stated that the intention of the service book was not to "impugn that freedom."[1] Huxtable's statement has been proved to be true; the United Reformed Church has been a prolific producer of liturgical resources over its lifetime and there is no one liturgy that defines the worship of the Church. Yet, as the historical survey demonstrates, freedom in worship concerns not only what, if any, liturgical material is used; it relates to how the Church understands its practice theologically, particularly in relationship to its identity as a church of the Free Church tradition. Also, although it is much emphasized, the corporate worship of the United Reformed Church is not characterized by freedom alone. It is the distinctive relationship freedom has with order and with participation and how these terms are understood in practice, historically and theologically, that allows for a theology of the Church's corporate worship to be articulated.

Methodology

In *Theology, Music, and Time* (2000), the theologian Jeremy Begbie explored theologically human freedom. Freedom can be defined as the state of being able to act without hinderance or restraint. However, Begbie recognized that in human freedom this cannot be the case. Human freedom, Begbie defined, is "mediated through and in relation to constraint."[2] Under this

---

1. United Reformed Church, *Book of Services*, 7.
2. Begbie, *Theology, Music, and Time*, 198.

condition constraint should not be understood as a method of confinement or form of hinderance, rather as a specificity that gives structure to prevent something from being indeterminate.[3] For example, human beings subject themselves to conditions which might be defined as constraints—frameworks, rubrics, structures—yet they enable experiences to be meaningful. It is possible that some constraints can run the risk of threatening human freedom. Nevertheless, without degrees of limitation humanity would never advance beyond chaos. Therefore, constraint ensures freedom because it gives a structure within which meaningful choices can be made,[4] as was evident in the Presbyterian approach to the development of a directory of worship.

Begbie stated, freedom "is not a thing or entity to be sought after, or a possession to be grasped. It qualifies arrangements of persons and things; it describes proper relationships and configurations between particularities."[5] Begbie went on to suggest an aid to understanding the truth about freedom flourishing through the engagement with and negotiation of constraints is to think about it through the lens of improvisation in "traditional jazz" music.[6] Begbie explained:

> At first sight, we might think that the only limit or constraint to consider is a musical structure or framework—a pattern of chords, a theme, or whatever. But improvisation involves larger networks of constraint, interacting in highly elaborate ways. The improvisor is *multiply* constrained, and as with all networks of constraints we can never exhaustively specify all the constraints. Some are purely passive, setting the boundary conditions; some are actively and directly causative; some are permissive, needing a particular happening in order to be activated; some are proximate, some distant; some are invariant and intransigent, some flexible and pliable.[7]

In improvisation there has to be an alertness to all these constraints, but not all define what happens musically. Some constraints can be rejected, for example a certain musical convention, in order to pursue something

---

3. Begbie, *Theology, Music, and Time*, 198.
4. Begbie, *Theology, Music, and Time*, 199.
5. Begbie, *Theology, Music, and Time*, 199.
6. Begbie, *Theology, Music, and Time*, 199.
7. Begbie, *Theology, Music, and Time*, 200.

A Theology of Freedom, Order, and Participation

that appears to be musically promising. This is never done without taking seriously that constraint and testing its implications on the overall composition.[8]

This analogy of improvisation for comprehending the truth about human freedom is also applicable to freedom in worship. However, in developing a theological understanding of corporate worship, as shown by the historical survey in the preceding chapters, freedom has to be considered in relationship to order and participation, both of which can be defined as constraints on freedom. They ensure that worship is not chaotic and that it is meaningful in its purpose and the participation of the congregation and God. It is how these three interrelate that make worship what it is. Therefore, to define corporate worship theologically, the interaction of these three needs to be discussed, analyzed, and evaluated theologically. To aid this discussion, and to continue the musical analogy, order and participation will also be considered in music. Order will be treated as *cantus firmus* (a pre-existing melody that form the basis of a polyphonic composition) and participation as the performers.

Dietrich Bonhoeffer wrote of how God in all aspects of life wants humanity to have a firm support, which has a distinct wholeness in its own right, and ensures nothing calamitous happens in the polyphony of life.[9] Although this was part of a Christological reflection on love, the musical analogy he used translates, *mutatis mutandis*, to a theological consideration of corporate worship in the interaction between freedom, order, and participation. Bonhoeffer described the "firm support" as the *cantus firmus*. To have a clear, plain *cantus firmus* means that a musical composition can develop to its limits without coming adrift from the melody that defines it.[10] When thought of in terms of something more than a fixed liturgy of words and ritual, order is the *cantus firmus* of an act of corporate worship. Without it, as was observed in the historical survey, worship can be chaotic, and its purpose unclear as aspects of worship come adrift from one another.

Cantus firmus is not musical terminology usually applied to traditional jazz music. Nevertheless, the sense and purpose of the *cantus firmus* is there. Every piece of jazz music has an "undergirding structure that makes improvisation possible."[11] In traditional jazz music this is provided by the

---

8. Begbie, *Theology, Music, and Time*, 200.
9. Bonhoeffer, *Letters and Papers*, 303.
10. Bonhoeffer, *Letters and Papers*, 303.
11. Benson, "Improvising Texts, Improvising Communities," 304.

meter (or syncopation), and harmonic sequence (or chord progression), maintained by the "rhythm section" of the band, and the melody from which improvisation is developed and shaped according to an idiom (or style).[12] Therefore, for the purpose of this theological exploration, it is appropriate to think of order in worship, analogously, as the *cantus firmus*.

Freedom and order might define and give content to an act of corporate worship but for it to be worship there has to be participation. Using the analogy, a piece of jazz music only becomes that when the foundational *cantus firmus* is subject to improvisation by a musician. That musician, or performer, has to have some technical competence and an understanding of musical theory, its rules of harmony, counterpoint, and acceptable conventions for the development of melody.[13] Considering participation in worship through the analogous lens of performer does put a particular inference on participation—those participating should have a level of understanding and sensitivity to the relationship between order and freedom in approaching worship as a whole. Theologian Frances Young, when talking about the performance of Scripture, observed that the performer needs to "have a sensitivity to the actual score of that work, its form, its themes and subjects, and their 'generative' potential."[14] In scriptural terms, this equates to a "philological competence [in] biblical [interpretation], linguistic skills, sensitivity to context, and ability to re-state without distortion but with imagination."[15] In the context of worship, this would be more appropriately applied to the minister or worship leader than the congregation. Yet, as has been argued throughout the historical survey, the congregation's understanding of worship and their place within it is just as important as that of the worship leader. They too are performers.

The *cantus firmus* and performers, using Begbie's definition, constrain improvisation in the sense that they make the resulting music meaningful and not just a cacophony of sound. Similarly, order and participation shape freedom to ensure worship fulfils its purpose in the life of the church. The *cantus firmus* and performers can constrain improvisation in different ways affecting the overall composition of the music heard. The same is true for corporate worship; it is dependent on the interrelationship between

---

12. Begbie, *Theology, Music, and Time*, 208; Benson, "Improvising Texts, Improvising Communities," 304.

13. Young, *Art of Performance*, 160.

14. Young, *Art of Performance*, 160.

15. Young, *Art of Performance*, 160–61.

A Theology of Freedom, Order, and Participation

freedom, order and participation. Begbie suggested that this resulted in three types of constraint: "occasional, cultural, and continuous." He described them as follows:

> Occasional constraints [are] unique circumstances which are specific to a social, spatial or temporal situation, in the case of improvisation, those pertaining to a performance—for example, the acoustics of a concert hall, the mood of a particular audience. Cultural constraints are frameworks and patterns of action brought to an improvisation by the improvisers and listeners, constraints which have developed from interactions with others, perhaps over many years—the harmonic sequence in blues is an example. They include the whole range of skills and musical experience which inevitably shape any particular performance. Continuous constraints are those which condition us by virtue of the fact that we all inhabit a "given," physical world with its own integrity—for example, the way strings vibrate, bodily competence, etc.[16]

When considering these types in the context of worship, these constraints translate as tradition (cultural constraint), embodiment (continuous constraint) and response (occasional constraint). These three constraints will now be explored and used to develop a theology of corporate worship in the United Reformed Church, through the analogies for freedom, order and participation of improvisation, *cantus firmus* and performers.

Tradition

The early church was recorded in Acts 2 as having "devoted themselves to the apostles' teaching and fellowship, to the breaking of bread and the prayers."[17] These actions of the New Testament Church are the foundation of corporate worship, and it was with these words of Scripture the European Reformers of the sixteenth century began their approach to reforming the worship of the church. John Calvin (1509–64) wrote:

> There are in sum three things which our Lord has commanded us to observe in spiritual assemblies, namely, the preaching of his Word, the public and solemn prayers and the administration of his sacraments (cf. Acts 2:42).[18]

16. Begbie, *Theology, Music, and Time*, 201.
17. Acts 2:42.
18. Maag, *Lifting Hearts to the Lord*, 144.

The *cantus firmus* which Acts 2 offers has continued to underwrite approaches to corporate worship, particularly in the United Reformed Church, whose Basis of Union when describing the ministry of the Church, states:

> This service is given by worship, prayer, proclamation of the Gospel, and Christian witness; by mutual and outgoing care and responsibility, and by obedient discipleship in the whole daily life, according to the gifts and opportunities given to each other.[19]

Although this suggests an orderly approach, it does not formally order corporate worship. It gives a *cantus firmus* that ensures there is something in the life of the Church that is recognizable as worship, but it does not constrict worship in such a way that there is no freedom of interpretation which comes from the interaction of the "performers" through "improvisation." Despite this, the *cantus firmus* of Acts 2, was only the starting point for sixteenth century European Reformers and can only be identified as rooting the practice of worship in the United Reformed Church. Over the centuries, as shown by the historical survey, approaches taken to worship have been revised as the relationship between freedom, order and participation has become apparent and the understanding of these terms has developed and changed. The *cantus firmus* has come to have more substance as "tradition" has grown and become an important narrative in the Church's approach to worship.

Prescribed or fixed liturgy was dispensed with by the United Reformed Church's Puritan antecedents in the seventeenth century, yet a liturgical tradition has developed over the centuries which is rooted in the form of worship Calvin determined for the churches in Geneva and Strasbourg from original liturgies by William Farel and Martin Bucer.[20] Calvin noted that Jesus "foresaw that [the ceremony of worship] depended upon the state of the times, and he did not deem one form suitable for all ages."[21] Therefore, it is the general rules that are found in the Scriptures, and any disciplines or ceremonies believed necessary for the order and decorum of worship should be tested against these.[22] This is why Calvin's liturgies were refinements of what had been used before and why Calvin did not discount

---

19. United Reformed Church, "Basis of Union," clause 19.
20. Spinks, *Freedom or Order*, 9.
21. Calvin, *Institutes*, 4.10.30.
22. Calvin, *Institutes*, 4.10.30.

A Theology of Freedom, Order, and Participation

formal, prescribed liturgy. To remain faithful to the principles of worship, that *cantus firmus*, words and formulae might alter, although some fixed elements are required in specific situations. In a letter to the Protector Somerset, dated October 22, 1548, which commented on reforms needed in the English church, Calvin recognized that there may be a case for written liturgy that bound ministers, although he believed the catechism would serve equally well as a check upon people and their practices:

> Indeed, I do not say that it may not be well, and even necessary, to bind down the pastors and curates to a certain written form, as well for the sake of supplementing the ignorance and deficiencies of some, as the better to manifest the conformity and agreement between all the churches; thirdly, to take away all ground of pretence for bringing in any eccentricity or new-fangled doctrine on the part of those who only seek to indulge an idle fancy; as I have already said, the Catechism ought to serve as a check upon such people. There is, besides, the form and manner of administration of the sacraments; also the public prayers.[23]

For Calvin, a form of liturgy was a way in which the church could honor the holy ordinances ensuring it is known "what they contain, what they mean, and to what purpose they tend, in order that their observance may be useful and salutary, and in consequence rightly regulated."[24] As the historical survey shows, when considering how to approach its corporate worship, the United Reformed Church and its antecedent church traditions have made this an aim in the various publications produced in order to guide the worship of the church. For example, this is demonstrated in the inclusion of explanatory notes about worship as a whole and the different elements included in an act of worship which are part of the introductions or prefaces to *A Book of Public Worship compiled for the use of Congregationalists* (1949), the Congregational Church of England and Wales's *An Order of Public Worship* (1970), and the United Reformed Church's *Book of Order for Worship* (1974) and *A Book of Services* (1980).[25] Although the folklore of nonconformity suggests a break from liturgy, the historical survey reveals that what has been before has not stopped the development

---

23. Baird and Binney, *Chapter on Liturgies*, 23; Calvin, *Letters*, 191–92.

24. Maag, *Lifting Hearts to the Lord*, 144.

25. Huxtable et al., *Book of Public Worship*, xiii–xxii; Congregational Church of England and Wales, *Order of Public Worship*, 29–32; United Reformed Church, *Order for Worship*, 3–9; United Reformed Church, *Book of Services*, 10–15.

of liturgy. Instead, it has informed it and ensured that the ordinances set out in Scripture—the *cantus firmus* for all worship—are maintained even though there has been and continues to be improvisation. Liturgies have been updated with regard to cultural change and, as Geoffrey Wainwright observed, as a cause for the revision of corporate worship, from a perceived gap between current practice and that of earlier and classical periods of the church's history.[26] Wainwright's remark echoed Baptist theologian Neville Clark's view:

> Liturgy is not, cannot be, a sudden artificial construction, because it ever has been, ever must be, the product and deposit of the on-going life and experience of the Body of Christ, there every new venture must be positively related to tradition and must, in some sense, stem from the practice of years.[27]

In the context of the jazz analogy, Begbie can be seen as supporting this process, while offering an important caveat:

> The informal ways in which jazz has been gathered, passed on, improvised and re-improvised can remind us of a similar process in the development of tradition, and of the dangers of unduly restrictive ways in which the Church has understood the sources of "valid" themes for improvisation.[28]

In improvisation, tradition can only point beyond itself insofar as the one improvising is prepared to trust and inhabit it.[29] This means that tradition has to be understood and fully defined. It is possible to turn tradition into themes within the church that unduly restrict freedom or make freedom "freer" than it truly is in the context of the church. In the preface to the *Service Book* published by the United Reformed Church in 1989, Colin Gunton acknowledged the tradition of the Church's worship:

> The forms of worship offered in this book reach back through Christian history both to those biblical beginnings and to their development in the early centuries of the Church's life. But it is to the Reformation, and perhaps especially to John Calvin, that they owe their particular shape. For Calvin, the Church was to be found wherever the Word was truly preached and the sacraments

---

26. Wainwright, *Doxology*, 324.
27. Clark, *Call to Worship*, 12.
28. Begbie, *Theology, Music, and Time*, 216–17.
29. Begbie, *Theology, Music, and Time*, 219–20.

of Baptism and the Lord's Supper were duly administered, and this book maintains that two-fold emphasis. One of its ancestors is the [Westminster Assembly's *Directory for the Public Worship of God*], approved by the Commonwealth Parliament in 1645. Revealing influences from Geneva, Scotland and the Netherlands, it listed the necessary components of worship, gave instructions on prayer and preaching, but also allowed flexibility and encouraged free prayer. Influences on this present book are not only that tradition, but more recent developments within and without the [United Reformed Church].[30]

However, as with the *Book of Services* published in 1980 and *Worship: From the United Reformed Church* published in 2003, it was a tradition of freedom that was emphasized when consideration was given to how worship leaders and churches might use this book.[31] Of course, it can be said that a traditional element of jazz music is improvisation, but to constrain it in such a way is nonsensical. Even in the genre of "free-jazz" where the improvisation is supposedly free from all constraints or influences, there is an inheritance from the past and influences from different musical styles are evident.[32] As Begbie stated, "the intelligibility of any music depends on indwelling proven traditions of practice, interpretation and belief, ranging from the small-scale to the corporate memories which form the large-scale interpretative grids of a cultural group."[33] And this is true for the corporate worship of the church. For it to be intelligible there are indwelling traditions of practice, interpretation and belief that are natural conditions of worship, particularly around the concept of freedom.

The United Reformed Church belongs within the Free Church tradition in the United Kingdom. The identifier of "free" is predominantly understood in the context of a denomination's relation to the state—it is not connected to the state and therefore free from its control in its worship and practice. Although this freedom does not relate to every operation of the Church; there are legal requirements it must meet (e.g., related to Charity status, safeguarding, etc.). As revealed by the historical survey, this understanding is rooted in the events of the seventeenth century, influenced by controversies between the church and state and theological thought of the

30. United Reformed Church, *Service Book*, vii.
31. United Reformed Church, *Book of Services*, 7; United Reformed Church, *Worship*, Foreword.
32. Begbie, *Theology, Music, and Time*, 217.
33. Begbie, *Theology, Music, and Time*, 217.

sixteenth century. Ernest Payne described Free churches as coming "into existence because the life-giving spirit broke out with new power from within structures and polities, ceremonies and conventions, which were in danger of becoming too restrictive."[34] Perhaps Payne's view reflected the strength of nineteenth/early twentieth century nonconformity for whose adherents it was convenient to see the Ejectment as the result of conscience more than legal prescription and exclusion. Nevertheless, as a Baptist, Payne would have seen the Anabaptists and the "Spiritual Reformers" of the sixteenth century as influential and the subsequent radical groups of the seventeenth century providing a courageous witness that should not be overlooked.[35] This focus on conscience as a particular narrative of freedom has developed other freedom narratives within the life of the church which in turn have come to define churchmanship.[36] It is also evident that this traditional interpretation of freedom in the church is a notion linked with lordship and ruling over choices and actions. In viewing freedom in terms of lordship, theologian Jürgen Moltmann observed that everyone finds in others "a competitor in the struggle for power and possession."[37] Taking the position that the individual is master of choice and action suggests that the only perspective the individual holds is that of self. There is no sense of freedom of another person, although the ideal is that as a society of individuals no other person disturbs another—everyone equally having the right to be free.[38] If through freedom a better social outcome is sought, Moltmann suggested that freedom has to be an activity of a community or fellowship.[39] In community, freedom goes beyond the limits of self and there is unhindered solidarity which is important in the consideration of how the church worships corporately.[40] Although community broadens the limits, there continued to be boundaries to freedom which are those traditions of practice, interpretation and belief that in community are the "checks and balances" on actions.

---

34. Payne, *Free Churchmen*, 2–3.

35. Payne, *Free Church Tradition*, 45.

36. Payne lists these freedoms as including freedom from State connection and control, freedom from essential dependence on a priestly succession, freedom from fixed liturgical forms, freedom of conscience and inquiry (Payne, *Free Churchmen*, 3).

37. Moltmann, *Trinity and the Kingdom*, 215.

38. Moltmann, *Trinity and the Kingdom*, 215.

39. Moltmann, *Trinity and the Kingdom*, 216.

40. Moltmann, *Trinity and the Kingdom*, 216.

A Theology of Freedom, Order, and Participation

In the church, freedom cannot only be defined in human terms. God is a part of the community. Therefore, freedom is also a creative initiative that transcends the present and directs the future.[41] In the Christian faith this relates to the activity of the Holy Spirit. To be free is to participate in the creative Spirit of God.[42] This necessitates a distinctive understanding of freedom as it is no longer about the chosen actions of the human individual or community, but what the Holy Spirit inspires within them. This translated into traditions of practice which were believed to be inspired by the Holy Spirit.[43] It could be argued that an example of this is extemporary prayer, but the meaning is more nuanced than this. None of the church's traditions should be born of what the people want but of how the Spirit leads. That is why although the Holy Spirit might be perceived as having ultimate freedom—like the wind, the Spirit blows where it chooses[44]—in the context of the church the Holy Spirit structures, or orders, the church's freedom so that it is meaningful.

Martin Bucer (1491–1551), although holding to the importance of Scripture in the life and practice of the church as other first-generation reformers in sixteenth-century Europe, held the view that the Holy Spirit was also essential to the Christian life. This was based on John 6:63 where Jesus is quoted as saying, "it is the Spirit which gives life." Bucer formulated the perspective that "it is by the Spirit that those who are children of God are led (Rom 8:14), and [God] will teach them that they should always observe with their deeds what they teach in words."[45] Therefore, God's people will only come truly to worship God through the indwelling of the Holy Spirit, and it is the Holy Spirit that enables the church to worship as God desires—in spirit and in truth as identified in John 4 verses 23 to 24.[46] As theologian Ottomar Cypris summarized from *Grund und Ursach*, Bucer's defining work which was influential on liturgies across the Reformed and Protestant churches of the sixteenth century, including those of John Calvin (1509–64), John Knox (1514–72) and Thomas Cranmer (1489–1556):

> The servants of the Spirit are enabled through the Spirit to render to God the spiritual worship which is acceptable to Him, a

---

41. Moltmann, *Trinity and the Kingdom*, 216–17.
42. Moltmann, *Trinity and the Kingdom*, 217.
43. Payne, *Free Churchmen*, 4.
44. John 3:8.
45. Cypris, *Ground and Reason*, 111.
46. Poll, *Liturgical Ideas*, 16–17; Cypris, *Ground and Reason*, 24.

worship which concerns itself not with external matters but with inner spiritual realities.[47]

The Holy Spirit, therefore, inspires and is the means of achieving and participating in the worship that God desires from humanity.[48]

By understanding the Holy Spirit as being how the church achieves and participates in the worship God desires, Bucer determined that praise and prayer should be spontaneous. This view was not without scriptural root. Bucer wrote:

> Since we know that only the Spirit of God can know divine things (1 Cor 2:10–11), and further that the Scriptures of God contain nothing but good (2 Tim 3.16), therefore in the congregation of God we used neither songs nor prayers which are not based on Holy Scripture.[49]

Although, Cypris stated, "Bucer looked upon spontaneity in worship and the expression of the freedom of the spirit as an ideal," there was an orderly form to worship that Bucer believed congregations should follow.[50] This too was argued on the basis of Scripture.[51] But, interrelated to this was Bucer's understanding of Christian freedom. Bucer encouraged the church in Strasbourg to move away from the medieval practices that had become superstitious, were not understood by ordinary people, and were not described in Scripture. However, to force any to observe or not observe a particular practice without attendance to an individual inner conviction, Cypris determined, for Bucer was a transgression against Christian freedom.[52] Therefore, although Bucer spoke out against the elevation of the bread and cup in the Lord's Supper, the making of the sign of the cross, and other customs and practices of medieval piety, if they were beneficial to the spiritual wellbeing of an individual, were understood and remained as signs and took on no other significance, Bucer did not see them as harmful. Bucer wrote:

> We ask all those who love the Gospel that they should regard with faithful and simple eyes all the reasons . . . for the changes which

---

47. Cypris, *Ground and Reason*, 24.
48. Hardy and Ford, *Jubilate*, 120.
49. Cypris, *Ground and Reason*, 176.
50. Cypris, *Ground and Reason*, 62.
51. Cypris, *Ground and Reason*, 139–41.
52. Cypris, *Ground and Reason*, 24.

have been made among us, according to the Scriptures of God, and should make use of Christian freedom in external things in such a way that their first concern should always be those things which are edifying and useful; and further to take to heart that even though the idols are nothing, all external ceremonies are free in themselves, yet there are very few who will recognize these things as nothing and free in truth, even though they may have said so for a long time.[53]

The tradition of freedom in worship established by Bucer allows for freedom in approach but only if it gives due regard to the Word of God and is led by the Holy Spirit. This is the only way to ensure true worship. John Calvin, as a pupil of Bucer, reinforced that God alone has the authority over humanity's right and fitting approach to worship and Christian conscience should be such that it is bound by the Word of God.[54] Calvin's argument, like Bucer's, was based on Scripture. From the letter to the Colossians, Calvin reasoned:

We are not to seek from men the doctrine of the true worship of God, for the Lord has faithfully and fully instructed us in how he is to be worshipped. To prove this, [Paul] says in the first chapter that the gospel contains all the wisdom by which the man of God is made perfect in Christ [Col 1:28]. At the beginning of the second chapter he states that all treasurers of wisdom and understanding are hidden in Christ [Col 2:3]. From this he subsequently concludes that believers ought to beware lest they be seduced from Christ's flock through empty philosophy, according to the constitutions of men [Col 2:8]. But at the end of the chapter he condemns with greater confidence all self-made religion, this all feigned worship, which men have devised for themselves or received from others, and all precepts they of themselves dare promulgate concerning the worship of God [Col 2:16–23]. We therefore consider impious all constitutions in whose observance the worship of God is feigned to consist.[55]

Like Bucer, Calvin allowed for a freedom in observances in corporate worship which were believed useful and would build up the congregation. Without stating it, this could have included some ceremonial rites.[56] Calvin

---

53. Cypris, *Ground and Reason*, 179.
54. Calvin, *Institutes*, 4.10.8.
55. Calvin, *Institutes*, 4.10.8.
56. Calvin, *Institutes*, 4.10.32.

did emphasize that the ways of worship should be those set out in Scripture and with the "least possible admixture of human invention."[57] The Holy Spirit does empower and enable new possibilities, yet the church should be aware of how easily worship described as being from the freedom of the Spirit can become worship that is pleasing to individual worshippers and the church but not God.

Tradition can give shape and understanding to how worship in the church creatively incorporates freedom, order, and participation. It is through tradition that the *cantus firmus* enables the performer to improvise successfully. However, without knowledge of tradition, inherited ideas or thoughts on how individuals and congregations worship come to lack true understanding. This in turn can lead to corporate worship being meaningless.

Embodiment

The exploration of tradition has shown that worship in the United Reformed Church inhabits a narrative of freedom within order. For some congregations this means that every act of corporate worship starts from the premise of the *cantus firmus* of Acts 2 verse 42 or possibly expounds Calvin's ecclesiology in the *Institutes of Christian Religion* that is based around worship:

> Wherever we see the Word of God purely preached and heard, and the sacraments administered according to Christ's institution, there, it is not to be doubted, a church of God exists [cf. Eph 2:20]. For his promise cannot fail: "Wherever two or three are gathered in my name, there I am in the midst of them" [Matt 18:20].[58]

Other congregations will have more elaborate prescribed orders which have developed over their lifetimes as traditions. A need for continuity and the natural cycle of change meld together in their worship. Moltmann described these rhythms and memories which are fundamental for a community as rituals, and they have the potential of becoming fixed.[59] Whatever approach is taken, these are the anchors that Bucer spoke of as being required for the spiritual wellbeing of an individual or community. A

---

57. Thompson, *Liturgies*, 194.
58. Calvin, *Institutes*, 4.1.9.
59. Moltmann, *Church in the Power*, 263.

A Theology of Freedom, Order, and Participation

liturgy that is acceptable to the present Christian community and faithful to its past does more than just encourage spiritual wellbeing. Wainwright observed that it also enables worshippers to "identify themselves with a continuing community and enter into the 'story' of that community."[60] Such a perspective is offered by Huxtable about the liturgies drafted in *A Book of Services* (1980):

> We believe most of these services reflect the ethos of our Church and of its inherited traditions.[61]

Given that it was seen as "desirable" that the United Reformed Church had a service book from early in its life, this statement by Huxtable could be read to mean that through *A Book of Services* the United Reformed Church's identity was made evident.[62] However, the Church was formed in the hope that it would encourage further organic union in the church.[63] In fact, what *A Book of Services* did, James Todd observed in his reflection on the draft of the first order of Holy Communion presented to the 1973 General Assembly, was to provide the United Reformed Church with a text which did justice to the tradition inherited, took account of new liturgical insights "by which all branches of the church [were] being enriched," and enabled congregations "to worship God in freedom, with confidence and joy."[64] This process drew the congregations of the United Reformed Church into the bigger story which goes beyond the local and denominational—the church universal.

Moltmann took the definition of the community with which people can identify themselves through worship beyond the confines of a local congregation or denomination. The church has to be a messianic fellowship, organized in "accordance with the gospel, its promises and its challenges."[65] In this context, worship that identifies worshippers with that community and enables them to be a part of the "story" takes a unique shape. Moltmann wrote:

> A "religious" church which aims to "look after" people will always stylize its services into fixed ceremonials and will understand

---

60. Wainwright, *Doxology*, 344.
61. United Reformed Church, *Book of Services*, 7.
62. United Reformed Church, *Book of Reports, 1973*, 24.
63. Huxtable, *New Hope*, 33.
64. Todd, "Tradition and Change," 18.
65. Moltmann, *Church in the Power*, 275.

them quite generally as being anthropologically founded rituals with social functions, adapted to people's particular needs in certain social situations. But a messianic fellowship of the people will see itself as the subject of its assemblies, and will hence mould them into feasts of the divine history.[66]

If the church understands itself as the body of Christ and is open to being drawn into the community of God through incorporation into Christ in the Holy Spirit, then its worship will become shaped around the church's indwelling in God. Yet, if too much human history is molded into divine history, Bucer and Calvin's fears of human invention in worship becomes a reality. That said, for worship to be of the people for the glory of God it needs to be identifiable and owned by the community who are offering that act of corporate worship. In Begbie's analogy of the jazz improvisation this relates to the musical instrument in the hands of the musician. The instrument is not a mere tool "for making pre-conceived sounds."[67] Just as a musical instrument has its own properties, characteristics, and features that have to be respected and understood by the musician for them to create that improvised jazz melody, a congregation has its own characteristics and traditions that should be explored, honored, and incorporated in worship. In jazz, successful performance relies on the performer not only knowing how they can develop a melody but being one with their instrument, knowing its sound and limitations and allowing that to be part of the performance. Similarly, if corporate worship is to retain what Wainwright described as its etymology—the sense of being "the work of the people"—then it must embody the identity of a congregation, reflecting and embracing all that congregation has to offer to God and in fellowship with one another.[68]

As something that comes from the church's indwelling in God, worship cannot only be an expression of the people. It has to be of and in relation to God. Begbie suggested that faithful worship is that which is properly orientated—"primarily to God, and, in the power of the Spirit, to others with whom [the church] worship, and to the world [the church] represent and to which [the church] are sent."[69] This orientation is possible because of that connection of the church with Christ through Christ's humanity and the understanding of the church as a messianic fellowship. Christ ensures

66. Moltmann, *Church in the Power*, 275.
67. Begbie, *Theology, Music, and Time*, 232.
68. Wainwright, *Doxology*, 8.
69. Begbie, "Faithful Feelings," 336.

A Theology of Freedom, Order, and Participation

that the church's worship is true to God's character and purpose.[70] This is only fully true when Christian freedom is understood as coming from the knowledge and acceptance that Christ has made people free.[71] It is not the lordship of one's own identity. The freedom that the church has before God is given by God's own grace through Christ and by the sacrifice of Christ on the cross.[72] Begbie wrote, the Spirit "brings about that particularity-in-relation which constitutes [Christian] freedom and which has already been actualized in the Son."[73] This cements the idea that the freedom of the performer in worship requires the agency of both themselves and God. Although Christ makes it possible for humanity to worship, God too acts through the Holy Spirit.

The epistles show how the Spirit can inspire and facilitate aspects of worship. In the letter to the Romans, the apostle Paul wrote: "Likewise the Spirit helps us in our weakness; for we do not know how to pray as we ought . . ."[74] In the letter of Jude, there is the encouragement to "pray in the Holy Spirit."[75] The work of the Holy Spirit is related specifically to how the church prays in these Scriptures. Yet, they demonstrate how the Holy Spirit can be described as both leader and enabler of worship.[76] The Holy Spirit also does more than this. The Holy Spirit draws humanity into the divine. In Isaiah 11:2 the affinity between the divine and human spirit can be observed. The Spirit acts as the contact point between God and humanity, making the *koinonia* (fellowship/communion) in Christ real to believers.[77] The activity of the Spirit entwinning humanity and God in Christ, enables God through the Spirit to shape "human character and conduct the divine model and purpose."[78] Therefore, as theologian Alan Kay reflected, worship is the uniting of the church with God "in heart, will, mind, and deed" through Christ:

> The union of heart is a uniting of the worshipper with God in all the feelings that are created by love. The union of will is a true

---

70. Begbie, "Faithful Feelings," 336.
71. Payne, *Free Churchmen*, 10.
72. Cypris, *Ground and Reason*, 105; Forsyth, *Faith, Freedom, and the Future*, 61.
73. Begbie, *Theology, Music, and Time*, 240.
74. Rom 8:26.
75. Jude 20.
76. Wainwright, *Doxology*, 91.
77. Kärkkäinen, *Spirit and Salvation*, 25.
78. Isa 11:2; Wainwright, *Doxology*, 93.

> sacrifice, not merely a delighting of God, but a desire and determination to those things that please Him. The union of mind is a waiting upon the word of God that we may know who He is, what is His will, and how it may be done—a learning of the mind of Christ. The union of deed is not only practised in our work and life during the week, but finds its place also in our worship when we make requests both for ourselves and others, and thus co-operate with God by faith in the transforming of the world.[79]

Begbie echoed this view in his conclusion of faithful worship as a uniting activity:

> To be re-directed to the Father through the Son by the Spirit is to discover the love that is eternally given and received between Father and Son, the love with which [humanity] can be bound together (John 17:21). All worship in the Spirit builds up the Body of Christ and encourages unity (1 Cor 14:5, 12, 26).[80]

Theologian Alan Torrance summarized this as worship being part of the "human-Godward movement that belongs to God and takes place within the divine life."[81] Begbie stated "to participate, through the Spirit, in what Christ has done and is doing for us in relation to the Father, is to participate in God's gratuitousness and his inner life of exchange."[82] Therefore, by the Holy Spirit the church is brought into and within God to participate through the gift of grace realized in Christ. The church's worship, when "in the Spirit" becomes a sign of a God who is immanent without forfeiting a transcendent nature. Elizabeth Welch, theologian and Moderator of the United Reformed Church's General Assembly from 2001 to 2002, expressed this in the way she concluded that, because of the Holy Spirit, worship is at the heart of transformation in individuals and the church:

> Worship offers visibility for the Holy Spirit's transformative activity. This transformative work of the Spirit takes place in the moments of visible offering of worship and contributes to the ongoing process of transformation. The regularity of the offering of worship itself points to the developmental aspects of transformation. This is not something that happens in the moment and is then

---

79. Kay, *Nature of Christian Worship*, 41.
80. Begbie, "Faithful Feelings," 337.
81. Torrance, *Persons in Communion*, 314.
82. Begbie, *Theology, Music, and Time*, 254–55.

A Theology of Freedom, Order, and Participation

forgotten. Worship contributes to the development of transformation in the person and the church.[83]

God is among and within the people to transform them in order that they become "sharers in the divine nature" and subsequently agents of transformation in the world as "partners in [God's] enterprise for the whole world."[84] The performer receives the *cantus firmus*—those givens of meter, harmony, melody, idiom—and through improvisation "returns an equivalent different gift."[85] This, Begbie wrote, results in:

> The giving back here usually includes passing it on in an equivalent but different (and unpredictable) form to an audience of some sort, who themselves (unpredictably) receive it in countlessly different (and unpredictable) ways, and who themselves pass it on unpredictably (perhaps in no other form than an increased joy in their lives). Alternatively, the improvisation may be taken up by other musicians on subsequent occasions. As we have seen, in traditional jazz the improvisation itself (relying on its underlying, prior gift of harmonic progression) can function as the subject of further (unpredictable) improvisation, resulting in improvisation on improvisation.[86]

There results a cascade of response that makes the performance something dynamic and alive that has the potential of continuing for generations.

Response

Theologian Catherine Mowry LaCugna and Moltmann shared the view that "worship is essentially something which 'we do,' a task which we perform, in response to what 'God has done and is doing.'"[87] Although this has been demonstrated as being a result of the embodiment of the church in God which leads to worship, it is also suggestive of worship being subjective. Worship can be an anthropological response, or a consequence of, "the human perception of the divine joy."[88] Moltmann derived this from the experience of salvation, which when known can only find "expression in

---

83. Welch, *Holy Spirit and Worship*, 222.
84. 2 Pet 1:4; Wainwright, *Doxology*, 352; Begbie, "Faithful Feelings," 337.
85. Begbie, *Theology, Music, and Time*, 249.
86. Begbie, *Theology, Music, and Time*, 249.
87. Torrance, *Persons in Communion*, 317.
88. Torrance, *Persons in Communion*, 311.

thanks, praise and adoration."[89] Humanity's encounter with and knowledge of God leads to doxology which is more than mere thanks by the receiver to the giver; it extols the giver because they are good.[90] Moltmann suggested that adoration goes beyond thanksgiving and praise, "it is totally absorbed into its counterpart, in the way that [humanity is] totally absorbed by astonishment and boundless wonder."[91] A similar account, relating to what constitutes corporate worship in the United Reformed Church, is evident in Gunton's perspective on worship in the Church found in the preface of the *Service Book* (1989):

> In response to the presence of Christ, made known by the Spirit especially in Scripture and the preaching of the Word, the Church gives praise to God by offering its life and the life of the world in prayer, hymn, and sacrament.[92]

But worship is not just a task of the church. It is also a gift that the church participates in through priesthood of Christ.[93] Begbie wrote:

> Christ, as fully human, embodies and enables faithful worship. He is "faith-ful," full of faith in the Father, not only in his earthly life of loving and obedient self-offering to the Father, culminating in crucifixion, but also in his continuing risen life—he is now the human High Priest who, on the ground of his atoning work, leads us in our worship (Heb 2.12; 4.14; cf. Rom 8.34). In him, our humanity has been taken, and through the Holy Spirit re-formed, re-turned to God, so that now with him we can know his "Abba, Father" as *our* Abba, Father. So the church's worship is united with the one perfect response of the incarnate Son, with his once-for-all offering of worship on the cross, and with his ongoing worship of the Father in our midst as High Priest. And this is possible through the same Spirit who enabled and undergirded Christ's own earthly self-offering. Worship, in short, is a sharing by the Spirit in the Son's communion with the Father by the Spirit.[94]

In this context, therefore, corporate worship is the Spirit-inspired response of the church to the revelation of the triune God in which praise is rendered

---

89. Moltmann, *Trinity and the Kingdom*, 152.
90. Moltmann, *Trinity and the Kingdom*, 153.
91. Moltmann, *Trinity and the Kingdom*, 153.
92. United Reformed Church, *Service Book*, vi.
93. Torrance, *Persons in Communion*, 311.
94. Begbie, "Faithful Feelings," 336–37.

A Theology of Freedom, Order, and Participation

"to the Father, through the Son and in the Spirit."[95] This is also evident in Gunton's description of worship in the United Reformed Church—it is where God and God's people meet and both parties respond and act.

Theologian Nicholas Wolterstorff observed that the sixteenth century Reformers saw corporate worship as God's action and the church's faithful reception of that action.[96] To participate in worship was to enter into the sphere of God's acting, not just God's presence, and for the church "to appropriate God's action in faith and gratitude through the work of the Spirit."[97] This is demonstrated in Huldrych Zwingli's (1484–1531) approach to worship. Theologian Bard Thompson stated in Zurich "churchgoers were not expected to rush into the traditional activities of worship—seeing and doing, making adoration and oblation to the righteous God—but to wait in stillness and repose upon the loving heavenly Father, that they might 'hear' His Word and 'receive' His gift of forgiveness and sonship."[98] Equally Bucer believed that true worship only occurred when the Word went forth in the church and the church made its response of prayer and praise. It was then "in this context that the Spirit of the Lord [worked within] the congregation, bringing [people] to faith and thence to true piety in Christ."[99] The Holy Spirit is the central agent of God's action. It is the Holy Spirit who impresses the external word of the sermon on the hearts of the congregation and makes it the living Word of God. The Holy Spirit calls the church to repent, impels it to prayer and assures it that those prayers are heard by God, and provides the church with the spiritual gifts for mutual priesthood that serve both God and neighbor.[100] Therefore, the Holy Spirit "stands at the head of the cascade of giving that flows through the material world and nourishes the creativity of the artist" or performer.[101] Embodiment feeds response because it is the inspiration of the Holy Spirit which fosters in the performer the musicality that enables them in their improvisation to bring an "old score and present experience into creative interaction."[102] This might suggest that because the performer's experience of inspiration

---

95. Chan, "Liturgy as the Work of the Spirit," 47.
96. Wolterstorff, "Reformed Liturgy," 290.
97. Wolterstorff, "Reformed Liturgy," 291.
98. Thompson, *Liturgies*, 144.
99. Thompson, *Liturgies*, 162.
100. Thompson, *Liturgies*, 162.
101. Guthrie, *Creator Spirit*, 146.
102. Young, *Art of Performance*, 162.

is beyond personal conscious control or something that is in spite of themselves, that any response to the performance or as part of the performance is passive. Frances Young suggested, through consideration of what happens with pieces of artwork, this is not the case. The artist produces their own artwork.

> The response of hearer or reader is more than merely passive since the "recipient" of the "revelation" has to discern in the "symbol," the meaning or meanings that ring bells or create new discernment. The authority of such artistic creation is inherent in the work, and yet has no impact on the "blind" or "deaf"—only on those who see the signs and believe.[103]

This demonstrates further how multi-dimensional worship is in its meaning and practice, particularly when framing it as something that is free. The anthropological aspect of worshippers' response—their participation as performers in the performance of worship—cannot be lost sight of because the truth of worship and the struggle for true worship would cease to be. This is highlighted by Young's discussion on whether there can be a definitive performance if the Scriptures presented Christ as both fulfilment of all the complexities of existence and a critical challenge to it. Young stated that there can never be a single adequate doctrine of biblical authority or a single adequate theology of biblical inspiration.[104] "Like 'faith and works,' 'grace and freewill,' and many other areas of Christian thought," Young wrote, "the truth does not lie where the tension or paradox is resolved."[105] It is in the struggle to perform that an appreciation of the range of dynamics is exploited.[106]

Improvisation cannot be seen as one-sided. The performer, the one improvising, has to be working with something that already exists.[107] This is the *cantus firmus* but, from the Christian perspective, it is also the guidance of the Holy Spirit. Zwingli, Bucer and Calvin were of the same opinion that for worship to be true the invocation of the Holy Spirit was required. In the church in Zurich, Zwingli began an act of worship with a plea for God, by the Holy Spirit, to open God's holy and eternal Word to himself and the congregation and to establish within them the knowledge of God's

---

103. Young, *Art of Performance*, 180.
104. Young, *Art of Performance*, 181.
105. Young, *Art of Performance*, 181–82.
106. Young, *Art of Performance*, 182.
107. Benson, "Improvising Texts, Improvising Communities," 303.

will, directing all who err in the right way, so that all might live according to God's divine pleasure.[108] Bucer and Calvin took the approach that worship should begin with the confession of the congregation to bring them to a place of openness to the grace of God. In the prayers of confession they used, this was to be brought about through the action of the Holy Spirit. An example of a confession used by Bucer is:

> Almighty, eternal God and Father, we confess and acknowledge that we, alas, were conceived and born in sin, and are therefore inclined to all evil and slow to all good; that we transgress the holy commandments without ceasing, and evermore corrupt ourselves. But we are sorry for the same, and beseech thy grace and help. Wherefore have mercy upon us, most gracious and merciful God and Father, through thy Son our Lord Jesus Christ. Grant to us and increase in us thy Holy Spirit, that we may recognise our sin and unrighteousness from the bottom of our hearts, attain true repentance and sorrow for them, die to them wholly, and please thee entirely by a new and godly life. Amen.[109]

The confession Calvin used in the Geneva and Strasbourg was:

> O Lord God, eternal and almighty Father, we confess and acknowledge unfeignedly before thy holy majesty that we are poor sinners, conceived and born in iniquity and corruption, prone to do evil, incapable of any good, and that in our depravity we transgress the holy commandments without end or ceasing: Wherefore we purchase for ourselves, through the righteous judgement, are ruin and perdition. Nevertheless, O Lord, we are grieved that we have offended thee; and we condemn ourselves and our sins with true repentance, beseeching thy grace to relieve our distress. O God and Father most gracious and full of compassion, have mercy upon us in the name of thy Son, our Lord Jesus Christ. And as thou dost blot out our sins and stains, magnify and increase in us day by day the grace of the Holy Spirit: that as we acknowledge our unrighteousness with all our heart, we may be moved by the sorrow which shall bring forth true repentance in us, mortifying all our sins, and producing in us the fruits of righteousness and innocence which are pleasing unto thee; Through the same Jesus Christ &c. [our Lord. Amen][110]

---

108. Thompson, *Liturgies*, 147.
109. Thompson, *Liturgies*, 168.
110. Thompson, *Liturgies*, 197–98.

Although neither of these prayers invoke the Holy Spirit directly, they suggest the need of the Holy Spirit which Bucer and Calvin perceived as essential in the congregation to participate in and offer true worship. Theologian G. van de Poll stated that in Bucer's opinion, it is the Holy Spirit that "renders God's Word transparent and prepares [the people] for the service of God."[111] A similar understanding of the work of the Spirit is demonstrated in Calvin's theology:

> That the Word may not beat your ears in vain, and that the sacraments may not strike your eyes in vain, the Spirit shows us that in them it is God speaking to us, softening the stubbornness of our hearts, and composing it to that obedience which it owes the Word of the Lord. Finally, the Spirit transmits those outward words and sacrament from our ears to our souls.[112]

Therefore, before the reading of Scriptures and the preaching of the sermon, both Bucer and Calvin would offer prayers of illumination. Other *epicletic* prayers were included as part of the sacraments emphasizing an awareness of the continued need for divine interruption and transformation within worship to ensure that it is the best it can be and fulfils its purpose. Theologian Matthew Myer Boulton argued that "the *epicletic* character of Christian worship should be conceived and enacted as a recognition of worship's own destitution and malformation, its urgent need for the Spirit's gracious, transformational presence."[113] This probably takes the Reformers perspective on how the *epiclesis* should shape worship further, but it takes us full circle to their view that worship is lacking if based solely on human invention. Calvin wrote:

> Every chance invention, by which men seek to worship God, is nothing but a pollution of true holiness.[114]

Jean-Jacques von Allmen wrote:

> It is absolutely essential that the act of worship should be open towards God, that God may intervene in His saving power. It must not be self-justifying, in other words, the element of *epiclesis* is of vital necessity. We must be free from prejudices or enviousness.[115]

---

111. Poll, *Liturgical Ideas*, 77.
112. Calvin, *Institutes*, 4.14.10.
113. Boulton, "Adversary," 77.
114. Calvin, *Institutes*, 4.10.25.
115. Allmen, *Worship*, 288.

A Theology of Freedom, Order, and Participation

Theologian Simon Chan suggested worship as being "both truly the work of the people and truly the work of God."[116] What becomes evident is how the Holy Spirit causes and enables response—aiding and bringing about a congregation's participation—so that worship is the work of God in and through the work of the people. As theologian Steven Guthrie wrote:

> Because God gives to make us givers, each participant in the cascade of giving contributes its own voice, its own gifts, to the onward movement.[117]

Conclusion

Theologian Bruce Ellis Benson suggested that although improvisation on the tune is what is thought to make jazz music unique, it is also the improvisation on musical styles, which are both historical and ontologically prior, that is key to how jazz music operates and is created.[118] Benson goes on to say that the development of jazz is in fact "the story of continual improvisation upon itself."[119] Given all that has been discussed, the same can be said about corporate worship. Worship is constantly being reshaped. It is being given new emphases without loss of historical knowledge or its importance in the life of the church. There has been that cascade of giving with each generation, yet also a constancy, through worship being both rooted in Scripture and God because of the church's relationship with Christ in the Holy Spirit. To limit the evolution of corporate worship to be solely about freedom, not only misinterprets exactly what happens in improvisation—the givens and constraints that are essential to create music of any genre—it requires freedom to be thought of in very specific terms. The analogy of improvisation has demonstrated that freedom in worship is more complex and wider consideration must be given to what happens when Christians gather for corporate worship.

If freedom was the only consideration in how the church worships corporately, the definition of freedom would need to align with Moltmann's perspective:

---

116. Chan, "Liturgy as the Work of the Spirit," 53.
117. Guthrie, *Creator Spirit*, 146.
118. Benson, "Improvising Texts, Improvising Communities," 308.
119. Benson, "Improvising Texts, Improvising Communities," 308.

> Freedom means the unhindered participation in the eternal life of the triune God himself, and in his inexhaustible fullness and glory. "Our hearts are restless until they find rest in thee," said Augustine. And when we think of freedom we may surely say: "Our hearts are captive until they become free in the glory of the triune God."[120]

This might be how the church should understand its freedom and be the underlying principle to the freedom that ensures worship is truly directed to God and of God, but it does dismiss what is understood and known of human freedom. The historical survey has shown that, for the church, human freedom is as important as divine freedom when it comes to worshipping corporately. But what can happen is that the church ends us with two approaches to freedom. Theologian John McIntyre described them as:

> One [approach] holding that the sovereignty of the Spirit is supreme and irresistible—all is of God and nothing is of the human spirit, which is in any case too sinful to accept God's goodness; the other, that it is wrong to eliminate human responsibility and freedom, because the dehumanising of persons, even if the results are the highest and the best of them, is too high a price to pay, and persons are open and free themselves to decide on acceptance or rejection of God's offer.[121]

In corporate worship these two approaches have to be held in tension with one another. This is achieved by the interrelationship with and constraint of order and participation on freedom.

There are three potential ways in which this tension can be understood and engaged within the context of worship: tradition, embodiment, and response. Tradition is the inherited ideas and thoughts that cement the importance of freedom while demonstrating why order and participation cannot be dismissed. Tradition gives the formulae from which corporate worship can develop and evolve from generation to generation. Embodiment brings the human and divine together. However, the church and God do not only meet in corporate worship. Through Christ and the Holy Spirit, the church is part of the divine life and, therefore, the activities of the church should reflect this. Yet in worship this relationship between humanity and God finds its greatest expression. Welch wrote: "In worship the nature of human dependency in God is emphasized, and in this relationship

---

120. Moltmann, *Trinity and the Kingdom*, 222.
121. McIntyre, *Shape of Pneumatology*, 188.

of dependency, God is known."[122] Response is the working together of the human and divine in worship. Response is born out of what is given by God and the people's gift back to God. Therefore, tradition, embodiment, and response do not singularly describe how divine and human freedom in worship are brought together through their relationship with order and participation. As Wainwright reflected:

> Into [worship] the people bring their entire existence so that it may be gathered up in praise. From [worship] the people depart with a renewed vision of the value-patterns of God's kingdom, by the more effective practice of which they intend to glorify God in their whole life.[123]

They all add to a theology of worship that encourages the church to see corporate worship as an ongoing process of reforming activity which is crucial to the life and identity of the church as it participates both in the life of God and of the community.

---

122. Welch, *Holy Spirit and Worship*, 139.
123. Wainwright, *Doxology*, 8.

6

Conclusion

THE CENTRALITY OF WORSHIP in the life of the church makes it an anchor for identity, being both a place of teaching and an expression of who a gathered community of believers are in God. Therefore, there is a desire and need for continuity in worship as this ties the generations of the church to one another. However, the development of tradition (i.e., denomination), era, and encounter with God mean that worship is always changing if it is a true expression of a common life that is attentive to Scripture and open to the Holy Spirt in the search for God's kingdom. Whether the manner of worship is dictated or not by a prescribed liturgy, this is evident in how freedom, order, and participation interrelate in worship. It is in how each of these, together, have come to be understood in and through the worship of the church that the life of the church is revealed.

Freedom, Order, and Participation in the United Reformed Church

The United Reformed Church with its antecedents (English Presbyterianism, English, Welsh, and Scottish Congregationalism, and the Churches of Christ) affiliate with the global Reformed tradition and the national Free Church tradition. Both traditions have influenced the Church's approach to worship, instilling the idea that there should be freedom in worship but not to the detriment of order. All corporate worship has to have an order to enable worship to fulfil its role within the life of the church: drawing the community of disciples together in communion with God, to glorify God, and learn more of God. However, worship is not only an action of the church

CONCLUSION

toward God; in worship humanity and God encounter one another. The United Reformed Church overtly emphasizes freedom—freedom in worship is cherished and no book of services is to "impugn that freedom."[1] But for worship to be meaningful and for it to fulfil its true purpose in the life of the Church, freedom has to be bound. Understanding the limits to freedom in worship has developed over time as theological thought has expanded. For the United Reformed Church and its antecedents that understanding has also been influenced by history.

Freedom

The Westminster Assembly, in the drafting of the *Directory for the Public Worship of God* attempted to move the worship of the English church away from a rigid liturgy to worship that was scriptural and orderly while being free to engage the gifts of the minister in response to the Holy Spirit. It was recognized that worship should embrace both human and divine freedom, where the divine, through the Holy Spirit, would guide and illuminate the Word of God. This was to be manifested in the preaching and prayers of the minster, as well as the praise and petition of the congregation. However, following the events of the Great Ejectment in 1662, freedom in worship became predominantly thought of in terms of human freedom. As individuals and church communities dissented from being subject to the measures enforced by Parliament on the English church by the *Act of Uniformity* (1662), (establishing the Church of England), so the opinion that worshipping communities were best placed to know and decide how they should worship God became more influential. The domination of human freedom, particularly the concept of the liberty of conscience, has continued. This is evident in how scripted liturgies have come to be used by some congregations of the United Reformed Church. The freedom to alter and vary those liturgies has been maintained and at times actively encouraged. Some authors of worship resources connected with the United Reformed Church have even suggest that their material should be adapted to "meet the taste" of the user (i.e., worship leaders and/or congregation).[2]

---

1. United Reformed Church, *Book of Services*, 7.

2. Presbyterian Church of England, "General Assembly Records 1964," in *General Assembly Records, 1954–1972*, 424; Hilton, *Lent & Easter*, 3; Forester and Smith, *New Start*, 11.

A Historical Theology of Worship

The dominance of human freedom has caused divine freedom to be misinterpreted or considered through the lens of human freedom. There has been no acknowledgement in the discourses that humanity must surrender its freedom for the divine to truly act freely. Theologian Daniel Jenkins illustrated this in his observation on Congregational worship:

> In contrast to churches with a fixed liturgy, Congregationalism has always been disposed to emphasize the free and active movement of the Spirit in worship, valuing sincerity and spontaneity of expression more than the due performance of a rite. It cannot always claim to have understood the right relation between the free movement of the Spirit and fixed forms, although it sometimes has, and it has often had a naïve conception of what constitutes sincerity and spontaneity. This has exposed it to grave dangers.[3]

Jenkins identified here how a human understanding of freedom can misinform humanity's understanding of divine action in worship. It is often believed that the Holy Spirit only acts when corporate worship allows for spontaneity, primarily of the worship leader, therefore making worship truly sincere. There is a naivety in this understanding of the divine and, as Jenkins suggested, discounts God's ability to act and enable sincere worship through fixed forms of liturgy.

Human factors may be prevalent in the United Reformed Church's approach to worship but divine freedom, particularly that of the Holy Spirit, is theologically central to United Reformed Church worship. The importance of and reliance on the Holy Spirit has been reiterated over the centuries. Without the Holy Spirit, the worship of the Church would be worthless and without foundation, as summarized in the preface to the *Service Book*:

> Worship takes its reality from the presence of the risen Christ in the congregation; through him the Holy Spirit lifts the people up to God the Father, creator, ruler, and redeemer of all things. Thus it is that "The worship of the local church in an expression of the worship of the whole people of God" (*Basis of Union*). In response to the presence of Christ, made known by the Spirit especially in Scripture and the preaching of the Word, the Church gives praise to God by offering its life and the life of the world in prayer, hymn, and sacrament.[4]

---

3. Jenkins, *Congregationalism*, 90.
4. United Reformed Church, *Service Book*, vi.

Conclusion

As well as reinforcing the Reformed nature of the Church, it demonstrated how the United Reformed Church understands that its worship is both an action of the divine and human. Therefore, corporate worship of the United Reformed Church holds true to the theologian David Fergusson's definition of worship:

> A performative action in which both the Church and God participate. It is not merely a human acknowledgement of who God is or what Christ has done. Worship is an event by which God is known and Christ communicated; it is not of our own making for it is dependent upon the grace of God. In this regard, the act of worship is not merely a human recollection or bearing witness although it includes these. It is also an event in which God's grace works for us in repeated, regular and dependable ways, albeit in a manner that refers us to the once for all action of Christ.[5]

Worship is where the community of the church can be built up in relationship with God. It is where God can speak to the people and the people of God can make a response to God. Understanding worship to be that place of participation by both the divine and humanity reminds the church of how it dwells in God and God dwells within it. In turn, this is essential for faithful worship.[6]

Participation

Although worship is an entwinement of divine and human action, discussion of participation in corporate worship has come to be thought of practically in terms of human actions. In the United Reformed Church and its antecedent traditions how participation in corporate worship has evolved over time reflects the Church's response to societal change and includes the incorporation of worship practices of other church traditions thus embracing the breadth and diversity of the Church. Critically, the choice of language has been an important factor in ensuring corporate worship is inclusive, and therefore intelligible by all members of a congregation. Responsive litanies and prayers have been written with specific groups in mind to directly encourage their participation in worship. However, reflection of societal changes has not been constrained to the language spoken

---

5. See David Fergusson, "The Theology of Worship: A Reformed Perspective," in Forrester and Gay, *Worship and Liturgy*, 72–73.
6. Torrance, *Persons in Communion*, 314; Begbie, "Faithful Feelings," 337.

and used in liturgy and hymns. The Congregationalists and Presbyterians both recognized the importance of the presence of children and young people in worship and so included a "children's address" in all acts of worship. In the United Reformed Church, this terminology has ceased to be used and the term "theme introduction" favored. Within an act of worship, this remains the time where the minister or worship leader is encouraged to speak directly to children and young people.[7] Yet, the change in terminology signifies how the Church has tried to shift toward a model of worship that considers all generations during the entirety of an act of worship. Emphasis on this has increased since the adoption of the *Charter for Children*.[8] In the Charter, the United Reformed Church is called to recognize that children are equal partners in the life of the Church and are included in the concept of the "priesthood of all believers." Therefore, children and young people should not be thought of or spoken to at only one point in a service. Consideration should be given to their inclusion and participation throughout a whole act of corporate worship.

The expanse of resources for use in corporate worship by congregations of the United Reformed Church demonstrates how freedom in worship has enabled liturgical evolution focused on participation.[9] New and alternative ways of worship enhancing participation, including the use of liturgy from other church traditions and the use of silence, have been encouraged in corporate worship with diversion from what principally might be considered as the Church's approach to worship. This is a strength in United Reformed Church worship especially as the Church is broad. An overemphasis on human action, though, has the possibility of making corporate worship purely humanity's response to God. This is demonstrated in the opening prayer of the 2020 edition of the *Prayer Handbook*:

> From our hearts to yours, O God,
> from our hearts to yours.
> All that sits and bubbles within—
> The naked truth of who we are
> and what we feel,
> born of joys and fears
> and hopes and disappointments,
> challenges and frustrations
> and pain.

---

7. United Reformed Church, *Book of Services*, 22.
8. United Reformed Church, *Book of Reports*, 1990, 102.
9. Colechin, "Worship of the United Reformed Church," 284–320.

Conclusion

No "right words";
no "correct way";
no pomp,
no ceremony,
no norms or etiquette.

Just a pouring forth of
all we are
in response to what we sense
of you.

From our hearts to yours, Gracious God.
From the hearts of your people
to you.[10]

A beautiful prayer that reflects the theme of the *Prayer Handbook*, yet shows how easy, when free to do so, worship can become one-dimensional (e.g., only humanity's response to God), rather than a multi-dimensional encounter between God and humanity, where both receive, act, and respond.

Order

Order has been the means over the centuries to ensure that the worship of the church fulfils its place in the life of the church. Order gives worship the structure it needs to educate those gathered in the Christian faith. It also demonstrates "faith's embodiment in prayer, proclamation, and the patterns of community life."[11] Even in periods of history when the antecedent traditions of the United Reformed Church were without published orders, corporate worship followed an order that was fairly constant from Sunday to Sunday.[12] This might be explained by the recognition that even though it can be asserted that if God is free to act worship will be as God wills, human freedom can skew what happens in practice. Whether order in corporate worship of all congregations of the United Reformed Church demonstrates this action of human freedom over divine freedom, it cannot be concluded. Nevertheless, the concept of "orderly freedom" has been exhibited and encouraged denominationally in the ways the United Reformed Church has approached and worded service books over the years.

10. Campbell and Fosten, *Prayers from the Heart*, 3.
11. Ellis, *Gathering*, 1.
12. Anonymous, "Bury Street Church Records," 333–42.

Although not imposed, the liturgies within the United Reformed Church service books are fully formulated with limited expressions of the minister or worship leader having the options to use other words than those printed. This greatly differs from how "orderly freedom" was demonstrated by the Westminster Assembly in the *Directory for Public Worship of God* and in the early directories for worship published by the Presbyterian Church of England, which, though not without examples of the words that might be said or prayed, were far more instructive on how to order worship.

Order has had another role in the corporate worship of the United Reformed Church. It has been how continuity in worship has been assured over the generations. There has been evolution, particularly in content. But the shape and form of the worship of the United Reformed Church can be traced back to Martin Bucer (1491–1551) and his reformation of the worship in the church in Strasbourg. The church in Strasbourg was where he laid the ground for understanding worship to be ordered and free. Over the centuries, there have been subtle variations but essentially Bucer's model of worship has continued to be used. Worship begins with actions (prayers, psalms, and hymns) that prepare the congregation to hear God's Word. God's Word is then listened to and heard through the reading of Scripture and the preaching of a sermon. Finally, the congregation is led in response to God's Word through prayer, possibly the proclamation of an affirmation of faith and the singing of hymns. This basic pattern has given worship freedom, encouraged participation, and allowed worship to evolve while ensuring it fulfils its purpose in the life of the Church.

Conclusion

Freedom, order, and participation in corporate worship of the church are an expression of the church's nature, faith, and order. They can be thought of practically, in relation to a specific denomination. Yet, there is a universality to them, as freedom, order, and participation in corporate worship are about how the church is encountering God as a community and responding always "in spirit and in truth."[13] Exploring freedom, order, and participation from historical and theological perspectives demonstrates how worship is the thread that connects the generations of the church. The surveying of worship in these terms also shows how worship is how the

---

13. John 4:24.

Conclusion

church evolves in its ministry to the world as ordained by God through Jesus Christ.

This book has demonstrated what the consideration of worship in terms of freedom, order, and participation through the lens of a specific denomination or church does for the general theological understanding of worship in the life of the church. It has also shown the impact of worship on the knowledge of a church of its identity and vice versa. The method used, which could be described as a derivative of liturgical theology although it does not follow the principle rigidly, is applicable to any church of the Free Church tradition in Britain. However, if the corporate worship of a church is attentive to Scripture and open to the Holy Spirit, then that worship, whatever the church's tradition, can be described in terms of freedom, order, and participation. It does not matter whether liturgy is firmly prescribed or completely free to be whatever God or the congregation believe is required. Worship that is a communal encounter between those gathered and God is free and ordered. It is a reforming activity that is crucial to the life and identity of the church as the church strives to be a community of disciples expressing the sovereignty of God in their common life.

> What should be done then, my friends? When you come together, each one has a hymn, a lesson, a revelation, a tongue, or an interpretation. Let all things be done for building up.
> (1 Cor 14:26)

Bibliography

Abba, Raymond. *Principles of Christian Worship: With Special Reference to the Free Churches.* London: Oxford University Press, 1957.
Acheson, R. J. *Radical Puritans in England, 1550-1660.* London: Longman, 1990.
Adams, Jonathan. *The Dairy of Jonathan Adams, Minister of Scotts Lane Independent Chapel, Salisbury, 1772-1804.* Diary. 541/1. Wiltshire and Swindon History Centre. Archives of Salisbury United Reformed Church.
Allmen, Jean-Jacques von. *Worship: Its Theology and Practice.* London: Lutterworth, 1965.
Allon, Henry. *Church Song in Its Relation to Church Life: A Lecture.* London: Morgan & Chase, 1862.
Ames, William. *Conscience with the Power and Cases Thereof.* Anno: Anno, 1639. http://www.digitalpuritan.net/Digital%20Puritan%20Resources/Ames,%20William/Conscience.pdf.
Andrew, Edward G. *Conscience and Its Critics: Protestant Conscience, Enlightenment Reason, and Modern Subjectivity.* Toronto: University of Toronto Press, 2001.
Anonymous. "From the Bury Street Church Records." *Transactions of the Congregational History Society* 6 (1914) 333-42.
Appleby, David J. *Black Bartholomew's Day: Preaching, Polemic, and Restoration Nonconformity.* Manchester: Manchester University Press, 2007.
Argent, Alan. *The Transformation of Congregationalism, 1900-2000.* Nottingham: Congregational Federation, 2013.
Baillie, Robert. *The Letters and Journals of Robert Baillie, A.M. Principal of the University of Glasgow, 1637-1662.* Vol. 2. Edinburgh: Ogle, 1841.
Baird, Charles W., and Thomas Binney. *A Chapter on Liturgies: Historical Sketches.* London: Knight & Son, 1856.
Banyard, Edmund. *Straws in the Wind.* London: United Reformed Church, 1992.
Baxter, Richard. *The Autobiography of Richard Baxter.* Edited by N. H. Keeble and J. M. Lloyd Thomas. London: Dent and Sons, 1985.
———. "Christian Ecclesiastics." In *The Practical Works of Rev. Richard Baxter: With a Life of the Author, and a Critical Examination of his Writings*, edited by W Orme, 5:1-246. London: Duncan, 1830.
———. *One Sheet for the Ministry against the Malignants of All Sorts.* London: White, 1657.
Beddington, David W. *Evangelism in Modern Britain: A History from the 1730s to the 1980s.* Florence: Taylor & Francis, 2005.

Bibliography

Begbie, Jeremy S. "Faithful Feelings: Music and Emotion in Worship." In *Resonant Witness: Conversations between Music and Theology*, edited by Jeremy S. Begbie and Steven R. Guthrie, 323–54. Grand Rapids: Eerdmans, 2011.

———. *Theology, Music, and Time*. Cambridge: Cambridge University Press, 2000.

Benson, Bruce Ellis. "Improvising Texts, Improvising Communities: Jazz, Interpretation, Heterophony, and the Ekklesia." In *Resonant Witness: Conversations between Music and Theology*, edited by Jeremy S. Begbie and Steven R. Guthrie, 295–319. Grand Rapids: Eerdmans, 2011.

Beynon, Graham. *Isaac Watts: Reason, Passion, and the Revival of Religion*. London: Bloomsbury T. & T. Clark, 2016.

Binney, Thomas. *The Service of Song in the House of the Lord*. London: Jackson, Walford, Ward & Co., 1849.

Bonhoeffer, Dietrich. *Letters and Papers from Prison*. Enlarged ed. London: SCM, 1971.

Boulton, Matthew Myer. "The Adversary: Agony, Irony, and the Liturgical Role of the Holy Spirit." In *The Spirit in Worship—Worship in the Spirit*, edited by Teresa Berger and Bryan D. Spinks, 59–77. Collegeville, MN: Liturgical, 2009.

Bradbury, John P. "Non-conformist Conscience? Individual Conscience and the Authority of the Church from John Calvin to the Present." *Ecclesiology* 10 (2014) 32–52.

———. *Perpetually Reforming: A Theology of Church Reform and Renewal*. London: Bloomsbury T. & T. Clark, 2013.

Branch, Lori. *Rituals of Spontaneity: Sentiment and Secularism from Free Prayer to Wordsworth*. Waco, TX: Baylor University Press, 2006.

Breward, Ian. *The Westminster Directory being a Directory for the Public Worship of God in the Three Kingdomes*. Bramcote: Grove, 1980.

Brown, Stewart J., et al., ed. *The Oxford Handbook of the Oxford Movement*. Oxford: Oxford University Press, 2017.

Browne, John. *History of Congregationalism and Memorial of the Churches in Norfolk and Suffolk*. London: Jarrold and Sons, 1877.

Brownell, Kenneth G. "Voluntary Saints: English Congregationalism and the Voluntary Principle, 1825–1962." PhD diss., University of St. Andrews, 1982.

Burgess, John H., ed. *In Word and Spirit: Discussion Papers on the Theology of Worship*. Exeter: Spiritualseekers, 2016.

Burroughs, Jeremiah. *Gospel-Worship, or, The Right Manner of Sanctifying to Name of God in General and Particularly in These Three Great Ordinances: 1. Hearing the Word. 2. Receiving the Lords Supper. 3. Prayer*. 1653. Reprint, Morgan: Soli Deo Gloria, 1990.

Bury St. Edmunds Independent Church. *Church Book, 1646–1801*. Duncan, 1961.

Cadoux, Cecil J. *A Pilgrim's Further Progress: Dialogues on Christian Teaching*. Oxford: Basil Blackwell, 1943.

Calvin, John. *Institutes of Christian Religion*. Translated by John T. McNeill. Philadelphia: Westminster, 1960.

———. *Letters of John Calvin, Compiled from Original Manuscripts and Edited with Historical Notes*. Vol. 2. Translated by Jules Bonnet. Philadelphia: Presbyterian Board, 2014.

Campbell, Karen, and Ian Fosten. *Prayers from the Heart: Prayer Handbook 2020*. London: United Reformed Church, 2019.

Camroux, Martin. *Ecumenism in Retreat: How the United Reformed Church Failed to Break the Mould*. Eugene, OR: Wipf & Stock, 2016.

Bibliography

Cannadine, David, et al., eds. *Oxford Dictionary of National Biography*. Oxford: Oxford University Press, 2016.

Carruthers, S. W. *1844: A Tale of Faith and Courage*. London: Presbyterian Church of England, 1944.

———. *Fifty Years, 1876–1926: Being a Brief Survey of the Work and Progress of the Presbyterian Church of England since the Union*. London: Presbyterian Church of England, 1926.

Cashdollar, Charles D. *A Spiritual Home: Life in British and American Reformed Congregations, 1830–1915*. University Park, PA: Pennsylvania State University Press, 2000.

Chan, Simon. "The Liturgy as the Work of the Spirit: A Theological Perspective." In *The Spirit in Worship—Worship in the Spirit*, edited by Teresa Berger and Bryan D. Spinks, 41–57. Collegeville, MN: Liturgical, 2009.

Chapman, G. R., ed. *The Rodborough Bede Book*. Rev. ed. Woodchester: Arthurs, 1971.

Charnock, Stephen. *The Works of the Late Learned Divine Stephen Charnock, B.D. Being Several Discourses upon the Existence and Attributed of God. His Discourse of Divine Providence: and a Supplement of several Discourses on Various Divine Subjects*. 3rd ed. London: Anon Dom, 1699.

The Church of Scotland. *Book of Common Order of the Church of Scotland*. London: Oxford University Press, 1940.

Clark, Neville. *Call to Worship*. London: SCM, 1960.

Clarkson, David. "Public Worship to Be Preferred before Private, 1696." https://web.archive.org/web/20200708121439/https://www.covenanter.org/reformed/2015/8/18/david-clarksons-sermon-on-public-worship-to-be-preferred-before-private.

Cleal, Edward E., and T. G. Crippen. *The Story of Congregationalism in Surrey*. London: Clarke & Co, 1908.

Clifford, Alan C. *The Good Doctor: Philip Doddridge of Northampton—A Tercentenary Tribute*. Norwich: Charenton Reformed, 2002.

Colechin, Elaine S. "Praising God: Worship in the United Reformed Church." In *Traditions and Transitions: Studies in the History and Theology of The United Reformed Church*, edited by David Cornick and Robert Pope, 221–34. London: United Reformed Church, 2022.

———. "The Worship of the United Reformed Church: A Historical Theology." PhD diss., Anglia Ruskin University, 2021.

Common Close Congregational Church. *Church Minute Book*. Minutes. 2103/2. Wiltshire and Swindon History Centre. Archives of Warminster Congregational Church.

The Congregational Church in England and Wales. *A Declaration of Faith*. Hull: Independent, 1967.

———. *An Order of Public Worship*. London: Oxford University Press, 1970.

Congregational Union of England and Wales. *Book of Congregational Worship*. London: Congregational Union of England and Wales, 1920.

———. *A Book of Services and Prayers*. London: Independent, 1959.

———. *Congregational Church Hymnal*. London: Congregational Union of England and Wales, 1887.

———. *Congregational Hymn Book*. London: Congregational Union of England and Wales, 1836.

———. *Congregational Hymnary*. London: Congregational Union of England and Wales, 1916.

Bibliography

———. *Congregational Praise*. London: Independent, 1951.
———. *Congregational Yearbook, 1863*. London: Congregational Union of England and Wales, 1863.
———. *Congregational Yearbook, 1874*. London: Congregational Union of England and Wales, 1874.
———. *Congregational Yearbook, 1876*. London: Congregational Union of England and Wales, 1876.
———. *Congregational Yearbook, 1897*. London: Congregational Union of England and Wales, 1897.
———. *Congregational Yearbook, 1920*. London: Congregational Union of England and Wales, 1920.
———. *Congregational Yearbook, 1936*, London: Congregational Union of England and Wales, 1936.
———. *Declaration of the Faith, Church Order, and Discipline of the Congregational or Independent Dissenters*. London: Jackson and Walford, 1833.
———. *New Congregational Hymn Book*. London: Hodder & Stoughton, 1859.
Cornick, David. "Catch a Scotchman Becoming an Englishman . . . Nationalism, Theology and Ecumenism in the Presbyterian Church in England, 1845–1876." *Journal of the United Reformed Church History Society* 3 (1985) 202–15.
———. "The Disruption in London: English Presbyterians and the Scottish Disruption of 1843." In *Modern Christianity and Cultural Aspirations*, edited by David Beddington and Timothy Larsen, 288–308. London: Sheffield Academic, 2003.
———. *Under God's Good Hand: A History of the Traditions Which Have Come Together in the United Reformed Church in the United Kingdom*. London: United Reformed Church, 1998.
Cousland, Kenneth H. "The Significance of Isaac Watts in the Development of Hymnody." *Church History* 17 (1948) 287–98.
Cypris, Ottomar Frederick. *Martin Bucer's Ground and Reason: A Commentary and Translation*. Yulee, FL: Good Samaritan, 2016.
Dale, R. W. *History of English Congregationalism*. 2nd ed. London: Hodder and Stoughton, 1907.
———. *The Holy Spirit in Relation to the Ministry, the Worship, and the Work the Church*. 2nd ed. London: Hodder and Stoughton. 1869.
———. *A Manual of Congregational Principles*. London: Hodder and Stoughton, 1884.
———. *Nine Lectures on Preaching Delivered at Yale, New Haven, Connecticut*. 11th ed. London: Hodder and Stoughton, 1900.
Davies, Horton. *Worship and Theology in England*. 5 vols. Edited by Horton Davies. Grand Rapids: Eerdmans, 1996.
———. *The Worship of the English Puritans*. Westminster, London: Dacre, 1948.
Deconinck-Brossard, Françoise. "The Art of Preaching." In *Preaching, Sermon, and Cultural Change in the Long Eighteenth Century*, edited by Joris van Eijnatten, 95–130. Leiden: Brill, 2009.
Dell, William. *The Stumbling-Stone, or, A Discourse Touching that Offence which the World and Worldly Church do take against 1. Christ Himself. 2. His True Word. 3. His True Worship. 4. His True Church. 5. His True Government. 6. His True Ministry.: Wherein the University is reproved by the Word of God. Delivered partly to the University-congregation in Cambridge, partly to another in the same town. Together with a brief touch in the epistle (for the present) on the late quarrelsom, weak, and erroneous*

Bibliography

Animadversions of one Mr. Chambers, called Doctor in Divinity, and Pastor of Pewsy in Wiltshire. London: Calvert, 1653.
DeVries, Dawn. "Calvin's Preaching." In *The Cambridge Companion to John Calvin*, edited by Donald K. McKim, 106–24. Cambridge: Cambridge University Press, 2004.
Ditchfield, G. M. *The Evangelical Revival*. London: UCL, 1998.
Dix, Gregory. *The Shape of the Liturgy*. 2nd ed. London: Dacre, 1945.
Doddridge, Philip. *The Works of the Rev. P. Doddridge, D.D. in ten volumes*. Vol. 5. Leeds: Bains, 1803.
Doodson, Alberta J. *The Presbyterians in Liverpool: A Social and Religious Survey up to 1972*. London: United Reformed Church, 2004.
Dryness, William A. *A Primer on Christian Worship: Where We've Been, Where We Are, Where We Can Go*. Grand Rapids: Eerdmans, 2009.
Drysdale, A. H. *History of the Presbyterians in England: Their Rise, Decline, and Revival*. London: Presbyterian Church of England, 1889.
Duck, Ruth C. *Worship for the Whole People of God*. 2nd ed. Louisville: Westminster John Knox, 2021.
Duncan, John. "The Presbyterians in Bury St. Edmunds: A Summary." *Journal of the Presbyterian History Society* 12 (1963) 100–109.
Earle, Jabez. "The Nature of Singing." In *Practical Discourses of Singing in the Worship of God: Preach'd at the Friday Lectures in Eascheap*, edited by Jabez Earle et al., 1–18. London: Darby, 1707.
Ellis, Christopher J. *Gathering: A Theology and Spirituality of Worship in Free Church Tradition*. London: SCM, 2004.
England Parliament. *The Humble Advice of the Assembly of Divines concerning A Confession of Faith*. London: Tyler, 1647.
———. *The Solemn League and Covenant for the Reformation and Defence of Religion, the Honour and Happiness of the King, and the Peace and Safety of the three kingdoms of Scotland, England, and Ireland*. Edinburgh: Tyler, 1643.
Fagerberg, David W. *Theologia Prima: What Is Liturgical Theology?* 2nd ed. Chicago: Hillenbrand, 2004.
Fenn, J. E. "Worship in the Mid-Twentieth Century." In *Papers to Committee on Public Worship and Aids to Devotion*, 1968. Paper. PCE/HMC/WAD/A. Westminster College, Cambridge. Archives of the Presbyterian Church of England.
Fisherton Congregational Church. *Scotts Lane Chapel and afterwards at Endless Street, and afterwards at the New Congregational in Fisherton Street, Salisbury, Church Book*, 1852–1895. Minutes. 1279/2. Wiltshire and Swindon History Centre. Archives of Salisbury United Reformed Church.
Forrester, Duncan B., and Doug Gay. *Worship and Liturgy in Context: Studies and Case Studies in Theology and Practice*. London: SCM, 2009.
Forster, Michael, and Simon Smith. *A New Start in All-Age Worship: Service Outlines for the Millennium and Beyond*. Stowmarket: Mayhew, 1999.
Forsyth, P. T. *Faith, Freedom, and the Future*. 2nd ed. London: Independent, 1955.
Fraser, Donald. *The Presbyterian Church of England: An Outline of Its Doctrine, Worship, Polity, History*. London: Presbyterian Church of England, 1890.
The General Assembly of the Church of Scotland. "Claim, Declaration, and Protest, 1842." *Reformed Books Online*. https://reformedbooksonline.com/scottish-theology/free-church-of-scotland/claim-declaration-and-protest-1842/.

BIBLIOGRAPHY

Goodwin, Thomas. *The Works of Thomas Goodwin, D.D.* Edited by Thomas Smith. Edinburgh: Nichols, 1865.

Grieve, A. J., and W. Marshall Jones. *These Three Hundred Years: Being the Story of Congregational Work and Witness in Bury St. Edmunds, 1646-1946.* London: Independent, 1946.

Guthrie, Steven R. *Creator Spirit: The Holy Spirit and the Art of Becoming Human.* Grand Rapids: Baker Academic, 2011.

Hall, C. Newman, ed. *Free Church Service Book: Five Short Services, with Supplementary Collects and Anthems, selected from the Book of Common Prayer.* London: Snow and Co., 1866.

Hambrick-Stowe, Charles E. "Practical Divinity and Spirituality." In *The Cambridge Companion to Puritanism*, edited by John Coffey and Paul C. H. Lim, 191-205. Cambridge: Cambridge University Press, 2008.

Hardy, Daniel W., and David F. Ford. *Jubilate Theology in Praise.* London: Darton, Longman, and Todd, 1984.

Henry, Matthew. "A Method of Prayer." In *The Select Works of the Late Revd Mr Matthew Henry. Being a Complete Collection of all his Practical Pieces. Together with An Account of his Life, and A Sermon preached on the Occasion of his Death*, edited by William Tong, 143-94. Edinburgh: Gray and Alston, 1772.

Hilton, Donald. *Celebrating Lent & Easter, Book 2.* Redhill: National Christian Education Council, 1990.

Howe, John. "A Treatise of Delighting in God." In *The Whole Works of the Rev. John Howe, M.A. with a Memoir of the Author in Eight Volumes*, edited by John Hunt, 2:7-207. London: Westley, 1822.

Hunt, Arnold. *The Art of Hearing: English Preachers and Their Audiences, 1590-1640.* Cambridge: Cambridge University Press, 2010.

Hunter, John. *Devotional Services for Public Worship.* 8th ed. London: Dent & Co., 1903.

Huxtable, John. *A New Hope for Christian Unity.* Glasgow: Fount Paperbacks, 1977.

Huxtable, John, et al. *A Book of Public Worship Compiled for the use of Congregationalists.* 2nd ed. London: Oxford University Press, 1949.

James, T. T. *The Work and Administration of a Congregational Church.* London: Congregational Union of England & Wales, 1925.

Jenkins, Daniel. *Congregationalism: A Restatement.* London: Faber and Faber, 1954.

Jennings, John. "Two Discourses of Preaching Christ, and of Particular and Experimental Preaching." In *Instructions to Ministers: In Three Parts*, edited by D. Jennings and Isaac Watts, 15-71. London: Jennings, 1744.

Jones, R. L. *Derby Street Congregational Church: The Church Meets for Worship.* Bolton: Derby Street Congregational Church, 1943.

Jones, R. Tudur. *Congregationalism in England, 1662-1962.* London: Independent, 1962.

Jordon, M. D. "The Early Independents and the Visible Church." *Transaction of the Congregational History Society* 8 (1922) 258-66.

———. "The Early Independents and the Visible Church." *Transaction of the Congregational History Society* 8 (1923) 296-304.

Kärkkäinen, Veli-Matti. *Spirit and Salvation.* Grand Rapids: Eerdmans, 2016.

Kavanagh, Aidan. *On Liturgical Theology: The Hale Memorial Lectures of Seabury-Western Theological Seminary, 1981.* Collegeville, MN: Liturgical, 1992.

Kay, J. Alan. *The Nature of Christian Worship.* London: Epworth, 1953.

Bibliography

Kaye, Elaine. *The History of the King's Weigh House Church: A Chapter in the History of London*. London: Allen & Unwin, 1968.

Keeble, N. H. *The Restoration: England in the 1660s*. Oxford: Blackwell, 2002.

Knox, R. B. "The Links between Irish and English Presbyterianism between 1840 and 1976." *Bulletin of the Presbyterian History Society of Ireland* 9 (1979).

Maag, Karin. *Lifting Hearts to the Lord: Worship with John Calvin in Sixteenth-Century Geneva*. Grand Rapids: Eerdmans, 2016.

Macleod, Donald. *Presbyterian Worship: Its Meaning and Method*. Richmond: Knox, 1965.

MacLeod, George. *We Shall Re-build: The Work of the Iona Community on Mainland and on Island*. Glasgow: Iona Community, 1962.

Manning, Bernard L. *The Hymns of Wesley and Watts*. London: Epworth, 1942.

Marvin, Ernest. *Shaping Up: Reforming Reformed Worship*. London: United Reformed Church, 2005.

Matthews, A. G., ed. *The Savoy Declaration of Faith and Order, 1658*. London: Independent, 1959.

McGraw, Ryan M. *A Heavenly Directory: Trinitarian Piety, Public Worship, and a Reassessment of John Owen's Theology*. Göttingen: Vandenhoeck & Ruprecht, 2014.

McIlhagga, Donald. "Experimental Worship." In *Symposium on Worship*. 1971. Paper. PCE/HMC/WAD/B. Westminster College, Cambridge. Archives of the Presbyterian Church of England.

McIntyre, John. *The Shape of Pneumatology: Studies in the Doctrine of the Holy Spirit*. Edinburgh: T. & T. Clark, 1997.

McNally, Frederick W. "The Westminster Directory: Its Origin and Significance." PhD diss., University of Edinburgh, 1958.

Micklem, Nathaniel, ed. *Christian Worship: Studies in Its History and Meaning*. Oxford: Clarendon, 1936.

Middlemiss, J. T. *How Far Is a Directory of Worship Necessary or Expedient?* Sunderland: Campbell & Co., 1893.

Millard, Benjamin A. *Congregationalism*. London: Constable & Company, 1912.

Miller, John. *After the Civil Wars: English Politics and Government in the Reign of Charles II*. Harlow: Longman, 2000.

Moltmann, Jürgen. *The Church in the Power of the Spirit*. 2nd ed. London: SCM, 1992.

———. *The Trinity and the Kingdom of God: The Doctrine of God*. London: SCM, 1981.

Moore-Keish, Martha L. *Do This in Remembrance of Me: A Ritual Approach to Eucharist Theology*. Grand Rapids: Eerdmans, 2008.

Morgan, D. Densil. "Spirituality, Worship, and Congregational Life." In *The Oxford History of Protestant Dissenting Traditions: The Nineteenth Century*, edited by Timothy Larsen and Michael Ledger-Lomas, 3:502–23. Oxford: Oxford University Press, 2017.

Murray, Douglas M. "Disruption to Union." In *Studies in the History of Worship in Scotland*, edited by Duncan B. Forrester and Douglas M. Murray, 87–106. 2nd ed. Edinburgh: T. & T. Clark, 1996.

———. "High Church Presbyterianism in Scotland and England." *Journal of the United Reformed Church History Society* 3 (1985) 225–34.

Newman, John. "Sermon XIII: On the Nature of Hearing the Word." In *Eastcheap Lectures containing Twenty-four Practical Discourses on the Duties of Hearing the Word and Reading the Scriptures: Delivered at the Weigh-House, in Little Eastcheap*, edited by Benjamin Grosvenor et al., 2:5–82. London: Brown, 1816.

BIBLIOGRAPHY

Nichols, James H. *Corporate Worship in the Reformed Tradition*. Eugene, OR: Wipf & Stock, 1968.

Nuttall, Geoffrey F. *The Holy Spirit in Puritan Faith and Experience*. Oxford: Basil Blackwell, 1947.

———. *Visible Saints: The Congregational Way, 1640–1660*. 2nd ed. Weston Rhyn: Quinta, 2001.

Old, Hughes Oliphant. *The Reading and Preaching of the Scriptures in the Worship of the Christian Church: Moderatism, Pietism, and Awakening*. Vol. 5. Grand Rapids: Eerdmans, 2004.

———. *The Reading and Preaching of the Scriptures in the Worship of the Christian Church: The Modern Age*. Vol. 6. Grand Rapids: Eerdmans, 2007.

Orchard, W. E. *The Order of Divine Service for Public Worship*. 2nd ed. London: Oxford University Press, 1926.

Owen, David. *Sharers in Worship*. Redhill: National Christians Education Council, 1980.

Owen, John. *John Owen on the Holy Spirit: Pneumatologia*. Cedar Lake, MI: Waymark, 2012.

———. "The Nature and Beauty of the Gospel Worship, 1721." *The Highway*. https://www.the-highway.com/GospelWorship_Owen.html.

Panel on the Worship of the Church of Scotland. *Book of Common Order of the Church of Scotland*. 2nd ed. Edinburgh: St. Andrew, 1996.

Parker, Joseph. *The Paraclete: An essay on the personality and ministry of the Holy Ghost with reference to current discussions*. London, 1874.

Payne, Ernest A. *The Free Church Tradition in the Life of England*. London: SCM, 1944.

———. *Free Churchmen, Unrepentant and Repentant, and Other Papers*. London: Kingsgate, 1965.

Pearsall, John S. *Public Worship: The best method of conducting it*. London: Jackson, Walford, and Hodder, 1867.

Peel, Albert. *A Brief History of English Congregationalism*. London: Independent, 1931.

Peel, David R. *Reforming Theology: Explorations in the Theological Traditions of the United Reformed Church*. London: United Reformed Church, 2002.

Perkins, William. *The Art of Prophesying and the Calling of the Minister*. Rev. ed. Edinburgh: Banner of Truth Trust, 2011.

The Presbyterian Church of England. *The Directory for the Public Worship of God, on the basis of that agreed upon by the Assembly of Divines at Westminster, A.D. 1644. Recommended for use in the Presbyterian Church of England by the Synod, 1898*. London: Presbyterian Church of England, 1898.

———. *Directory for the Public Worship for Use in the Presbyterian Church of England*. London: Presbyterian Church of England, 1921.

———. *General Assembly Records, 1921–1923*. London: The Publications Committee of the Presbyterian Church of England, 1923.

———. *General Assembly Records, 1944–1949*. London: The Publications Committee of the Presbyterian Church of England, 1949.

———. *General Assembly Records, 1954–1972*. London: Presbyterian Church of England, 1972.

———. *Minutes of the Committee on Public Worship and Aids of Devotion, 1954–1972*. Minutes. PCE/HMC/WAD/1. Westminster College, Cambridge. Archives of the Presbyterian Church of England.

Bibliography

———. *The Presbyterian Church of England: A Memorial of the Union*. London: Nisbet & Co., 1877.

———. *Synod Records, 1885–1898*. London: Presbyterian Church of England, 1898.

———. *Synod Records, 1913–1920*. London: Publishing Office of the Presbyterian Church of England, 1920.

———. *Yearbook, 1970*. London: Presbyterian Church of England, 1970.

The Presbyterian Churches of England and Wales. *The Presbyterian Service Book for Use in the Presbyterian Churches of England and Wales*. London: Presbyterian Church of England, 1948.

———. *The Presbyterian Service Book for Use in the Presbyterian Churches of England and Wales*. London: Presbyterian Church of England, 1968.

Price, Ernest J. *A Handbook of Congregationalism*. London: Congregational Union of England and Wales, 1924.

Poll, G. J. van de. *Martin Bucer's Liturgical Ideas: The Strasburg Reformer and His Connection with the Liturgies of the Sixteenth Century*. Assen: Van Gorcum & Comp, 1954.

Pope, Robert, ed. *T. & T. Clark Companion to Nonconformity*. London: Bloomsbury T. & T. Clark, 2016.

Randall, Ian M. "Emmanuel Congregational Church, Cambridge, 1874–1924: A 'Representative Church'?" *Journal of the United Reformed Church History Society* 10 (2018) 73–93.

Rice, Howard L., and James C. Huffstutler. *Reformed Worship*. Louisville: Geneva, 2001.

Rivers, Isabel. *Reason, Grace, and Sentiment: A Study of the Language of Religion and Ethics in England, 1660–1780—Whichcote to Wesley*. Vol. 1. Cambridge: Cambridge University Press, 1991.

Ross, Nella. "On the Use of Silence in Presbyterian Worship." In *Symposium on Worship*. 1971. Paper. PCE/HMC/WAD/B. Westminster College, Cambridge. Archives of the Presbyterian Church of England.

Routley, Erik. *I'll Praise My Maker: Studies in English Classical Hymnody*. London: Independent, 1951.

———. *Into a Far Country: Reflections upon the Trajectory of the Divine Word, and upon the Communication, in Affairs Human and Divine, of the Imperative and the Indicative*. London: Independent, 1962.

———. "A New Book of Worship for a New Church." *Worship* 48 (1974) 413–20.

———. *The Story of Congregationalism*. London: Independent, 1961.

Rushworth, John. "Historical Collections: December 1641." In *Historical Collections of Private Passages of State*, edited by John Rushworth, 4:436–71. London: Browne, 1721. British History Online. https://www.british-history.ac.uk/rushworth-papers/vol4/pp436-471.

———. "Historical Collections: Parliamentary and Civil Occurrences, 1645." In *Historical Collections of Private Passages of State*, edited by John Rushworth, 6:141–228. London: Browne, 1722. British History Online. https://www.british-history.ac.uk/rushworth-papers/vol6/pp141-228.

———. "Historical Collections: Passages Relating to Scotland, 1642–43." In *Historical Collections of Private Passages of State*, edited by John Rushworth, 5:387–504. London: Browne, 1721. British History Online. https://www.british-history.ac.uk/rushworth-papers/vol5/pp387-504.

Bibliography

Rutherford, Mark. *Autobiography of Mark Rutherford, edited by his friend Reuben Shapcott*. 2nd ed. London: Hard, 1881.

Ryrie, Alec. *Being Protestants in Reformation Britain*. Oxford: Oxford University Press, 2015.

———. *Protestants: The Radicals Who Made the Modern World*. London: Collins, 2017.

Saliers, D. E. "Liturgical Theology." In *A New Dictionary of Christian Theology*, edited by Alan Richardson and John Bowden, 336-37. London: SCM, 1983.

Sanford Street Congregational Church. *Church Meeting Minutes, 1877-1895*. Minutes. 1471/1. Wiltshire and Swindon History Centre. Archives of Sanford Street Congregational Church, Swindon.

Scotland Parliament. *The Directory for Publick Worship of God*. 1645. Reprint, Brooksville, FL: Westminster Society, 2017.

Schmemann, Alexander. *Introduction to Liturgical Theology*. New York: St. Valadimir's Seminary Press, 1966.

Schaeffer, John D. "Tropical Latitude: Prophecy, Orality, and the Rhetoric of Tolerance in Jeremy Taylor's *The Liberty of Prophesying*." *Studies in Philology* 101 (2004) 454-70.

Selderhuis, Herman J. *The Calvin Handbook*. Grand Rapids: Eerdmans, 2009.

Sell, Alan P. F. "Living in the Half Lights: John Oman in Context." In *John Oman: New Perspectives*, edited by Adam Hood, 3-63. Milton Keynes: Paternoster, 2012.

Simpson, P. Carnegie. *The Character of Presbytery*. Manchester: Aikan & Son, 1936.

Smith, Gary S., and P. C. Kemeny, eds. *The Oxford Handbook of Presbyterianism*. New York: Oxford University Press, 2019.

Spinks, Bryan D. *Freedom or Order? The Eucharistic Liturgy in English Congregationalism, 1645-1980*. Allison Park, PA: Pickwick, 1984.

Srawley, J. H. *The Liturgical Movement: Its Origin and Growth*. London: Mowbray & Co., 1954.

Statter, Chris. "Managing the Disruptions: The Ministry of J. Oswald Dykes." *Journal of the United Reformed Church History Society* 10 (2018) 59-72.

Taylor, William M. *The Ministry of the Word*. London: Nelson and Sons, 1876.

Temperley, Nicholas. "The Music of Dissent." In *Dissenting Praise: Religious Dissent and the Hymn in England and Wales*, edited by Isabel Rivers and David L. Wykes, 197-228. Oxford: Oxford University Press, 2011.

Templeton, Julian, and Keith Riglin, eds. *Reforming Worship: English Reformed Principles and Practices*. Eugene, OR: Wipf and Stock, 2012.

Thomas, David. *A Biblical Liturgy: for the use of churches, schools, homes and hospitals*. 12th ed. London: Charles Higham, 1881.

———. *The Ministry and the Church: The Inaugural Address delivered before the Annual Assembly of the Congregational Union of England and Wales, May 9th 1865*. London: Jackson, Walford, & Hodder, 1865.

Thomas, Keith. *In Pursuit of Civility*. New Haven: Yale University Press, 2020.

Thompson, Andrew C., ed. *The Oxford History of Protestant Dissenting Traditions*. Vol. 2, *The Long Eighteenth Century c. 1689-c. 1828*. Oxford: Oxford University Press, 2018.

Thompson, Bard. *Liturgies of the Western Church*. Philadelphia: Fortress, 1980.

Thompson, David M. "Remembering 1662." *Journal of the United Reformed Church History Society* 9 (2013) 154-70.

———. *What We Believe: The Faith of the United Reformed Church*. London: United Reformed Church, 1996.

Bibliography

Thorogood, Bernard. *Our Father's House: An Approach to Worship*. London: United Reformed Church, 1983.

Todd, James M. "On Spontaneity on Prayer." In *Symposium on Worship*. 1971. Paper. PCE/HMC/WAD/B. Westminster College, Cambridge. Archives of the Presbyterian Church of England.

———. "Tradition and Change: Worship in the United Reformed Church." *Liturgical Review* 5 (1975) 1–18.

Tomkins, Stephen. *The Journey of the Mayflower: God's Outlaw and the Invention of Freedom*. London: Hodder and Stoughton, 2020.

Torrance, Alan J. *Persons in Communion: An Essay on Trinitarian Description and Human Participation with Special Reference to Volume One of Karl Barth's Church Dogmatics*. Edinburgh: T. & T. Clark, 1996.

Tucker, Tony. *Reformed Ministry: Traditions of Ministry and Ordination in the United Reformed Church*. London: United Reformed Church, 2003.

Underhill, Evelyn. *Worship*. 2nd ed. London: Nisbet & Co., 1937.

The United Reformed Church. *Book of Order for Worship*. London: United Reformed Church, 1974.

———. *A Book of Services*. Edinburgh: St. Andrew, 1980.

———. *General Assembly Book of Reports, 1973*. London: United Reformed Church, 1973.

———. *General Assembly Book of Reports, 1990*. London: United Reformed Church, 1990.

———. "Section A: Basis of Union." In *The Manual*. London: United Reformed Church, 2015. https://urc.org.uk/images/the_manual/A_The_Basis_of_union.pdf.

———. *Service Book*. Oxford: Oxford University Press, 1989.

———. *Service of Thanksgiving for the Inauguration of the United Reformed Church*. Westminster Abbey, London, October 5, 1972. Service Sheet. PCE/IDR/JPC/26. Westminster College, Cambridge. Archives of the Presbyterian Church of England.

———. *Wholly Worship: Resource Material to Develop Worship in the Local Churches*. London: United Reformed Church, 1999.

———. *Worship: From the United Reformed Church*. London: United Reformed Church, 2003.

van Dixhoorn, Chad. *God's Ambassadors: The Westminster Assembly and the Reformation of the English Pulpit, 1643–1653*. Grand Rapids: Reformation Heritage, 2017.

Vincent, Thomas. *An Explicatory Catechism: Or, An Explanation of the Assembly's Shorter Catechism*. Edinburgh: Brown and Company, 1723.

Wadsworth, K. W. *The Yorkshire Congregational Union and Home Missionary Society 1872–1972*. N.p., 1972.

Wainwright, Geoffrey. *Doxology: The Praise of God in Worship, Doctrine, and Life*. London: Epworth, 1980.

———. "Theology of Worship." In *The New SCM Dictionary of Liturgy and Worship*, edited by Paul F. Bradshaw, 454–57. London: SCM, 2013.

Wakefield, Gordon S. *Puritan Devotion: It's Place in the Development of Christian Piety*. London: Epworth, 1959.

Walkden, Peter. *A Diary from January 1733 to March 1734*. Otley: Smith Settle, 2000.

Wallace, Valerie. *Scottish Presbyterianism and Settler Colonial Politics: Empire of Dissent*. Cham: Palgrave Macmillan, 2018.

Warfield, Benjamin B. *The Westminster Assembly and Its Work*. New York: Great Christian Books, 2015.

Bibliography

Watts, Isaac. *Guide to Prayer; or, A Free and Rational Account of the Gift, Grace, and Spirit of Prayer; with Plain Directions how every Christian may attain them.* Bungay: Brightly and Childs, 1816.

———. "An Humble Attempt towards the Revival of Practical Religion among Christians." In *The Works of the Rev. Isaac Watts, D.D.*, 4:583–635. London: Forgotten, 2015.

———. *Hymns and Spiritual Songs.* 6th ed. London: J. H., 1718.

———. *The Psalms of David, Imitated in the Language of the New Testament, And applu'd to the Christian State and Worship.* 4th ed. London: Clark and Ford, 1722.

Watts, Michael R. *The Dissenters: From the Reformation to the French Revolution.* Vol. 1. Oxford: Clarendon, 1978.

Watson, J. R. *The English Hymn: A Critical and Historical Study.* Oxford: Clarendon, 1997.

Welch, Elizabeth A. *The Holy Spirit and Worship: Transformation and Truth in the Theologies of John Owen and John Zizioulas.* Eugene, OR: Pickwick, 2021.

Westminster Assembly. *A Directory for Church-Government and Ordination of Ministers, to be Examined Against the Next Generall Assemblie.* Edinburgh: Tyler, 1647.

———. *The Minutes and Papers of the Westminster Assembly, 1643–1652: Introduction.* Edited by Chad van Dixhoorn and David F. Wright. Vol. 1. Oxford: Oxford University Press, 2012.

———. *The Minutes and Papers of the Westminster Assembly, 1643–1652: Minutes, Sessions 199–603 (1644–1646).* Edited by Chad van Dixhoorn and David F. Wright. Vol. 3. Oxford: Oxford University Press, 2012.

———. *The Westminster Larger Catechism (with scripture proofs).* Great Britain, 2019.

———. *The Westminster Shorter Catechism (with scripture proofs).* Great Britain, 2020.

Winship, Michael P. *Hot Protestants: A History of Puritanism in England and America.* New Haven: Yale University Press, 2018.

Wolterstorff, Nicholas. "The Reformed Liturgy." In *Major Themes in the Reformed Traditions*, edited by Donald K. McKim, 273–304. Grand Rapids: Eerdmans, 1992.

Young, Frances. *The Art of Performance: Towards a Theology of Holy Scripture.* London: Darton, Longman, and Todd, 1990.

Zachman, Randall C. *The Assurance of Faith: Conscience in the Theology of Martin Luther and John Calvin.* Louisville: Westminster John Knox, 2005.

Zakai, Avihu. "Religious Toleration and Its Enemies: The Independent Divines and the Issues of Toleration during the English Civil War." *Albion: A Quarterly Journal Concerned with British Studies* 21 (1989) 1–33.

Name/Subject Index

Abba, Raymond, 73, 74, 78
acts of parliament,
    Act of Uniformity, 22, 23, 65n5, 161
    Blasphemy Act, 26
    Corporation Act, 25
    Doctrine of the Trinity Act, 26
    Religious Worship Act, 25
    Test Act, 25
    Toleration Act, 19, 26
Adams, Jonathan, 47
Allmen, Jean-Jacque von, 156
Allon, Henry, 93
Ames, William, 31–32
anabaptists, 22, 142
Anne, queen, 24
Argent, Alan, 72

Baillie, Robert, 48–49, 110
Banyard, Edmund, 11
Barrett, G. S., 82, 84, 95
barrowists, 22
Baxter, Richard, 21, 28, 22, 33, 38–39
Beart, John, 58
Bebbington, David, 28
Beddome, Benjamin, 59–60, 62
Begbie, Jeremy, xii, 133–34, 136–37 140, 141, 148, 149, 150, 151, 152
Bell, John, 131
Benson, Bruce Ellis, 157
Beynon, Graham, 40
Binney, Thomas, 83, 84, 91, 92
Bonhoeffer, Dietrich, xii, 135
Boulton, Matthew Myer, 156

Branch, Lori, 43
Briggs, John, 27
brownists, 22, 111
Bucer, Martin, xi, 120, 138, 143–45, 146, 148, 153, 154, 155, 156, 166
Burroughs, Jeremiah, 43, 56, 57
Bury, Samuel, 27–28

Cadoux, Cecil, 70
Calvin, John, 9, 29, 30, 31, 32, 34, 37, 51, 52, 54, 110, 120, 137, 138, 139, 140, 143, 145, 146, 148, 154, 155, 156
Camroux, Martin, 7, 8
cantus firmus, 135–36, 137, 138, 139, 140, 146, 151, 154
Carruthers, S. W., 102, 104, 105, 114
Cashdollar, Charles, 87
Chan, Simon, 157
Charles II, king, 22, 24
Charnock, Stephen, 33
Churches of Christ, xi, 7
Church of England, 18, 20, 22, 23, 24, 25, 26, 85, 86, 118, 161
    Book of Common Prayer, 19, 20–21, 23, 43, 47, 49, 90
Church of Scotland, 20, 102, 103, 104, 118–19, 131 *also see* Kirk
    Book of Common Order, 116, 131
Clark, Neville, 140
Clarkson, David, 53–54
Clifford, Alan, 61

Name/Subject Index

communion
    in Christ, 148–49
    of saints, 51–54, 57, 60, 82, 92, 96
    with God, 51–55, 82, 91–92, 96
community, identified by worship, 146–47
congregationalism, 52, 92, 102, 123, 125
    in England, 64–72, 107, 123
    and freedom, 64, 66, 68, 71, 72
Congregational Church in England and Wales, xi, 7, 72, 92, *also see* Congregational Union of England and Wales
Congregational churches
    Carrs Lane, Birmingham, 71
    Common Close, Warminster, 81
    Derby Street, Bolton, 90
    Fisherton Street, Salisbury, 95
    Emmanuel, Cambridge, 95–96
    Sanford Street, Swindon, 83
Congregational Federation, 72
Congregational Union of England and Wales, 67, 69, 72, 77, 79, 91
    and worship books, 87–91
    and hymn books, 94
    declaration of faith, 69, 72, 92
Congregational Union of Scotland, xi, 7
conscience
    and morals, 29, 32–33
    Christian, 29, 145
    freedom of, 24, 29–33, 63, 142
    liberty of, 4, 5, 22, 29, 30, 161, *also see* freedom of
Cornick, David, 27
County Unions, 66, 67
Cranmer, Thomas, 143
Cromwell, Oliver, 21, 22, 31, 36
Cypris, Ottomar, 143–44

Dale, R. W., 66, 68, 69, 74, 75–76, 77–78, 80, 87
Davies, Horton, 11, 23, 50, 90, 95, 99, 109, 115, 116
Declaration of Breda, 22

Dell, William, 33
dissent, 18, 24, 65n5
    as traditions of, 5, 28, 103
Dix, Gregory, 6
Dixhoorn, Chad van, 39, 49
Doddridge, Philip, 29, 40, 42, 44, 45, 46, 58, 59, 61, 62
Duncan, John, 28
Durber, Susan, 15, 16

Earle, Jabez, 56n174, 59, 60
Eastcheap lectures, 56, 56n174, 59
Ecumenical Movement, 2, 85, 88, 97, 118–19, 131
Ellis, Christopher, 3, 4
epiclesis, 156
embodiment, 137, 146–51, 153, 158–59
encounter, in worship, 2, 4, 13, 15, 17, 131, 152, 160, 161, 165, 167
Evangelical Revival, 28, 65, 65n7

Farel, Guillaume, *also referred to as* William, 120, 138
familists, 22
Fergusson, David, 6, 163
Forsyth, P. T., 74, 75
Fraser, Donald, 106, 108–9, 127
Free Church, as tradition, 5, 141, 167
Free Church of Scotland, 103
freedom, 134, 142, 157–58
    divine, 73, 97, 158, 159, 161, 162, 163, 165
    human, 133–34, 135, 158, 161, 162
    in worship, 9, 10, 11–12, 73–81, 96, 97, 113, 118, 123, 125, 126, 127, 160
    of religion, 25, 80
    also see liberty, of choice

Gaunt, Alan, 14
George I, king, 24–25
Gillespie, George, 49, 110
glorification, of God, 15, 51, 55, 59, 60, 61, 63, 100, 159, 160
Goodwin, Thomas, 31, 36, 48n140
Gordon, Alexander, 28

Name/Subject Index

great ejectment, 19, 23, 65n5, 161
Gunton, Colin, 140–41, 152, 153
Guthrie, Steven, 157

Hall, Christopher Newman, 84–85, 90
Hambrick-Stowe, Charles, 55
Henry, Matthew, 39, 41, 42, 46
Hilton, Donald, 10
Holy Spirit
    and conscience, 29, 46
    and freedom, 4, 9, 10, 23, 33, 63, 73–77, 97, 127, 143–46
    and scripture, 32, 34–26, 53, 155
    and preaching, 36–41, 53, 56, 75–79, 153
    and prayer, 53, 77–79, 153, 155
    and the church, 53, 149
    in worship, 5, 17, 86–87, 127
hymnody,
    and doctrine, 59, 61–62
    as edification, 59, 60, 61
    use of, 14–15, 58–62, 93–94
Howe, John, 34–35, 39
Hunt, Arnold, 36, 37
Hunter, John, 84, 85
Hussey, Joseph, 57
Huxtable, John, 80, 133, 147

improvisation, 134, 135–37, 138, 140, 141, 148, 151, 153, 154, 157
independent churches, and chapels, 27, 28–29, 31, 32, 53, 57, 65, 66, 75
    Bury St Edmunds, 27, 54–55, 58
    also see United Reformed Church
    Scotts Lane, Salisbury, 47
Iona Community, 11, 115–16

James II, king, 24, 25
James, T. T., 76, 77, 91
jazz, 17, 134, 135–36, 140, 141, 148, 151, 157
Jenkins, Daniel, 73, 74, 94, 162
Jenkins, Jill, 14
Jennings, John, 39–40
Jesus, xi, 12, 25–26, 33, 36, 138, 143

and the church, xi, 4, 13, 54, 62, 77, 79, 109, 123, 166–67
as word of God, 61, 127
Johns, Evan, 27–28
Jones, R. Tudur, 70
Jordon, Dorothea, 52

Kavanagh, Aidean, 1
Kay, J. Alan, 149–50
kirk, 102–3
Knox, John, 109, 110, 143
Knox, R. Buick, 100n5

LaCuga, Catherine Mowry, 151
liberty, of choice, 10, 32, 77, 96, 123, 124, 126, 127
Liturgical Movement, 85, 91, 96, 128
liturgy, 90–91, 94, 129
    as prescribed, 63, 79–80, 106, 109, 112–13, 138
    as order, 9, 11, 46–47, 63, 81, 82–83, 84–87, 106, 139, 161, 166
    distrust in, 46, 82, 83–84
Locke, John, 32
Lutheran Church, 5, 25

Macleod, Donald, 127, 130
MacLeod, George, 115–16
Manning, Bernard Lord, 62, 71, 94
March, Septimus, 86
Marsh, John, 80
McClure, John, 78, 80, 91, 93, 94
McIlhagga, Donald, 130
McIntyre, John, 158
Melville, Andrew, 109
methodism, 28
Micklem, Nathaniel, 71, 75, 84
Micklem, Romilly, 80
Middlemiss, J. T., 106, 109, 110–11, 111–12, 126
Millard, Benjamin, 70
Milton, John, 31, 34
Moltmann, Jürgen, xii, 142, 146, 147–48, 151–52, 157–58
Morgan, G. Campbell, 75

Newman, John, 56
nonconformity, 24, 25, 29

Name/Subject Index

Nuttall, Geoffrey, 32, 36
Nye, Philip, 45, 50

Old, Hughes Oliphant, 39
Orchard, W. E., 90
order,
    in the life of the church, 8–9, 68, 70, 71, 113, 131
    with freedom, 11, 46, 64, 82, 87, 97, 99, 122–27, 146, 165, 166, 167
orderly, worship, 10, 11, 49, 106, 110, 112, 118, 127, 131, 144, 165
Owen, John, 31, 44, 53–54
Oxford Movement, 85, 86

Parker, Joseph, 76, 91–92
participation,
    and liturgy, 128–30, 163
    and order, 128, 132
    and the vernacular, 51
    of the congregation, 6, 15, 82, 90, 91, 94, 95, 127, 128, 129, 130, 135, 157, 163
    of God, 5, 163
    through the Holy Spirit, 149, 150
Parry, K., 78
Paul, the apostle, 4, 5, 11, 14, 37, 53, 59, 92, 145, 149
Payne, Ernest, 4, 5, 140, 142
Pearsall, John Spencer, 78–79
Peel, Albert, 69, 70
Peel, David, 11
Peirce, James, 26
performance, xii, 131, 136, 137, 148, 151, 154
performer(s), 135, 136, 137, 138, 146, 148, 149, 151, 153, 154
Perkins, William, 38
Poll, G. van de, 156
prayer, 41–46, 95–96, 125
    conceived, 45–46, 50, 78n71
    extempore *or* extemporary, 12, 42, 43, 45–46, 50, 77–79, 109, 124, 125, 130, 143 *also see* prayer, free
    free, 50, 77–79, 84, 90, 141
    personal, 41–42
preaching, 39, 55–58, *also see* sermon
    extemporarily, 38, 76
presbyterianism, 101–2, 123
    in England, 99, 100–106
    Presbyterian Church of England, xi, 7, 100–106
    and worship books, 107–22
    Parkgate group, 116
priesthood, of all believers, 92, 130, 164
psalmody, 58–59, 61
puritanism, 16–17, 18–19, 34, 48, 55, 58
Price, Ernest, 64

Reformed, as a tradition, xi, 8–9, 11, 13n 100n4, 106, 115, 119, 120, 128, 143, 160, 163
Reformed Presbyterian Church of Scotland, 104
response, 137, 151–57, 158, 159
Roman Catholic Church, 5, 24, 49, 85
Routley, Erik, 10, 14, 15, 26, 61, 62, 67, 70, 79
Rutherford, Mark, 87
Ryrie, Alec, 21

Salters' Hall, 26
    controversy of, 26–27
Savoy Assembly, 31
Savoy Conference, 22
Savoy Declaration, 30, 31, 34, 36, 54, 57, 65n5, 69
separatists, 19–20, 65n5
sermon, 37, 38–39, 40–41, 55, 75–77, 91, *also see* preaching
    extempore, 38, 39, 40
Shillito, E., 75
Simpson, Carnegie, 101–2, 122–23
Smith, John Pye, 69
Spinks, Bryan, 90
spontaneity, in worship, 12–13
Solemn League and Covenant, 19, 20, 23

Taylor, William, 76–77, 81, 82, 92, 96

Name/Subject Index

testimonies, as responses in worship, 57–58
theology, liturgical, 3–4, 6, 167
Thomas, David, 84, 92
Thompson, Bard, 153
Thorogood, Bernard, 12, 14
Todd, James, 9, 80, 125, 147
Torrance, Alan, 150
tradition, 137–46, 158, 159
trinity, doctrine of debate, 25–27
true church, 51–52

Underhill, Evelyn, 6
unitarianism, 27
    and english presbyterianism, 27, 100
unitarian church, Bury St Edmunds, 27–28
United Presbyterian Church of Scotland, 104
United Reformed Church, xi, 7–8, 16, 18, 100, 119, 125, 133, 137, 138, 139, 140, 141, 146, 147, 152, 153
    and liturgy, 9–10
    and hymnody, 14
    Basis of Union, 8, 138
    Bury St Edmunds, 27, *also see* independent churches, and chapels
    Prayer Handbook, 13–14
    worship of, xii, 8–16, 17, 160–66
unity, of the church, 7, 18

voluntarism, 32, 52, 69, 73

Wainwright, Geoffrey, 2, 140, 147, 148, 159
Watson, J. R., 59, 62
Watts, Isaac, 40, 41–42, 43, 44–45, 58, 59, 60, 61, 62
Watts, Michael, 24
Westminster Assembly, 19, 20, 31, 48, 52
    and Directory for Public Worship, 20–21, 22, 29, 33, 37, 40, 41, 42–43, 45, 47, 48–51, 99, 107, 108, 109, 119, 129, 161, 166
    Confession of Faith, 20, 30, 34, 54, 105
    Catechisms 20, 55, 60, 100
Welch, Elizabeth, 150, 158
Whale, John, 71
White, William Hale, 87–88
William of Orange, king and queen Mary II, 24, 25
Wilson, John, 23
Wolterstorff, Nicholas, 153
word, of God, 4–5, 17, 19, 33, 34–41, 46, 48, 51–52, 56, 57, 61, 68, 74, 75, 76, 77, 96, 98, 119, 120, 127, 145, 146, 150, 153, 161
worship
    and God, 6, 15–16
    and the church, xi, 1, 2
    and the freedom of, 4–5, 51, 63
    and theology, 1–2
    as human response, 6, 13
    as transformative, 150–51
Wren, Brian, 14
Wright, David, 49

Young, Frances, xii, 136, 154
Young, Thomas, 48n140
Zwingli, Huldrych, 120, 153, 154

Scripture Index

OLD TESTAMENT

Genesis
1:27	39

Psalms
47:7	61
66:16	58
73:25–26	37
90	37

Isaiah
11:2	149

Joel
2:28	33

NEW TESTAMENT

Matthew
5:22–24	12
12:34	44
18:20	146
20:1–7	58

Luke
17:11–19	xi
24:49	33

John
3:8	143
3: 14, 15	58
4:23–24	143
4:24	33, 166
6:63	143
15:18, 19	58
17:21	150

Acts
2:6–9	36
2:42	137–38, 146
8:26–39	36

Romans
6	58
7:26	44
8:14	143
8:26	149
8:34	152
12:5	2

1 Corinthians
2:10–11	144
14: 5, 12, 26	150
14:40	11
14:26	167
15	37

2 Corinthians
3:17	4, 5
13:5	37

Scripture Index

Galatians
3:13	58

Ephesians
2:18	53
2:20	146
2:21–22	53
4.11–13	92
5:19	14

Colossians
1:28	145
2:3	145
2:8	145
2:16–23	145
3:12–17	36
3:16	1, 14, 59

2 Timothy
3:16	144

Hebrews
2:12	152
4:14	152

2 Peter
1:4	151

1 John
1:7	58

Jude
20	149

www.ingramcontent.com/pod-product-compliance
Lightning Source LLC
Chambersburg PA
CBHW051741230426
43670CB00012B/2115